Success and Failure of Countries at the Olympic Games

The Olympic Games is undoubtedly the greatest sporting event in the world, with over 200 countries competing for success. This important new study of the Olympics investigates why some countries are more successful than others. Which factors determine their failure or success? What is the relationship between these factors? And how can these factors be manipulated to influence a country's performance in sport? This book addresses these questions and discusses the theoretical concepts that explain why national sporting success has become a policy priority around the globe.

Danyel Reiche reassesses our understanding of success in sport and challenges the conventional explanations that population size and economic strength are the main determinants for a country's Olympic achievements. He presents a theory of countries' success and failure, based on detailed investigations of the relationships between a wide variety of factors that influence a country's position in the Olympic medals table, including geography, ideology, policies such as focusing on medal-promising sports, home advantage, and the promotion of women.

This book fills a long-standing gap in literature on the Olympics and will provide valuable insights for all students, scholars, policy makers, and journalists interested in the Olympic Games and the wider relationship between sport, politics, and nationalism.

Danyel Reiche is an Associate Professor for Comparative Politics at the American University of Beirut and a Visiting Scholar at the Harvard University Institute for Quantitative Social Science (IQSS). He has also worked as a visiting Assistant Professor at the School of Foreign Services, Georgetown University, USA, and as a Postdoctoral Researcher at the Freie Universität Berlin, Germany. He is the author of numerous peer-reviewed articles, most recently in *European Sports Management Quarterly*, *International Journal of Sport Policy and Politics*, *Journal of Energy Policy*, *Sport in Society*, *Soccer & Society*, and *Third World Quarterly*.

Routledge Research in Sport, Culture and Society

Success and Failure of Countries at the Olympic Games

Danyel Reiche

Routledge
Taylor & Francis Group

NEW YORK AND LONDON

First published 2016
by Routledge
711 Third Avenue, New York, NY 10017

and by Routledge
2 Park Square, Milton Park, Abingdon, Oxon OX14 4RN

Routledge is an imprint of the Taylor & Francis Group, an informa business

British Library Cataloguing-in-Publication Data
A catalogue record for this book is available from the British Library

Library of Congress Cataloging-in-Publication Data
A catalog record for this book has been requested

ISBN: 978-1-138-79721-5 (hbk)
ISBN: 978-1-315-75730-8 (ebk)

Typeset in Times New Roman
by Wearset Ltd, Boldon, Tyne and Wear

MIX
Paper from
responsible sources
FSC   FSC® C013056
www.fsc.org

Printed and bound in Great Britain by
TJ International Ltd, Padstow, Cornwall

Contents

Figures

Tables

Acknowledgments

This book was only possible with the help of several people and institutions: I would like to thank the American University of Beirut (AUB) and the Faculty of Arts and Sciences (FAS) for granting me a paid research leave for the fall term 2014/2015. This grant exempted me from teaching and administrative work and gave me the opportunity to spend the semester in the United States, making it possible for me to solely focus on the completion of this book. During that time I was a Visiting Scholar at the Harvard University Institute for Quantitative Social Science (IQSS). I would like to thank IQSS for its hospitality, and in particular Dr. James Robinson, Professor of Government at Harvard University, affiliated faculty at IQSS and future University Professor at Chicago University, for inviting me to Cambridge, Massachusetts, and giving me the opportunity to spend time in such a stimulating intellectual environment. I returned as Visiting Scholar to IQSS in the summer of 2015 to finish this book, a trip made possible by a summer research travel grant of the American University of Beirut's Prince Alwaleed Bin Talal Bin Abdulaziz Alsaud Center for American Studies and Research (CASAR).

Two students made important contributions to this work: Alexander Brown, Graduate Assistant in the Department of Political Studies and Public Administration at the American University of Beirut, not only proofread my text but also supported me with my research, particularly by collecting data for the tables. Thomas Chekaiban, an undergraduate student majoring in business with a minor in political science who attended with great enthusiasm my "Politics of Sport" and "Politics of Emerging Countries" classes, helped me with the figures in this book and the PowerPoint presentations for talks I gave on topics related to this work.

We have exceptional students at the American University of Beirut, and I benefitted from our discussions in the "Politics of Sport" classes that I teach. Furthermore, it is always helpful to present research results at conferences and get the input from colleagues; particularly, I would like to highlight the feedback I got from the discussions after my following lectures: "Success and Failure of Countries at the 2014 Winter Olympics" at the North American Society for the Sociology of Sports (NASSS) 2014 Conference in November 2014 in Portland; "Motives to Participate in the Olympics" at the Sport & EU Conference 2014 at the German Sport University Cologne in June 2014; "Soccer at the Olympics: Interests, Issues, and Significance" at the conference "Soccer as the Beautiful Game: Football's Artistry, Identity and Politics" at Hofstra University in April 2014; and my two talks on Qatar, "Qatar's Motives for Hosting Mega Sport Events and Funding Elite Sports" at the SPLISS (Sports Policy factors Leading to International Sporting Success) Conference in Antwerp, Belgium, in November 2013 and "Qatar and the FIFA World Cup 2022: An Attempt to Gain Soft Power" in the Ash Institute Democracy Seminar Series at Harvard University in October 2014.

Although I completed my degree work on energy and environmental policy issues, my current position as Associate Professor of Comparative Politics at the American University of Beirut has given me the academic freedom to shift my research interests towards sport. A life-changing moment was when just before my appointment at AUB in Lebanon, I wrote a non-academic book in German language on my life as fan of the soccer team Hannover 96. The book was quite successful (it received considerable media coverage after it was presented at a press conference with the club president and a player legend, and the book quickly sold out) but I considered it a once in a lifetime event. After becoming a professor, I decided to gradually integrate my personal sport interest into my professional life by teaching "Politics of Sport" classes and starting to learn about the academic sports world. I published papers in leading journals in the field such as *European Sports Management Quarterly*, *International Journal of Sport Policy and Politics*, *Sport in Society*, and *Soccer & Society* and presented my work, among others, at the above-mentioned conferences.

My first academic book on sport is not the end of my journey in the academic world of sports, but an important first milestone. I am grateful to the luxury of my professional life to work on something I truly enjoy, and I am full of energy and ideas for future contributions.

1 Introduction

One of the first opinions I received from a friend in response to the idea of my book was that the Olympic Games are generally negative because of the notion that "Olympic athletes all ruin their health." Although this opinion might stem from a general bias against sport, I had to admit it might still be a valid question worth studying. However, such normative discussion is not the center of focus for this book. Rather than discussing whether elite sport is good or bad, I seek to analyze why winning medals at the Olympic Games has become a priority around the world. As a political science professor, I find it interesting to analyze this phenomenon because Olympic success has become an area of increased government involvement in many countries, with considerable resources from state budgets being channeled into policies that promote national success at the greatest international sporting event.

This book seeks to answer the following questions: how "Olympic success" is defined differently around the globe, why countries are aiming for success at the Games and its Winter and Summer editions, and which policy instruments are countries utilizing to achieve their sporting goals.

During the last decade I have worked as a professor in Lebanon and the United States, however my childhood in Germany played an important role for my interest in the topic of this book. After telling my father about plans to write a book on success and failure of countries at the Olympics, he was adamant that I discuss the role of the German Democratic Republic (GDR). The GDR, better known internationally as East Germany, was a sporting power despite its short period of existence. "We" in West Germany, the Federal Republic of Germany (FRG), had to acknowledge that our East German "brothers and sisters" outperformed us at the Olympic Games. Although there were severe travel restrictions from the West to the East (and even more restrictions vice versa), it remained possible to access East German TV in the northern German city of Hanover where I grew up. I can still remember East German commentators enthusiastically celebrating the successes of their athletes.

Despite being on paper dissolved in 1990, the GDR still ranks historically as a leading sporting power, ranked in the top 10 of the all-time Olympic medal rankings. This is a remarkable feat considering that the country participated in only six Winter and five Summer Olympics over a period of 20 years, from 1968 until

1988. While the GDR outperformed West Germany at the Olympic Games, it could not win against the "class enemy" ("Klassenfeind") beyond the sports field. The GDR only existed from 1949 until 1990, when the Berlin Wall fell, and the GDR's success as a major sporting power could not prevent its political downfall.

While the GDR was more successful overall than the FRG at the Olympics, it was unable to compete with West Germany in soccer, the sport most popular in both German countries. The GDR did have success by beating the FRG at the 1974 World Cup in the group stage. However, West Germany would later go on to win the world championship at the tournament, and the GDR's early win would become a marginalia in soccer history. Despite competition between East and West, when West German soccer clubs such as Bayern Munich had to play in European competitions in the GDR, many East Germans came to the stadium to cheer for the West German players. While this was in part a form of protest against the dictatorship in their country and a demonstration of their desire for German reunification, it also proved that sporting success is not that always easy to define: There are not only medal rankings, there are also the hearts and minds of the people, and for them a victory in a popular sport such as soccer often means much more than several medals in niche sports.

One scholar at Harvard University's Institute for Quantitative Social Science (IQSS) suggested in a discussion with me that there might be a simple answer to explain the success or failure of countries, simply by measuring the different number of a country's athletes in a particular sport. There might be cases that do prove this assumption. For example, Germany has the largest soccer association in the world (the German Football Association, DFB), and the men's team won the soccer world championship in Brazil in 2014. The German women's team is successful as well; winning two out of seven World Cups that took place from 1991 until 2015. However, when looking at the men's World Cups, there are also examples of small countries that have few athletes, but also have tremendous success: Costa Rica, a country with a population of less than five million people, made it to the quarter-finals in Brazil in 2014.

Still, there could be another simple explanation that the population size matters at the Olympics. In the recent history of the Olympic Games, China and the United States have been the most successful countries. Thus are more populated countries more successful at the Games than less populated countries? However, there are numerous exceptions such as the GDR with its 16 million people, which was more successful than more populated countries (such as West Germany). Cuba, for example, is still outperforming other far more populated Latin American countries such as Argentina, Brazil, and Mexico. China, the largest populated country in the world, has recently become an Olympic superpower, but why does India, a country with also more than one billion people, fail at the Games? Uruguay, a country with less than four million people, has won the men's soccer World Cup and Olympics each twice, as well as a record 15 wins at the prestigious South American Championship, the Copa America. Uruguay has achieved all of this success despite being surrounded by large soccer powerhouses such as Brazil and Argentina.

When discussing other macro variables such as GDP, the same pattern as in the case of population size can be observed: one finds some confirmations but also many deviations. For example, Saudi Arabia's per capita GDP is more than 17 times higher than Kenya's per capita GDP, but Kenya has won more than 17 times more medals than Saudi Arabia at the Olympic Games.

These examples show that explaining success and failure at the Olympic Games is a complex challenge, and while it might be helpful in many cases to study macro variables such as population size and GDP, they do not (1) explain outliers such as Uruguay in soccer, and Cuba and Kenya at the Olympics or (2) explain the less successful performance of similar countries (such as India and China, that have a similar population size). While in the cases of India and China one could argue that China has become economically more powerful than India, there are also cases of countries with similar population size and GDP but completely different performances at the Olympic Games, such as Bulgaria and Hungary, with the latter having won more than double the number of Olympic medals.

There are two bodies of literature on Olympic success. Whereas the first generation of studies have focused on general independent variables such as GDP, geography, and population size, the second generation of research has shifted toward investigating the policy level. One could argue that research has shifted away from quantitative measurement toward qualitative explanations of Olympic success. The problem with many studies of the first generation was that they investigated only a small number of explanatory variables such as GDP, and were not able to explain success cases of low-income countries like Cuba, Ethiopia, and Kenya. In this book I will attempt to explain the whole picture by discussing both the macro as well as the policy factors. By providing examples of outliers in the discussion of the macro variables, I attempt to prove that explanations relying only on macro variables are insufficient, and that it is necessary to study the policy level as well. Without investigating the policy level, success and failure of countries at the Olympics cannot be understood. If there exist favorable macro variables but insufficient sport policies there will be no Olympic success. However, Olympic success is still possible without favorable macro variables if there are effective policies. Thus, any country, whether small or large, economically strong or weak, can enjoy Olympic success to a certain extent.

According to De Bosscher et al., the impact of macro-level factors on elite sporting success remains high: "Macro-level determinants still account for more than 50% of Olympic success and this may be even higher in developing countries" (De Bosscher et al. 2006, 210). However, no evidence is given in the respective work for the ratio of "more than 50%," and I think one should be careful when introducing such numbers that give the impression that Olympic success is the result of a mathematical model that just needs to be applied.

I will introduce in this book what I call the "WISE formula," WISE standing for the promotion of women in sport (W), the institutionalization of the promotion of Olympic sports (I), the specialization in medal-promising sports (S) and the early adoption of trends such as sports newly added to the Olympic program

(E). The WISE formula is not meant as an accurate formula for precisely planning and calculating success and failure of countries at the Games. I agree that

> Uncertainties over the relationship between policies and international sporting success will always remain. The reason for this is that it is impossible to set up an experiment trying to explain a causal correlation of one factor leading to success while other factors are controlled.
>
> (De Bosscher et al. 2006, 209)

My work aims to contribute to a better understanding of forces impacting medal results that can be influenced by governments, with the WISE formula at the center of the analysis.

According to Pfau, the "inconsistency of country performances makes the use of simple econometric models more challenging." For the fluctuating share of medals by single countries he gives the following examples:

> Norway won 5 medals in 1988 and 20 medals in 1992, the United States went from 13 medals in 1998 to 34 medals in 2002 to 25 medals in 2006, Austria had 21 medals in 1992, 9 medals in 1994, and 17 medals in 1998, and so on.
>
> (Pfau 2006, 13)

Pfau made forecasts in his work for the 2006 Winter Olympics in Turin and compared them with the actual results. In his econometrics model he used data from the 1960 to the 2002 Winter Olympics to predict the medal ranking at the 2006 Games. His model was based on five explanatory variables: GDP per capita; population; serving as the host; number of medals won by each country in previous Olympics; and belonging to subsets of countries (such as Scandinavia) that have performed unusually well in the past and won more medals than would otherwise be justified by their economic and demographic characteristics.

While Germany and the United States did finish in the top two places in Turin, as predicted in Pfau's model, there were some surprises as Canada, Austria, and Russia performed better than expected, while Norway and Italy did not live up to expectations. The prediction that the 2006 Winter Olympics could be the most inclusive of all did not come to fruition, as of the 11 countries Pfau expected to win one medal, only Belarus succeeded.

Andreff aimed to predict in his work the number of medals Russia and China would win at the 2014 Sochi Games, but he failed to accurately predict those results. For China, Andreff expected the country to win at least 11 medals (China ended up with nine medals won in Sochi). Russia was the most successful country in Sochi according to all different rankings (more gold medals than any other country and more medals in total than any other nation-state), but Andreff predicted that Russia was "not likely to win the biggest number of medals at Sochi Winter Games" (Andreff 2013, 338). I agree with Andreff when he states, "Fortunately, economists are not capable to predict all the detailed Olympics results, otherwise why still convene the Games?" (Andreff 2013, 323).

The WISE formula is not a tool for predictions. It should be understood as a simple model with few explanatory variables that presents general guidelines for governments on how to develop elite sport policies. While detailed policies need to be adjusted to the country-specific context, it provides a framework for how a country can succeed at the Games. I will later explain that certain macro variables might apply to single sports (for example the wealth of a country in expensive sports such as sailing) but have only a limited explanatory power when the Olympics as a whole, with all its sports and events, are discussed. I do not claim that the variables represented in the WISE formula are the only factors that help to explain sporting success, but they certainly represent a substantial proportion of Olympic success. Applying the WISE formula is a precondition for overall success at the Summer and Winter Games. Countries that do not promote women in elite sports, which do not have institutions that support the elite sport sector, do not specialize in medal-promising sports and are not flexible to adopt new trends in global elite sport policies, fail at the Olympic Games.

Most research on Olympic success has focused on best practice cases such as Australia, Canada, the Netherlands, Norway, and the United Kingdom, among others. These countries share, apart from being successful at the Olympic Games, general characteristics such as being well-developed market economies and democracies. While reviewing research on these countries was beneficial for my own work, I am aiming to provide the reader with a more holistic picture that is also including success cases from developing countries such as Cuba, Ethiopia, and Kenya. Eighty-five nation-states (41.5% of all participating countries) won medals at the Summer Olympics in 2012. Before focusing on success factors in the second part of the book, I examine the motives for participation of countries, such as Lebanon and Syria, which belong to the majority of countries that did not win any medals in London (120, 48.5%) but still consistently send delegations to the Games. Most research has ignored cases of countries that mainly aim to raise the flag at the opening and closing ceremonies, despite the fact that these countries comprise the majority of countries at the Games.

When discussing Olympic success, I focus only on the output, the medals won. I am aware that this perspective ignores the input, meaning the processes that lead to the successes. I will argue later in the book that there is a global trend toward homogenization of elite sport policies; however, it is important to mention that the Olympic successes are reached in different environments under diverging conditions. In Western societies, everybody is free to choose a sport of his/her choice, while in more authoritarian countries such as China there is more pressure on children to practice sports for which they have favorable characteristics. While in Norway, for example, there are usually restrictions on talent identification concerning children under 13 years of age and rules aiming to prevent children from specializing in one particular sport too early, in China athletes leave their families at the age of 10 to live in specialized sport academies (Augestad et al. 2006, 293–313; Beech 2012). I am also ignoring the societal effects of Olympic success: does Olympic success go along with more activity at the grassroots sports level, preventing obesity and contributing to other health benefits? While I discuss in detail the motives of countries to invest in Olympic success, I do not make any statement on whether objectives such as improving health, societal cohesion, national pride, and gaining soft power are met.

My analysis helps to better understand why countries invest in elite sport but does not answer the question of whether it is worth the investment. However, from an overall perspective, it is certainly better to aim for outperforming other countries on the sports field than beating them on the battlefield. I would make the case that at the end of the day the Olympics help to bring people together and contribute to a more peaceful world, despite the prevalence of nationalism at the Games, a point that I will discuss later in the book.

I only look at the Summer and Winter Olympic Games and do not discuss other Games such as the Paralympic Games, the Youth Olympics or regional versions of the Olympics such as the very popular Asian Games. I do not limit my analysis to single Olympics such as Beijing 2008 and Vancouver 2010: fluctuating performances of countries at the Games would deform the results. There were also Games that were boycotted by some countries, for example the 1976 Summer Olympics in Montreal by African countries, the 1980 Games in Moscow by the United States and many of its allies, and the 1984 Summer Olympics in Los Angeles by the Soviet Union and many of its allies. Australia, France, UK, Greece, and Switzerland are, according to D'Agati's book on the Cold War and the Olympics, the only countries that never joined any boycott and participated in all Olympic Games (D'Agati 2013).

Therefore, I refer throughout the book to all-time statistics to be able to identify broader patterns and to make generalizations. The data in this book, such as medal statistics, covers all Olympic Games including the Summer Games in London 2012 and the Winter Games in Sochi in 2014. While I only look at the Olympics, the findings of this work might be transferable to other mega sporting events, particularly World Championships. Usain Bolt, for example, won six gold medals at the Summer Olympics and finished in first place at eight World Championships. There are only a few competitions at the Olympics where the results of the Games do not reflect those from World Championships, one of which is soccer. For example, Germany won the last World Cup in 2014 but did not even qualify for the London 2012 soccer tournament. That tournament was won by Mexico, a country with zero FIFA World Cup victories. Brazil has won the most FIFA World Cups but has never won the gold medal at the Olympics. Pele, considered by many people to be the greatest soccer player of all time, once joked that it is his fault that Brazil never won the Olympics since he never participated in the Games. This might be true, since FIFA has always restricted the eligibility for participation at the Olympics with frequently changing rules. Currently, there is an age limit with only three players older than 23 allowed on the team. However, in most sports, the best athletes compete in the World Championships as well as the Olympics, and international federations such as FIFA that restrict the access to the Olympics are in the minority.

As briefly mentioned above, I do not look at the individual success level. I understand the admiration for Olympic superstars such as sprinter Usain Bolt, and swimmer Michael Phelps who has won 22 Olympic medals, more than any other athlete in the history of the Games. While it might be certainly worth studying how those athletes became so successful, at the end of the day, I see their accomplishments as a result of an environment that recognized and promoted their talents from early on. Living in Lebanon, I personally see many athletes with passion and talent but none of them reach the top level. For example, there was a female student from the American University of Beirut who competed in table tennis for Lebanon at the London 2012 Olympics. Due to the absence of any state help, her father privately financed a coach from China who came every summer to practice with her. If this student, with her tremendous talent, had grown up in a country with a better sporting support structure instead of in a weak state such as Lebanon that lacks any strategic planning for elite sport success, she might have had much greater success at the Olympic Games.

An article in the *New York Times* published during the soccer Women's World Cup 2015 in Canada, reported that within the US team (which later won the tournament) 17 of the 23 players have older siblings. Research from the United States Soccer Federation reveals that 74% of the players on its women's youth national teams — from ages 13 to 23 — have at least one older sibling. The article also refers to a study involving 229 athletes and 33 sports in Canada and Australia that found that top athletes tended to be later-born children (Longman 2015). While such findings are interesting and help to better understand which athletes are representing a country at international sporting events, they do not provide relevant information for the comparative perspective of this book and do not help answer the question of why some countries are more successful than others.

The knowledge that this book provides is for the country level, explaining differences of Olympic success *between* countries. The book does not provide in-depth knowledge for success phenomena *within* countries. For example, in the United Kingdom, athletes from private schools – one-fifth of team GB and winners of one-third of the medals – are more successful at the Olympic Games than athletes from public schools. For Tozer, this is "one of the worst statistics of British sports" (Tozer 2013, 1436). In other countries such as China, it's the other way around, with athletes from a lower-class background being more likely to succeed. For example, when women's weightlifting became an Olympic sport, "scouts had been dispatched to the countryside, where parents were more likely than their urban counterparts to release their daughters into state care" (Beech 2012).

While in-depth research on a limited number of case studies can generate detailed information such as the different class and schooling background of Olympic athletes, the broader cross-country approach chosen in this work aims to contribute to a better understanding of success and failure at the Olympics. I aim to provide a blueprint for policy makers and contribute to the diffusion of best practices by providing information that better explains the elite sport policies of other nations. This will be accomplished by identifying patterns and making generalizations from country comparisons, by analyzing changes in countries over time, and by introducing the WISE formula.

The book proceeds in following order: In Chapter 2, the term success is discussed as it relates to the Olympic Games. There are different ways of counting medals, with the total medal count (AP method) and the gold first approach (IOC method), which uses silver and bronze medals only as a tiebreaker, as the most popular methods. While the first method is mainly used in the United States, the latter one is preferred in the rest of the world and by the International Olympic Committee. The *New York Times* has developed a compromise between both methods, by assigning points for different medals. While the AP, IOC, and NYT medal counts have relatively similar results, the outcome of two other ways of counting medals – medals per capita and medals by GDP – favor small countries (medals per capita) and nation-states with weak economies (medals by GDP). In the chapter I also present alternative suggestions for measuring Olympic success such as the market share model, looking at the costs of Olympic medals, or non-medal based measures of performance such as winning top eight places. Finally, I discuss weaknesses of medal rankings such as favoring individual over team sports, not taking the different popularity of sports into account, and ignoring the fact that not all sports popular in a country are part of the Olympic program. While the Olympic Games have become more inclusive, with more countries winning medals, the majority of medals are still concentrated among few countries, and most participating nation-states are unable to win medals at the Games.

Based on a case study of the upcoming Rio 2016 Olympics, Chapter 3 discusses the objectives of countries at the Olympics. While some countries such as China and Russia generally state that they want to be "sports superpowers," other countries have defined precise medal targets, either winning more medals than at the previous Summer Games in London 2012, or achieving a certain rank in the medal count. For example, Germany wants to exceed the number of medals won in London (44) and Great Britain wants to take home from Brazil at least one more medal than British athletes won in 2012, a remarkable objective given that the 2012 Games took place on Britain's home soil. Australia aims for a top five rank in the medal count, and Japan even wants to finish in the top three in Rio 2016. The analysis of Olympic objectives shows that countries have mainly quantitative medals targets (number of medals, rank in medal count), and there are only few cases of qualitative targets: Brazil and Nigeria are particularly aiming for success in soccer, the most popular sport in both countries. Kenya and Thailand want to achieve an increased number of participants and a stronger representation in some sports (and not only be successful in a particular sport, as is the case with Kenya and running).

After discussing the different definitions of Olympic success in Chapter 2 and the objectives of countries for Rio 2016 in Chapter 3, Chapter 4 analyzes the motivation of countries to participate in the Olympic Games and to aim for success in the largest sporting event in the world. The Olympics bring people from all over the world together, and the International Olympic Committee aims to contribute to a more peaceful world. While there are certainly some internationalist rituals at the Games, I argue that they are mainly a contest between nation-states. After the bloody wars of the nineteenth and twentieth centuries, the Olympic Games offer countries a nonviolent alternative to express nationalism. For this nationalism without war, I see four main drivers: First, the Olympic Games are a tool of legitimacy for countries. For example, for postcolonial or smaller countries participation in the Olympics offers a highly visible opportunity for recognition on the global stage, and is considered as a "sign of statehood" like a national currency or a national anthem. For countries such as Germany and Japan, the Olympic Games after World War II offered an opportunity to reintegrate into the international community. However, the goal of seeking legitimacy is something that applies to any country. All nation-states are witnessing external threats from cultural and economic globalization. Participating in the Olympics (and, if everything works well, outperforming other countries) proves to the domestic audience the capability of the national government.

My second argument is that Olympic success can unify divided countries. While this might hardly apply to relatively homogenous nation-states such as Japan and Norway, it can be important for more diverse countries such as Canada and Belgium, where people speak different languages, or Lebanon, a country without any single predominant religion like most other countries. For multinational countries like Spain, with regions such as Catalonia aiming for independence, the Olympic Games provide an opportunity to develop a common identity.

My third argument is that the Olympic Games are a tool for achieving statehood. The International Olympic Committee has more members than the United Nations (206 compared with 193 as of mid-2015). The five largest nations with a recognized National Olympic Committee by the IOC but without acceptance by the UN are Chinese Taipei (Taiwan), Hong Kong, Kosovo (the last recognized NOC in 2014), Palestine, and Puerto Rico. There were 51 UN members in 1945 and 193 in 2014. Given the ongoing desire of many nations to become sovereign states, the IOC might continue to be a popular tool for achieving statehood, and might be used by (so far) unrecognized National Olympic Committees such as Catalonia and Kurdistan.

My fourth argument is the power perspective. After World War II, the Olympics became a battleground for Cold War politics, and part of the competition for the supremacy of communism and accordingly capitalism. However, since the fall of the Berlin Wall, there are now for the first time more democratic than non-democratic countries in the world. According to the "democratic peace" theory, democracies are less likely to be at war with each other. However, their political weight in world affairs varies. Sport offers an arena to compete with each other and gain soft power. Small countries such as Norway and New Zealand have successfully used the Olympics to reach above their weight in global affairs, while the United States aims to showcase its dominance in the world, and Russia hopes to demonstrate its return to great power status. For others such as Brazil, the Olympics provide a chance to emerge on the global stage. I argue that "the new gold war" is certainly better than a military war where opponents meet on the battlefield rather than on the sports field.

In Chapter 5 I begin to discuss the factors explaining success and failure of countries at the Olympic Games. Figure 1.1 summarizes the original model that I present in this book: I am differentiating between general characteristics and the policy level, introducing for the latter what I call the WISE formula. Chapters 5, 6, and 7 discuss the importance of wealth, population size, and geography of countries for their success and failure at the Olympics. The fourth general characteristic I discuss in Chapter 8, ideology, is printed in the figure in italic because this macro variable has become more of a historic than a contemporary explanation since the end of the Cold War and the fall of the Berlin Wall in 1989.

After discussing the importance of four macro variables in Chapters 5–8, in Chapter 9 I discuss the policy level and introduce in Chapters 9, 10, 11, and 12 the WISE formula, WISE standing for the promotion of women in sport (W, Chapter 9), the institutionalization of the support of Olympic sports (I, Chapter 10), the strategic specialization on medal-promising sports (S, Chapter 11) and the ability to early adopt new trends in elite sport policies and be a pioneer in promoting sports newly added to the Olympic program (E, Chapter 12). Chapters 13 and 14 discuss two other policies, the naturalization of foreign-born athletes (Chapter 13), and hosting the Olympic Games to benefit from the home advantage (Chapter 14). Different from the policies summarized in the WISE formula in Chapters 9–12, these approaches are not accessible for all countries, and are therefore discussed separately. While in some cases the naturalization of foreign-born athletes and hosting

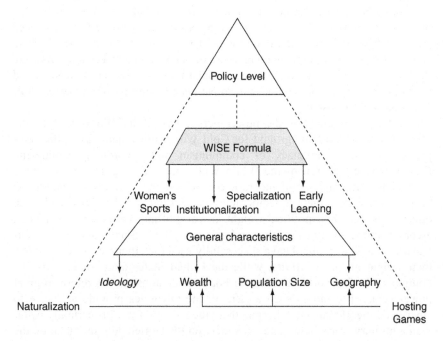

Figure 1.1 Success of Countries at the Olympic Games: The WISE Formula.

the Olympic Games contribute to Olympic success, these explanations for success and failure at the Games apply to only a limited number of countries and are therefore not included in the WISE formula.

In Chapter 5, the first macro variable I discuss is wealth. Many studies emphasize the correlation of GDP and Olympic success. I argue that the importance of wealth depends on the type of sport and Games. The wealth of a country matters more at the Winter than at the Summer Games because the Winter Olympics are more dependent on costly infrastructure. Presenting the cases of equestrian and marathon, I show the advantage of wealthier countries in sports that require expensive equipment. No country with a GDP below US$12,000 has ever won a medal in equestrian, while there are seven countries with a GDP below US$12,000 that have won marathon medals. While countries with a higher GDP are generally more likely than poor nation-states to have Olympic success, just looking at this variable does not explain outliers defined as unsuccessful wealthy countries such as Israel, and successful poor countries like Kenya.

Chapter 6 discusses another popular explanation for Olympic success, population size. Population size matters more at the Summer than at the Winter Games where sparsely populated Scandinavian countries belong to the most successful nation-states. It is evident that small countries have a disadvantage at the Olympic Games. For example, in London 2012 countries with a population below one million won only three medals, and the 102 countries with the smallest population accounted for just 11% of medals won (Houlihan and Zheng 2014, 1). However, this does not necessarily mean that there is a correlation between population size and Olympic success. There are only two countries in the world with more than one billion people, India and China. India has won only 26 Olympic medals at the Summer Games, while the largest nation-state China won 473 medals. Cuba has only the 10th largest population in Latin America, but has won more Olympic medals than any other Latin American country, including Argentina, Brazil, and Mexico. In Africa, Kenya has won almost four times more Olympic medals than the most populated African country Nigeria.

Chapter 7 discusses to what extent the geography of a country influences Olympic success. This factor is more influential for Winter Games and is only important for some sports in the Summer Games. While colder countries outperform warmer ones at the Winter Games, snow coverage is not a sufficient explanation for winter sport success. Without enough ski resorts and winter sport facilities even countries with high snow coverage fail, as the examples of Tajikistan and Kyrgyzstan demonstrate. For sports such as curling, ice hockey, and skating, the necessary infrastructure can be established even in countries without favorable winter sport conditions. One example is the Netherlands, where the highest "mountain" in the country is a hill with a height of 322.7 meters. However, the country is the leading skating nation at the Winter Olympics. For summer sports, sailing is an example of a sport where favorable geography is a precondition for Olympic success, as the 12 most successful sailing countries at the Games all have access to the sea.

Chapter 8 discusses ideology as an explanatory variable for Olympic success. Before the Cold War ended and the Berlin Wall fell in 1989, communist countries were very successful at the Games. For example, the GDR is still ranked in the top 10 of the all-time Olympic medal ranking, despite only participating in the Olympics from 1968 until 1988. Cuba, like East Germany, is a country with a small population base (11 million, compared with 16 million in the GDR). Cuba has remained successful even after the Cold War, while at the same time the performance of most other former allies of the Soviet Union has declined. China, a country that can maybe be best described as socialist market economy, has dominated recent editions of the Summer Olympics along with the United States. In academic literature, there are different explanations for the communist successes, among them are materialistic, capitalistic incentives for athletes, doping, providing women with equal access to sporting activities, and an early institutionalization of the promotion of elite sport. However, there were also differences in the performance of communist countries and some capitalist countries, such as Norway at the Winter Games, and West Germany, Great Britain, and others at the Summer Games, were able to compete with the leading communist countries.

After the relevance of general characteristics of countries such as wealth, population size, geography, and ideology have been discussed in Chapters 5–8, Chapters 9–12 introduce the WISE formula. Chapter 9 explains the first letter of the WISE formula: I argue that without the promotion of women in sport (W), a country cannot excel at the Olympics. China, which is the most successful country at recent Summer Olympics apart from the United States, has one of the highest female participation rates among all countries in the world. In contrast is the percentage of female athletes from Islamic countries. Brunei, Qatar, and Saudi Arabia included women in their Olympic squads for the first time at London 2012. Six of the nine countries with the lowest all-time women's participation at the Olympic Games are Muslim-majority countries. Before 1984, no Muslim women won an Olympic gold medal, and medals won by Muslim women are still an exception. For example, Iran has 60 medals in the history of the Olympic Games, all of them won by men. Muslim women face many major cultural obstacles, such as the dress codes required by the International Sport Federation. In beach volleyball female players are required to wear shorts of a maximum length above the knee. Given the new trend of mixed-gender events at the Olympics, the disadvantage for countries that do not promote women in sport might further increase.

Chapter 10 is about the second letter in my WISE formula: I argue that the institutionalization (I) of the elite sport sector is a precondition for Olympic success. Best practice cases of administrative capacities for Olympic sports are the Australian Institute of Sport (AIS), founded in 1981, and the Norwegian Olympiatoppen (OT), founded in 1988, both of which are classified by some authors as "medal factories." These institutions have served as blueprints for high performance policies around the world. However, pioneers for the institutionalization of Olympic sports were Soviet bloc countries in the 1960s and

1970s. Case studies on AIS and OT emphasize that the Australian and Norwegian institutions were particularly inspired by the systematic institutional framework in the GDR, among them a centralization of elite sport support, a highly scientific and professional elite sport regime with close links to the education system (and in some countries to the army), development of athletes of medal-winning potential, top-class facilities, and high-quality coaching. Many elite sport institutions (i.e. in China, Germany, Norway, Sweden, Switzerland, the Netherlands, and the United Kingdom) are funded by public lotteries to be independent from state budget up- and downturns. A recent trend is the promotion of sport in specific government departments. South Korea established a "Ministry of Sports" in 1983, and in the United Kingdom, "Sport" has been featured in the title of a government department since 1997.

Chapter 11 treats the third letter of my WISE formula: Specialization (S). Focusing on medal-promising sports has become a key strategy in Olympic policies around the world, and countries that have not introduced such a targeted approach are left behind in the medal rankings. A pioneer in specialization was the GDR, which had already introduced a respective policy in 1969 ("high-performance directive"). Countries usually specialize either by promoting sports where they have a historical comparative advantage or by heavily supporting new sports that were recently added to the Olympic program. An example for the latter is women's weightlifting that was added to the Olympic program in the year 2000. China has so far won half of all gold medals since the sport's introduction. Another example is South Korea's successful promotion of speed skating, winning 21 out of 48 gold medals since the sport was added to the program of the Winter Games in 1992. Good examples of focusing on historic strengths are Australia, which has won more than one-third of all its Olympic medals in swimming, and Austria, which has won more than one-third in alpine skiing. A targeted approach has become a key strategy adopted by different types of countries: from low-income countries such as Kenya and Ethiopia who invest in running, to communist countries such as Cuba (boxing) to the best developed countries in the world such as Denmark (track cycling) and Germany (luge at the Winter Games). Some individuals can win numerous medals for their countries such as the American Michael Phelps in swimming (22 medals) and the Norwegian Ole Einar Bjørndalen in biathlon (13).

Specialization is no coincidence, but is the result of a strategic approach by governments. A recent example is the United Kingdom that introduced a "no compromise system," concentrating public funding on the most medal-promising sports. Since moving to this "all or nothing" approach, the UK improved from rank 36 in the medal count in 1996 to a top five ranking at the 2008 and 2012 Summer Olympics. The United States has increased its overall lead in the Olympic medal count since moving to a performance-based funding system in 2000. In contrast, the examples of Sweden and Finland show what happens when countries do not specialize: Both countries have won a majority of their Olympic medals in the first half of the twentieth century, but have seen a decline since that time. Deeply rooted in the ideal of equality, they failed to make strategic choices in their funding systems in the second half of the twentieth century. However, more and more countries are joining the specialization trend. India, for example, introduced the "Target Olympic Podium Scheme" (TOPS) for the 2016 Olympics to support athletes who are medal prospects.

Chapter 12 explains the last letter of the WISE formula: E for early learning. Early learning has two dimensions: the first is the flexibility to quickly react to changes in the Olympic program, being an early adopter of sports that were newly added to the Olympic program. For example, South Korea and China have dominated short-track and won more than 60% of all gold medals since the sport was added to the program of the Winter Games in 1992. China's dominance of women's weightlifting is another example. After the decision was made to add rugby to the Olympic program starting in 2016 in Rio, Russia and China quickly made rugby part of the physical education curriculum in schools.

There is a trend toward homogeneity of elite sport policies that does not only apply to Western developed countries. China has introduced a lottery, and uses the revenues to promote Olympic athletes, taking after countries like Norway that have been successful with such policies at the Olympics long before China began to participate. This is the second dimension of early learning: the willingness to imitate the most successful elite sport regimes around the world, and a steady commitment to reforms. While there is little variation among the leading Olympic countries (all of them promote women's sports (W), have established institutions for the promotion of Olympic athletes (I), and are specializing in their most promising sports (S)), the challenge is to develop domestically slightly improved versions of the best practice cases that served as a model (E).

Chapters 13 and 14 discuss the naturalization of foreign-born athletes and the advantage of hosting the Olympic Games. Different to the policies summarized in the WISE formula in Chapters 9–12, these approaches are not accessible for all countries and therefore are discussed separately.

Chapter 13 focuses on the naturalization of foreign-born talents, a phenomenon at the Olympic Games that mainly occurs in countries with higher GDP levels. At the London 2012 Summer Games, 6.8% of all medals were won by immigrants, a statistically significant number higher than the general world's migrant population of 2.9% (Horowitz and McDaniel 2015, 19). There are some sports with above average numbers of migrant athletes: in table tennis, one-fifth of all players that participated from 1988 to 2012 at the Games were of Chinese origin (Heijmans 2015b). Similar to Chinese athletes in table tennis, the migration of runners from Kenya is a widespread phenomenon in track and field, with a recent trend of migrations toward the Middle East. While the main motivation for migrating athletes might be escaping poverty, another incentive is being eligible for the Olympics (and other mega sporting events such as World Championships) where usually only three athletes from one country can compete. This leaves out many world-class athletes such as Chinese table tennis players and Kenyan runners who are first class but not one of the three best in their countries. While some countries have transparent naturalization policies, such as Singapore's "Foreign Sports Talent Scheme," others such as Qatar try to hide their efforts, for example by giving Christian athletes from Kenya Arabic names. The IOC has introduced a three-year waiting period before athletes can compete for other countries.

Chapter 14 deals with the home advantage at the Olympic Games. Only 23 countries have ever hosted either the Summer and/or the Winter Olympics, and only a limited number of countries are even capable of hosting the largest sporting event in the world. Countries that host the Summer and Winter Olympic Games usually win more medals than at previous Games abroad. For example, Great Britain improved from 47 medals in 2008 in Beijing, to 65 in 2012 in London. In Sochi 2014, Russia won 33 medals, and was the most successful nation in the medal rankings. Four years earlier at the 2010 Games in Vancouver, Canada, Russia only won 15 medals and was 11th in the medal ranking. I argue based on previous research that I have conducted with Stephen Pettigrew (Pettigrew and Reiche 2016), that the academic literature largely ignores the importance of participation rates in explaining the home advantage. The qualification rules for athletes from host countries are significantly less strict, resulting in more medal opportunities for the host country. For example, Great Britain had 530 athletes competing at the London Games in 2012, compared to 304 in Beijing in 2008. Russia had 215 athletes in Sochi 2014, compared to 175 four years earlier in Vancouver. Looking at the Olympic Games from 1952 to 2014, in Summer Games the host country's team is on average 162.2 athletes larger than in the previous Summer Games. In Winter Games, the difference is 28.1 athletes. When we account for increased participation by looking at the ratio of medals to athlete, we find that the home advantage decays to almost zero.

In the conclusion (Chapter 15), I present an alternative model for measuring Olympic success by arguing that countries should evaluate the success of their Olympic programs not only in terms of the outcome (number of medals won, position in the medal count) but also in terms of the quality of the medals (popularity of the sport), and the social acceptance of elite sport policies which depends, among others, on the absence of doping. I proceed by discussing whether the desire for elite sport success around the world is good or bad for human development. I discuss the questions of whether governments should invest on the domestic level in areas such as education and health, rather than in elite sport policies, and whether, internationally, "the new gold war" contradicts Olympic objectives of peace and global harmony. To promote internationalism and cosmopolitism, I suggest introducing events at the Olympic Games that allow for teams composed of athletes from different countries.

2 Definition of Success

For the International Olympic Committee (IOC), "the Olympic Games are competitions between athletes in individual or team events and not between countries" (Olympic Charter 2015, 21). Therefore, according to the Olympic Charter, "the IOC and the OCOG (Organizing Committee of the Olympic Games) shall not draw up any global ranking per country" (Olympic Charter 2015, 99). However, the reality deviates from the ideals of the Olympic Charter. Newspapers across the whole world, and even the IOC itself, publish medal rankings during the Olympic Games.

The medal rankings are the main reference points for nation-states to consider the Games as a success or failure for their country.

What makes analyzing medal rankings contentious is that there are different ways of counting medals. The main controversy stems from counting the total number of medals won, or alternatively giving more preference to the gold medals won. For example, at the 2008 Beijing Olympics China won the most gold medals, while the United States won the most medals overall, yet "Organizers in both countries declared victory" ("Does the U.S. Lead the Winter Olympics – Or Does Germany?" 2014).

The AP (Associated Press) method looks at the overall number of gold, silver, and bronze medals a country has won. If country A wins 100 bronze medals and country B 99 gold medals, country A is ranked above country B according to the AP method.

Another way to view Olympic success is to look at the number of gold medals won, also called the IOC method. While the International Olympic Committee does not publish overall historical medal rankings to apply to its above quoted charter, it does publish rankings for every single Olympic Games on its website. These rankings weigh gold medals more than the total number of medals won. For example, if country A wins 100 silver medals overall, and country B wins only one medal but a gold one, country B is higher than country A in the IOC ranking. Only if countries win the same number of gold medals would silver or bronze medals play a role in the ranking, and the country with the higher number of silver medals would get a higher position in the medal ranking. If countries were tied in both gold and silver medals, then bronze medals would decide which country moves up in the ranking.

At the Asian Games 2014 in Incheon, South Korea, an event that is recognized by the IOC and one of the largest multi-sport event after the Olympic Games, the final medal ranking, conducted with the IOC method, had some extreme outcomes: Qatar was ranked 10th with 14 medals won, while Uzbekistan was ranked 11th with 44 medals won, the difference being that Qatar won one more gold medal. Myanmar finished 20th in the medal count with only four medals won, while Vietnam won 36 medals but ended behind Myanmar in the medal ranking at 21. Again, the difference between Myanmar and Vietnam was that Myanmar won two gold medals, but Vietnam only one gold at the Games (Olympic Council of Asia 2014).

There are also such examples from the Olympic Games: In Tables 2.1, 2.2, 2.3, and 2.4 I have listed four examples from Olympics Games between 1984 and 2006, three from Summer and one from Winter Olympic Games. In the first example from the 1984 Summer Olympic Games in Los Angeles, Great Britain won 37 medals in total, while New Zealand won only 11. However, the smaller country New Zealand with less than five million people (compared with about 60 million inhabitants in Great Britain) ended up three positions higher in the IOC ranking at 8th, because it won eight gold medals, compared with Great Britain's five.

At the 1988 Summer Olympics in Seoul, Sweden won more than five times as many medals as Turkey. However, since Turkey had two gold medals while Sweden won only silver and bronze medals, Turkey ended up five positions higher than Sweden in the medal rankings.

At the 2004 Summer Olympics in Athens, New Zealand once again benefitted from the gold-first methodology. Although Bulgaria won 12 medals, New Zealand was more successful in the IOC ranking with just five medals because it won one more gold medal than the southeastern European country. New Zealand was ranked nine positions higher than Bulgaria in the IOC ranking.

Table 2.1 Extreme Outcome of IOC Ranking at 1984 Summer Olympics

	Gold	Silver	Bronze	Total	IOC Rank
New Zealand	8	1	2	11	8
Great Britain	5	11	21	37	11

Source: Adapted from "A Map of Olympic Medals," *New York Times*, August 4, 2008. www.nytimes.com/interactive/2008/08/04/sports/olympics/20080804_MEDALCOUNT_MAP.html?_r=1&.

Table 2.2 Extreme Outcome of IOC Ranking at 1988 Summer Olympics

	Gold	Silver	Bronze	Total	IOC Rank
Turkey	1	1	0	2	27
Sweden	0	4	7	11	32

Source: Adapted from "A Map of Olympic Medals," *New York Times*, August 4, 2008. www.nytimes.com/interactive/2008/08/04/sports/olympics/20080804_MEDALCOUNT_MAP.html?_r=1&.

Table 2.3 Extreme Outcome of IOC Ranking at 2004 Summer Olympics

	Gold	Silver	Bronze	Total	IOC Rank
New Zealand	3	2	0	5	24
Bulgaria	2	1	9	12	33

Source: Adapted from "A Map of Olympic Medals," *New York Times*, August 4, 2008. www.nytimes.com/interactive/2008/08/04/sports/olympics/20080804_MEDALCOUNT_MAP.html?_r=1&.

Table 2.4 Extreme Outcome of IOC Ranking at 2006 Winter Olympics

	Gold	Silver	Bronze	Total	IOC Rank
Estonia	3	0	0	3	12
Norway	2	8	9	19	13

Source: Adapted from "A Map of Olympic Medals," *New York Times*, http://2010games.nytimes.com/medals/map/html.

At the 2006 Winter Olympics in Torino, Norway won more than six times as many medals as Estonia, but was ranked in the IOC medal ranking one position behind the Baltic nation-state because Estonia had won one more gold medal (three instead of two).

The total medal count is popular in the United States, while in the rest of the world most countries follow the IOC's gold-first approach. The *Wall Street Journal* quoted a Chinese sports official as saying, "One gold is worth a thousand silver" ("Does the U.S. Lead the Winter Olympics – Or Does Germany?" 2014).

The *New York Times* tried to develop a compromise between the two ways of counting medals by something the newspaper calls "medal points": one point for every bronze medal won, two points for every silver medal won, and four points awarded for every gold medal won. Such a system of weighting is a compromise that gives on the one hand more credit to countries who win more medals, while also awarding higher credit to more valuable medals. According to the newspaper, "medal points" are "a recognition of sport's traditional emphasis on the primacy of victory, combined with the AP's respect for those gifted athletes who win silver and bronze" (NYTimes.com 2008).

Apart from the AP, IOC, and NYT methods, other rankings have also been developed. The main reason is that the AP, IOC, and the NYT medal counts are criticized as favoring countries with strong economies and large populations. Therefore, alternative medal counts like medals per capita, and medals by GDP try to find a fairer way to reflect Olympic success. These rankings differ from the results of the AP, IOC, and NYT. For example, the all-time medals per capita ranking is led by Finland, a country of five million people that is 14th in the overall IOC Olympic ranking. Finland's leading rank per capita applies to all three medal-counting methods.

Per capita rankings are often used to compare the performances of rival countries of different size. For example, it was considered a success in New Zealand, but a failure in Australia that at the London 2012 Olympics New Zealand was on a per capita basis more successful that its bigger neighbor and main sporting rival Australia ("High Achievers to Get Olympic Games Cash" 2015). In 1984, New Zealand was even ranked higher than Australia in the total medal count. Prime Minister Jim Bolger would later claim that "New Zealand's sports men and women have established a reputation out of all proportion to our size" (Sam 2015, 6).

The total medals by GDP ranking favors, apart from developing countries such as Kenya, also nation-states such as North Korea, without Western-style capitalistic economies. However, the all-time GDP ranking is led by Jamaica, even though it is only 41st in the total medal count ("Olympic – Overall Medals by Country" 2014). Den Butter and Van der Tak investigated the number of medals won at the 1992 Summer Olympics per million dollars of national income. The result of this ranking was that Kenya won the Barcelona Games (as it did win the Seoul Games) with Hungary in second, and Cuba in third place: "These considerations demonstrate that it proves impossible to determine the true and only winners of the Olympic Games" (Den Butter and Van Der Tak 1995, 36).

In Tables 2.5 and 2.6 I present the winning countries according to the five different ranking systems for the 2012 Summer Olympics in London and the 2014 Winter Olympics in Sochi. In contrast to the example of the 2008 Olympics mentioned before, where China was first in the IOC ranking, but the United States was first in the AP ranking, the 2012 and 2014 Games had for the IOC, AP, and NYT ranking methods the same winners: for 2012 the United States, and for 2014 Russia. At the 2012 Summer Games, China was in second place in all three ranking systems, while there were two different countries, Great Britain and Russia, in third place.

At the 2014 Games, Norway was third in all three ranking systems, but there were different countries, the United States and Canada, in the second position.

The GDP and population weighted rankings had completely different results than the three most popular ranking systems IOC, AP, and NYT: for 2012, both rankings were won by Grenada, an island country in the Caribbean with an estimated population of about 110,000. The other countries listed at second and third place in the GDP and population weighted rankings – Jamaica, Bahamas, and North Korea – are, like Grenada, nation-states that are not listed on top of the IOC, AP, and New York Times ranking systems.

In Sochi, the population weighted ranking was led by Norway, a country that also finished in third place in the IOC, AP, and NYT ranking systems. Slovenia finished first in the GDP weighted ranking and second in the population weighted ranking. Apart from Norway, neither Slovenia nor the other countries ranked on top of the GDP and population weighted ranking systems for the 2014 Winter Games (Austria, Belarus, Latvia) were in first, second, or third place of the IOC, AP, and NYT ranking systems.

The different ranking systems show that it all depends on the way success is measured and which indicators are taken into consideration. While the IOC, AP, and NYT rankings have relatively similar results, the outcome of the GDP and population weighted rankings are completely different. Who decides which ranking is superior to other medal counting methods? Certainly, small countries with weak economies would favor the GDP and population weighted rankings while large, developed countries would have a preference for the IOC, AP, or NYT rankings. Maybe the best approach is to see the whole picture and take into consideration all rankings, even if it makes it more difficult to determine the "true" winner of the Olympic Games.

Apart from the five different ranking systems I have discussed before, there are some suggestions for alternative measures of Olympic success in the academic literature: One is to look at the "market share … identified as being a standardized measure which enables meaningful time series analysis to be conducted" (De Bosscher et al. 2008, 72). Looking as suggested at the market share model on proportional success (medals or points won in proportion of medals/points available to win) might give a more precise view of the performance of a country over time since "it is also possible for nations to improve their position

Table 2.5 Summer 2012 Olympic Medal Winners by Ranking Systems

Ranking Type	First Place	Second Place	Third Place
IOC Ranking	United States	China	Great Britain
AP Ranking	United States	China	Russia
NY Times Weighted Points Ranking	United States	China	Russia
GDP Weighted Ranking	Grenada	Jamaica	North Korea
Population Weighted Ranking	Grenada	Jamaica	Bahamas

Sources: Adapted from "Olympics 2012: The Alternative Medal Table," *Guardian*, www.theguardian.com/sport/datablog/2012/jul/30/olympics-2012-alternative-medal-table. "The World Factbook," *Central Intelligence Agency*, www.cia.gov/library/publications/the-world-factbook/rankorder/2119rank.html?countryname=Argentina&countrycode=ar&regionCode=soa&rank=33#ar. "London 2012 Olympic Medal Tracker Overall," *ESPN Summer Olympics*, http://espn.go.com/olympics/summer/2012.medals.

Table 2.6 Winter Olympic Medal Winners by Ranking Systems

Ranking Type	First Place	Second Place	Third Place
IOC Ranking	Russia	Canada	Norway
AP Ranking	Russia	United States	Norway
NY Times Weighted Points Ranking	Russia	Canada	Norway
GDP Weighted Ranking	Slovenia	Latvia	Belarus
Population Weighted Ranking	Norway	Slovenia	Austria

Sources: Adapted from "Sochi 2014 Olympics Medal Tracker Overall," *ESPN Winter Olympics*, http://espn.go.com/olympics/winter/2014/medals. "2014 Sochi Total Medals per Capita," *Medals Per Capita: Olympic Glory in Proportion*, www.medalspercapita.com/#medals-per-capita:2014. "2014 Sochi Total Medals by GDP," *Medals Per Capita: Olympic Glory in Proportion*, www.medalspercapita.com/#medals-by-gdp:2014.

in the ranking table simply by other nations performing less well" (De Bosscher et al. 2008, 47).

Since all rankings are based on medals won, a question is how to rank countries that did not have athletes on the podium. For example, this affects Arab countries such as Lebanon that did not win any medal at the recent Olympic Summer Games 2012 in London, nor at the Winter Games 2014 in Sochi. Nassif presented at the 2015 Conference of the International Society of Sport Sciences in the Arab World (I3SAW) a new annual ranking based on all annual results in events that are part of the Summer and Winter Olympic programs. The ranking is based on points, not on medals, and is a way to rank all countries and not only those that won medals. The points for each sport are multiplied by a coefficient based on its universality and popularity. While Lebanon is one of those 119 out of 204 countries that did not win any medal in London 2012 (and in Sochi it was one of the 62 out of 88 countries that did not win any medal), it is 95th in Nassif's ranking for the year 2014, which gives the country a better sporting profile rather than just being among 119 unsuccessful countries (International Sports Press Association 2015; Nassif 2015).

Other possible measures of success are the number of athletes posting seasonal best performances, achieving personal bests, or breaking national records; the number of athletes from a country that qualify to take part in the Olympics or the number of events that athletes from a nation-state qualify for a specific contest. For example, in men's super heavyweight boxing in London 2012, there were 16 competitors from 16 countries. This means that athletes from 188 countries were not able to qualify for that competition. Looking at the continental quota system (three from Africa, two from Asia, six from Europe, four from America, and one from Oceania) gives an idea of how difficult it is to participate in the Olympics. Another proposal is to measure the number of athletes that qualify for the final of an event. Finals in many competitions are often contested by eight athletes, and qualifying for them is a remarkable achievement: "This point is particularly true for smaller nations which have fewer athletes and resources to draw upon than larger more affluent nations" (De Bosscher et al. 2008, 66).

One could also compare how much money countries spent to achieve Olympic success and look for the most cost-efficient programs. For example, a study of federal investment in Australian sport found that "between 1980 and 1996 it cost the Australian taxpayer approximately $A37 million to secure each Olympic gold medal winner or, to put it another way, each Olympic medal won over this period involved an investment of $A8 million" (Green 2007, 930). It is estimated that China spent US$52 million on each gold medal won at the 1988 Summer Olympics, compared with US$9 million the host country South Korea spent for each of its gold medals won (Riordan and Jinxia 1996, 130–152). In the four years prior to the Athens Games (2004), the UK government invested GBP£70.1 million in Olympic sport development. With a haul of 30 total medals (nine gold medals), this meant that each medal cost the taxpayer approximately GBP£2.30 million each. For the Beijing Games the sum increased to GBP£75 million, and the total medals won increased to 47. This meant that each medal cost the taxpayer approximately GBP£1.6 million per medal (Grix and Carmichael 2012, 77). Forrest, a sports economist at the University of Salford, was quoted by the BBC that a British medal in Beijing cost GBP£10 million: "We spent an extra £165m and got 17 more medals, so that's about £10m a medal" (Anderson 2012).

The wide range of data for the case of Great Britain shows the difficulty in determining which nation achieves Olympic success in the most cost-efficient way. A problem is that there might be a lot of hidden costs in Olympic success, as the following examples from Sweden, Germany, and the United Kingdom show. Sweden claims to give priority to mass sport participation, and only putting a moderate amount of money into elite sport. However, there are 51 public elite sports schools with some 1,200 students in 30 sports in the country, funded by the education budget (Fahlén and Stenling 2015, 8). At the 2010 Winter Games in Vancouver, German athletes who are pro forma employed by the army, and whose costs are covered by the defense budget, won 57% of the country's medals (WAZ Rechercheblog 2012). Coming back to the British case, only a minority of the elite sport funding comes from the state budget (40%), while a majority of the money comes from a lottery (60%) (Anderson 2012). Therefore, a comparison of the official elite sport budgets does not tell much about how much a country spends in total for elite sport.

When analyzing historic successes at Olympic Games, there are rankings that combine the Summer and the Winter Games into one common ranking, while other rankings differentiate between the two Games. Figures 2.1 and 2.2 show the all-time top 10 Olympic medal count according to the IOC and AP method for both types of Games combined, while Figures 2.3 and 2.4 present separate histograms for the Summer (Figure 2.3) and Winter (Figure 2.4) Games, showing the top three countries at every single event since the Summer Olympics began in 1896, and the Winter Games in 1924.

Figures 2.1 and 2.2 show that the United States leads the all-time Olympic medal count in the two most popular ranking methods, the IOC as well as the AP ranking, and the Soviet Union is second in both rankings, a fact that is remarkable considering that the USSR only existed from 1922 until 1991. There are the same 10 nation-states in the top 10 of the IOC as in the AP ranking method, but there are differences in the sequence. For example, Germany is third according to the IOC, and fourth according to the AP method, while Great Britain is fourth according to the IOC, and third according to the AP method.

While there are only minor differences for the top 10 nation-states in Figures 2.1 and 2.2, there are some peculiarities in the all-time IOC ranking when looking beyond the top 10. In the IOC's gold-first approach, Burundi, a country that won only one Olympic medal, but a gold one (in Atlanta 1996 in athletics in the men's 5,000 meter running event), is ranked higher than the Philippines, which has won nine medals – two silver and seven bronze – but has never won a gold medal. The Philippines is the nation-state with the most Olympic medals but no gold. Second in this ranking is Puerto Rico with two silver and six bronze medals, and third is Moldavia with two silver and five bronze medals (Mallon 2014b).

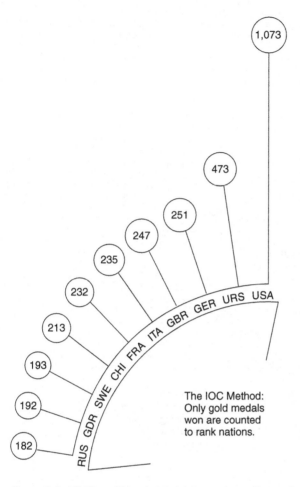

Figure 2.1 All-Time Olympic Medal Count According to the IOC Method (adapted from "Official Website of the Olympic Movement," accessed August 15, 2014, www.olympic.org/).

For the histograms in Figures 2.3 and 2.4, I used the most popular medal count method, the IOC ranking. The Summer Olympic histogram (Figure 2.3) shows that the United States was ranked in the top three of the medal count in all Games apart from 1980, when it boycotted the Moscow Games. While the United States was one of the three best nations in 26 out of 27 Summer Olympic Games, the country was less successful in the Winter Olympics, as Figure 2.4 shows. The United States was ranked in the top three in only 10 out of 22 Winter Games.

The United States is the leading country in Summer Olympics history, but not at the Winter Games. The Winter Games ranking is led by Norway. Figure 2.4 shows that Norway was ranked in the top three 14 times at the Winter Olympics. In the

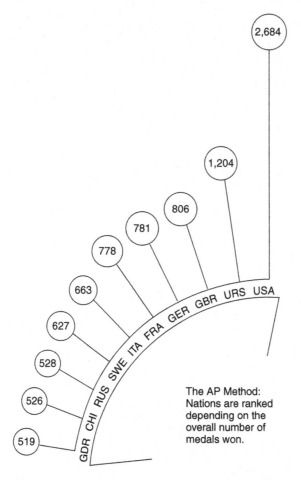

The AP Method:
Nations are ranked
depending on the
overall number of
medals won.

Figure 2.2 All-Time Olympic Medal Count According to the AP Method (adapted
from "Official Website of the Olympic Movement," accessed August 15,
2014, www.olympic.org/).

overall ranking of the total number of medals won at Summer as well as Winter
Olympics, Norway is at number 11, a rank that is still remarkable given the small
size of the country of about five million inhabitants. A total of 136 countries have
ever won an Olympic medal. While in the history of the Olympics 129 countries
have won a medal at the Summer Games, only 45 nation-states have won a medal
at the Winter Games ("Olympic – Overall Medals by Country" 2014).

One problem of all-time Olympic medal rankings is that they do not show
changes over time. Finland, for example, is still ranked 14th in the all-time
Olympic Summer medal ranking, a remarkable position for a country of 5.5 million
people. However, when looking at the Finnish case in detail, it is obvious that the

Ranking Using the IOC Method

Years · Winners · First runners-up · Second runners-up

Figure 2.3 Summer Olympic Games Histogram (adapted from "Official Website of the Olympic Movement," accessed August 15, 2014, www.olympic.org/).

Note
* EUN: The unified team, composed of 14 ex-USSR nations.

country had an impressive medal tally from 1908, the first time the country participated in the Games, until 1952, when the Summer Olympics took place in Finland's capital Helsinki. Finland won 302 medals at the Summer Games from 1908 until 2012; however, a vast majority (213 out of 302, 70.53%) of the medals were won in the first half of the twentieth century (1908–1952): "The difference between the golden age of Finnish elite sport (1907–1951) with an average of 23.8 medals in Olympic Games compared with the era of professionalism and an average of 3.7 medals, is striking" (Koski and Lämsä 2015, 5). One of the reasons

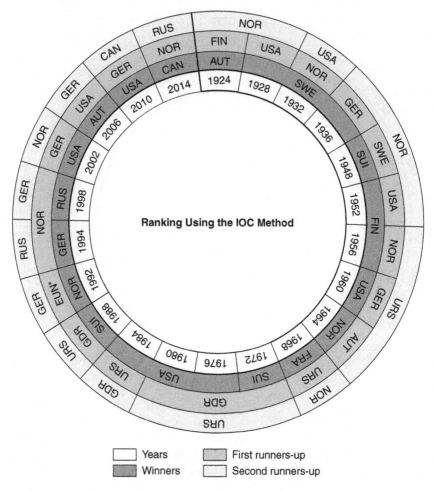

Ranking Using the IOC Method

Years   First runners-up
Winners   Second runners-up

Figure 2.4 Winter Olympic Games Histogram (adapted from "Official Website of the Olympic Movement," accessed August 15, 2014, www.olympic.org/).

Note
* EUN: The unified team, composed of 14 ex-USSR nations.

Koski and Lämsä give is that "Finland's success in the Olympic Games had been largely achieved through individual sports, such as long-distance running, wrestling and cross-country skiing, but over time young people within an increasingly urbanized Finland were attracted to team sports" (Koski and Lämsä 2015, 12).

The Olympic Games consist of many different sports. A weakness of total medal rankings is that they favor individual rather than team sports. A single athlete who dominates his/her sport can win numerous medals. An example is the American swimmer Michael Phelps, who won eight gold medals at the

Beijing Olympics in 2008. On the other hand, in team sports such as basketball, handball, soccer, field and ice hockey, a country can only win one medal in the men's and another one in the women's competition. A soccer team consists of 11 players, plus substitutes. An ice hockey squad is even larger. In the medal ranking, a Canadian gold medal in the team sport of ice hockey is equal to a German gold medal in an individual sport such as luge. This comparison also sheds light on another weakness of the currently practiced medal rankings, that they do not take into account the popularity of a sport as defined by how many people practice a sport, and how many people watch a sport live in the stadiums or on television. Returning to the previous example, ice hockey is by far the most popular sport in Canada, whereas even in the leading luge nation Germany there are only a couple of thousand athletes, and there is only limited public interest in that sport beyond the Olympic Games and World Championships.

Only few sports manage to be successful in both categories (number of athletes and spectators). Ski jumping, for example, is a sport at the Winter Olympics that is practiced only by a couple of thousand people in the whole world but people in many countries love to watch it on TV. Table tennis is the reverse example: it is globally practiced by millions of people but fails to attract large TV audiences in most parts of the world. Other sports such as women's weight-lifting are neither practiced nor watched by many people. Still, medals in all of those sports count equally in the medal count. This also applies to the few sports that manage to be practiced and watched by millions of people around the globe. The best example is soccer, which is the most watched as well as the most practiced sport in most countries. The population might be upset about the failure of a country in such a popular sport, even if the overall performance of the country is satisfactory. For example, the leading soccer nation, Brazil, has never won a gold medal in the Olympic competition. Winning the tournament at the home games in 2016 in Rio is an important objective for Brazilian sport, and might be more meaningful for the Brazilian population than several medals in individual niche sports. Mexico is not a leading Olympic nation, ranked only 48th in the overall historic medal count, but the Olympic gold medal in men's soccer in London 2012 was considered a huge national success. Medal rankings do not weigh the popularity of sports, but the public often does. For Canadians, ice hockey gold counts more than any other medal. Americans feel that a silver medal in basketball is a failure, whereas a silver medal in another sport without similar expectations is a huge success. Because basketball is so popular in the United States, a gold medal is expected (Binns 2009, 5, 58).

Whereas hockey-obsessed Canada and the basketball-crazed United States both perform well in team as well as individual sports (even if the population might value medals differently), all medal rankings are of a disadvantage for those countries with a sporting culture dominated by team rather than individual sports. Boria Majumdar and Nalin Mehta discuss India's problematic relationship with the Olympics in their book *India and the Olympics*. India, the most populated nation-state in the world after China, had only won 26 medals in all Olympic Games prior to the 2012 London Games. The authors explain this with the dominance of particular team rather than individual sports. India had already established itself by 1928, when the country won its first field hockey gold medal, as the world's foremost field hockey-playing nation, and the country has won 11 of its 26 Olympic medals in field hockey, among them eight gold medals. The second half of the twentieth century witnessed the "gradual rise of cricket mania in India," a sport that is not part of the Olympic program, and withdraws with its popularity potential athletes from other Olympic sports (Majumdar and Mehta 2010).

While field hockey as a team sport limits the number of medals won by India at the Summer Games, it is at least a recognized event at the Olympics. Other countries face the problem that their national sport is not even part of the Olympic program. While this also applies to India, where cricket has become over time the most popular sport, it is even worse for a country like Malawi. The nation-state in southeast Africa has never won an Olympic medal. One of the reasons is that netball, one of the most popular women's team sports in many countries in the world (particularly in countries belonging to the Commonwealth, an intergovernmental organization of countries which used to be territories of the former British Empire), is not part of the Olympic program. Malawi belongs to the leading netball countries in the world, ending up 5th and 6th at the last World Cups in 2007 and 2011, and would certainly have chances to win Olympic medals if the sport was an event at the Games.

Most dominant modern sports such as baseball, soccer, cricket, and rugby spread from the West to the "Rest," usually by "neo-colonial, military, missionary and mercantile circuits" (Kummels 2013, 13). However, there are also examples of how sports were exported to the West, such as judo from Japan that became an Olympic sport in 1964. In spite of this "multidirectional flows phenomenon" that leads to a global convergence of sporting cultures, there are also countries with popular indigenous sports such as in Afghanistan the equestrian game buzkashi. Such "pre-modern" and "traditional" sports "are denied recognition as agents of global sports development" (Kummels 2013, 17). Countries with sporting cultures dominated by indigenous sports are less competitive at the Olympics than those nation-states that focus on sports recognized by the IOC.

Given the different popularities of sports, one idea would be to develop a medal ranking that differentiates between high and low profile events. While most people in the world might agree to classify soccer (maybe the only true global sport, which also explains the popularity of the FIFA World Cup) as a high profile event, it might be more difficult with other sports. For example, handball is the second most popular sport in many European countries (such as Germany), but hardly known in North America. China would certainly classify table tennis as a high profile sport, something South American countries might not agree on. Ice hockey is the most popular sport in Canada and Russia, but most developing countries lack the facilities to play the sport and might there-fore oppose the idea to classify it as a high profile event. The same applies to alpine skiing, the leading sport in Austria that "has evolved over the course of the last 130 years into an economic, political and, not the least, symbolic reservoir for identification of national importance" (Müllner 2013, 660). On the contrary, in many developed countries long-distance running is not so popular as it is in Kenya and Ethiopia. The list of differences in the popularity of sports could be much longer, and the examples illustrate the difficulty in compiling a ranking that takes the relevance of sports into consideration in a fair way: "To try to weight the value of the medals won by the priorities of the games in which they were won is impossible because there would be no universal agreement among the countries as to the priorities" (Saaty 2010, 26).

A general trend is that more countries are achieving Olympic success, one of the reasons why in 2015 the first edition of the European Games took place in Baku, Azerbaijan. "The European Games was established to address the alarming decline of the continent's athletes at Olympic level – in 1988 Europe won 74 percent of the available medals, which was down to 37 percent by 2008" (Around the Rings 2015).

Table 2.7 shows the distribution of medals won at the Olympic Summer Games from the Games in Seoul in 1988 to the Games in London 2012. While the number of participating countries increased from 159 to 204 in that period of time, the number of countries winning at least one gold medal also increased from 31, 19.5% of all participating countries, to 54, 26.3% of all participating countries. If one also includes silver and bronze medals, 85 nation-states (41.5% of all participating countries) won at least one medal (Houlihan and Zheng 2013, 338–355). This means a majority of the 204 participating countries (58.3%) did not win any medal in London 2012. The last time that a majority of participating countries won a medal at the Summer Olympic Games was in 1960 (52%) (De Bosscher et al. 2015, 396).

Baimbridge concluded, "The games are an unequal competition between nations" (Baimbridge 1998, 162). He examined the uncertainty of Olympic medal winning, defined as the number of medal-winning nations in relation to those represented. His analysis covered the Summer Olympics from 1896 to 1996. The results were that this indicator fell from a peak national success rate of 90.9% at the London Games of 1908 to a low point of 32.7% 80 years later in Seoul. "The summer Games have become increasingly competitive and thus medals have become relatively harder to win" (De Bosscher et al. 2008, 42).

Two developments have contributed to a larger number of countries winning Olympic medals: New sports were introduced into the Olympic program such as judo (since 1964), table tennis (1988), and badminton (1992) that are popular in countries beyond the traditional Olympic powerhouses of Europe and North America that used to dominate the Olympic medal rankings. Furthermore, rule changes in certain sports such as boxing and judo, where each National Olympic Committee can enter only one athlete per event, are guaranteeing that four different countries will win a medal in each weight category (two bronze medals for both fighters that lost the semi-final) (De Bosscher et al. 2008, 46).

While the data proves that the Olympic Games have become more inclusive over time, there were still 120 participating countries at the London 2012 Summer Games that were not able to win one single medal. The International

Table 2.7 The Distribution of Medals at Summer Olympic Games 1988–2012

Olympic Games	Number of Participating Countries	Number of Countries Winning at Least One Medal	Percentage of Countries That Won at Least One Medal	Number of Countries Winning at Least One Gold Medal	Percentage of Countries That Won at Least One Gold Medal
1988	159	52	32.7	31	19.5
1992	169	64	37.9	37	21.9
1996	197	79	40.1	53	26.9
2000	200	80	40.0	52	26.0
2004	201	74	36.8	56	27.9
2008	205	86	42.1	54	26.5
2012	205	85	41.5	54	26.3

Source: Adapted from Houlihan and Zheng (2013).

Table 2.8 Concentration of Medals at Summer Olympic Games 1988–2012

Year	Total Medals Available	Number of Participating Countries	Number (%) Won by Top 20 Countries	Number (%) Won by Top 30 Countries
1988	739	159	661 (89)	700 (95)
1992	815	169	687 (84)	752 (92)
1996	842	197	599 (71)	706 (84)
2000	928	200	668 (72)	770 (84)
2004	928	201	683 (74)	769 (83)
2008	958	204	689 (72)	794 (83)
2012	962	205	683 (71)	787 (82)

Source: Adapted from Houlihan and Zheng (2013).

Olympic Committee has 206 members in 2016 but only 136 have ever won an Olympic medal (Houlihan and Zheng 2013, 338–355).

While 85 nation-states (41.5% of all participating countries) won at least one medal in London 2012, the Games are still dominated by fewer countries. Table 2.8 shows that the concentration of medals has slightly decreased from 1988 to 2012. While in 1988 in Seoul 89% of all medals were won by the top 20 countries, and even 95% by the top 30 countries, these percentages have decreased to 71% and 82% in 2012. However, this means that out of 962 total available medals, 683 are still won by the top 20, and 787 by the top 30 countries. This means that the other 55 countries that were able to win a medal in London won only 18% (175 medals) of all available medals at the Summer Olympics 2012.

At the London 2012 Olympics, 73.7% of the participating nation-states won no gold medal, and 58.5% of the participating countries won no medal at all. However, these numbers do not reflect the fact that some countries come close to the podium whereas others rank far from the top. An example of a country that closely missed a medal several times is Guatemala. Before the 2012 Summer Olympics, Guatemala had in its Olympic history three 4th place finishes, four 5th places (adding a fifth in London) and four more places between 6th and 8th. In London, Guatemala's bad luck ended and the country won a silver medal in the 20 km race walking (Heijmans 2015c).

Because of performances from countries such as Guatemala who are close to the top (different to nation-states such as Bolivia who end up far away from the podium) some researchers call for "other non-medal based measures of performance" such as winning top eight or top 16 places. For example, 56% of the participating nations won a top eight place at the London 2012 Olympics; 72% of the participating nations won a top 16 place. This is an increase from previous Games, while at the same time the number of participating nation-states increased. For example, in 1988 only 45% of the countries won a top eight place and 47% won a top 16 place. The data by Shibli et al. proves that more countries now invest in Olympic success (Shibli et al. 2013).

3 Olympic Targets

There is a significant number of countries that have very specific targets for the Olympic Games, as Table 3.1 shows. It lists the aims of nation-states for the 2016 Summer Olympics in Rio. The targets were in most cases declared by the respective National Olympic Committee (NOC). In some cases the objectives come directly from the responsible government department such as the ministry of sport. The table includes developing countries such as Afghanistan and Ethiopia, emerging countries such as Brazil and India, and developed countries like Australia and Germany. The table is the result of research I conducted in May 2015, more than one year ahead of the Games in Brazil. There might be more than the 19 country targets I was able to identify in my web search: Some countries might not have yet made their targets public; others might have not been published in English. While the number of my sample of 19 countries is small compared with the 204 participating National Olympic Committees in London 2012 (just 9.3%), the share is larger (22.35%) if a comparison is drawn with only those countries that won medals in London (85). It is obvious from my data that generally only countries that have won medals in the past give medal targets for the future. The table lists only one country that did not win one single medal in London, Nigeria. However, the West African country won 23 medals at previous editions of the Olympic Summer Games.

The most common objective for Rio 2016 is to improve from the previous Summer Olympics in London 2012. Apart from four countries (Kenya, Russia, Thailand, and Trinidad and Tobago), all countries are specifically aiming to increase their medal success. However, this does not mean that the other countries have no ambitions: Russia aims for "Russia's presence among sports superpowers." Russia's ambition is similar to a previously stated objective by China (that is not listed in the table). When China returned to the Olympics in 1984 after being absent for 32 years, it set the target of becoming "a top world sports power by the end of the century" (Riordan and Jinxia 1996, 130–152). Kenya is aiming for 60 participants at the 2016 Summer Olympics, with a "stronger representation in swimming, boxing, volleyball, and other sports disciplines." The case of Trinidad and Tobago is unique, because the twin island country has stated a goal for 2024, and just aims to win "as many gold medals as possible" in Rio 2016 to help meet its goal of winning 10 gold medals by 2024. Thailand

Table 3.1 Countries' Targets for Rio 2016

Country	Target	London 2012 Result
Afghanistan	To win more gold and silver medals	1 medal/IOC rank 79
Australia	One of the top five nations in the medal table	35 medals/IOC rank 10
Botswana	Win at least five medals	1 medal/IOC rank 69
Brazil	To finish the Olympic Games in one of the top 10 positions for the first time ever and winning first Olympic gold in soccer	17 medals/IOC rank 22
Canada	Top 12 finish in the medal table	18 medals/IOC rank 36
Ethiopia	Win 12 medals	7 medals/IOC rank 24
Germany	Exceeding the number of medals won (44) at the London 2012 Summer Olympics	44 medals/IOC rank6
Great Britain	Taking home at least 66 medals from Rio 2016, one more than British athletes won in London 2012	65 medals/IOC rank 3
India	Winning more than 10 medals	5 medals/IOC rank 55
Japan	Finishing third in the gold medal table	38 medals/IOC rank 11
Kenya	Stronger representation in swimming, boxing, volleyball and other sports disciplines by bringing at least 60 athletes	11 medals/IOC rank 28
Netherlands	Ranking among the top ten countries. For selected number of sport disciplines targets have been set to belong to the top eight countries	20 medals/IOC rank 13
New Zealand	Winning 14 medals	13 medals/IOC rank 15
Nigeria	Winning five gold medals, one of them in soccer	0 medals
Russia	Russia's presence among sports superpowers	82 medals/IOC rank 4
Singapore	Winning at least six medals	2 medals/IOC rank 75
South Africa	Winning 10 medals	6 medals/IOC rank 23
Thailand	Send at least 30 athletes and win at least one gold medal	3 medals/IOC rank 57
Trinidad and Tobago	Win as many gold medals as possible in Rio to help meet its goal of winning 10 gold medals by 2024	4 medals/IOC rank 47

aims to send at least 30 athletes to Rio. However, Thailand's goal of a certain number of participants is combined with the objective of winning "at least one gold medal."

Ten countries have declared that they want to win more medals than in London 2012. Afghanistan wants to win "more gold and silver medals." Since the country won only one bronze medal in 2012, and only two bronze medals in its entire Olympic history, this means Afghanistan wants to win in Rio its first silver and gold medals ever. Botswana wants to win five medals in Rio, after winning only one medal in London 2012. Ethiopia wants to improve from seven to 12 medals. Germany wants to win more medals than the 44 won at the London 2012 Summer Olympics. Great Britain's aim of bringing home at least 66 medals from Rio 2016, one more than British athletes won in 2012, is very ambitious, since the country was hosting the 2012 Games and was benefitting from having a much larger team than usual, since athletes from host countries get automatic spots and do not need to qualify for events. After winning five medals in London, India aims for "winning more than 10 medals" in Rio. New Zealand is more modest and wants to win 14 medals, compared with 13 medals at the last Summer Games. After not winning one single medal in London, Nigeria wants to win five gold medals in Rio. Singapore wants to improve from two to "at least" six medals, and finally, South Africa aims for 10 medals in Rio, after winning six medals in London.

Five countries want to move up in the IOC's gold medal count in Rio: Australia wants to move up from position 10 to a top 5 rank; Brazil from 22 to a top 10 rank; Canada from 36 to a top 12 finish; Japan wants to end up third in the gold medal count, after being ranked 11th in London, an ambition that goes along with Japan's vision to be "a world leading sport nation" (Yamamoto 2012, 278). The Netherlands wants to improve from 13 to a top 10 rank. The Australian and Dutch targets are remarkable, given the small size of the countries. Australia has a population of only about 20 million people; the population base in the Netherlands is even smaller (about 16 million). In contrast, Japan is one of the leading economies in the world with 127 million inhabitants. Therefore, its ambitious targets are less surprising than the Dutch and Australian ones.

There are only two countries that have specific goals for certain sports: Brazil and Nigeria state that one of the medals they are aiming for should be the gold medal in soccer, the most popular sport in both countries. There is a men's as well as women's soccer tournament at the Olympics, but both countries most likely refer to the men's competition. Brazil has won the FIFA World Cup five times but never the Olympics. To consider the home games in the domestic public perception as successful, gold in the main national sport seems to be crucial. Nigeria won the Olympic gold medal once in the men's soccer competition in 1996 and wants to repeat its triumph from Atlanta.

The table proves that countries mainly care about quantitative objectives such as the number of medals won or their position in the medal table. Qualitative targets are rare and can be found in only four out of 19 cases: Only Brazil and Nigeria are aiming for success in a specific sport popular in their country (soccer). Given that most countries have a national sport which is only in few cases an individual sport (for instance wrestling in Iran, running in Kenya and Ethiopia), but in most cases a team sport (for example rugby in Australia, New Zealand, and South Africa, soccer in Germany and the Netherlands, field hockey in India and Pakistan, etc.), it is surprising that success in these national sports has not become part of the countries' Olympic aims.

Kenya's objective of a "stronger representation in swimming, boxing, volleyball, and other sports disciplines by bringing at least 60 athletes" to Rio, and Thailand's aim of "sending at least 30 athletes" are other examples of going beyond the common medal (rank) objectives. Given how competitive it is to qualify for Olympic events, the stated aims make perfect sense for a country such as Thailand that is not an Olympic powerhouse, or one that is only good in few sports, such as Kenya in running. Hungary has also taken this same approach in the past. While the country had not yet made public its 2016 objectives at the time of this research, it had stated for the previous London 2012 Games the goal, apart from finishing in the top 20 of the medal table, of "obtaining the right to participate in 20–22 sports, and in the most competitive events possible, proving the versatility of Hungarian sport culture and the diversity of our Olympic traditions and ambitions" (Onyestyák 2013, 769).

Interestingly, no country aims for medals in a certain number of sports. The fact that spreading medals over various events is no objective should be kept in mind when later in the book one key strategy for Olympic success, the specialization of countries in the most medal-promising sports, is discussed. This strategy has become common even among the most developed nation-states.

For some nation-states such as the 75 who have never won a medal at any Olympic Games, there is a different motivation to participate than simply winning a gold, silver, or bronze medal. The next chapter discusses the motives for countries to participate at the Olympics, and includes analysis of sports powerhouses as well as countries that have never won an Olympic medal but aim to participate.

4   Motives

A growing number of countries are becoming increasingly ambitious when it comes to the Olympic Games, and are heavily increasing their elite sport budgets. For example, Houlihan and Zheng have investigated the elite sport policies of eight countries (New Zealand, Spain, Ireland, Norway, United Kingdom, South Korea, Japan, Sweden) and concluded: "In all the countries … there has been a substantial increase in funding allocated to elite sport" (Houlihan and Zheng 2013, 340). According to another comparative study on six countries (Belgium, Canada, Italy, the Netherlands, Norway, and the United Kingdom), the expenditure on sport increased in four of the six sample nations (De Bosscher et al. 2008, 122). In the Netherlands, there is an "increasingly powerful advocacy coalition for elite sport." Between 1999 and 2010, the sport budget multiplied by four (Waardenburg and van Bottenburg 2013, 465). According to Zheng's case study on sport in Hong Kong, there was a "sharp increase in government subvention for the London Olympiad" (Zheng 2015, 7). The German government announced at the end of 2014 that it would increase its budget for the elite sport sector by 15 million euro in 2015, arguing that German athletes would otherwise lose their competitiveness in Rio 2016 (Spiegel Online 2014).

An increasing amount of money is also being spent by the two Olympic superpowers, the United States and China: In China, the total sport budget (national and provincial) has risen dramatically since the mid-1970s. To advance to world sports power status, China has established the principle "Olympic success first" and channeled substantial investment, including over 97% of the national sport budget, into the Olympic sport system (Tan and Houlihan 2012, 146). The total sport budget in China, including national and provincial levels, has almost doubled every five years since 1976 (Tan and Green 2008, 327). Money spent on athletes has also more than doubled in the United States, and this has helped US athletes remain at the top of individual sports (Binns 2009, 50).

Why do nation-states allocate more and more resources into their desire for Olympic success, and participate in the "global sporting arms race?" (Bingham and Shibli 2008). A common argument is that of a "virtuous cycle" in sport: National success in elite sports leads to a higher sport participation, which in turn contributes to public health and widens the pool for talent identification, which contributes again to elite success (see Figure 4.1).

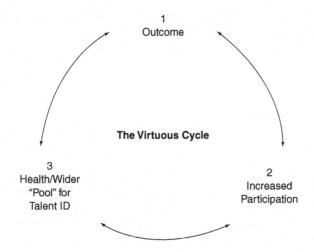

Figure 4.1 The Virtuous Circle (adapted from Grix and Carmichael 2012, 76).

The belief in the "virtuous cycle" is in the interest of many Olympic sports that cannot be operated on a professional level without public support. Only a few sports, such as tennis, are profitable, and have athletes who do not need public funding. A majority of sports, such as bobsleigh, need the status of being an Olympic sport that promises medals to get financial support by the government. However, while some sports such as running attract a mass audience, the example of bobsleigh shows the limits of a trickle-down effect in many Olympic sports. While being one of the leading countries in the sport of bobsleigh, there are for instance less than 10,000 members in the German bobsleigh and skeleton federation ("Bob- und Schlittenverband für Deutschland" 2015). Many authors argue that the so-called "trickle-down effect" lacks empirical foundation: "... The elite sport–participation causality sounds eminently sensible, but there is little evidence to support it" (Ronglan 2014, 4). According to Grix and Carmichael, "the academic literature on the topic provides limited evidence that explores the relationship between elite performers and mass participation in sport" (Grix and Carmichael 2012, 84). When asked in an interview for a book (edited by Haut) on elite sport success about the trickle-down effect, Grix responded: "I have not yet seen any scholarly evidence for a clear connection between the position of a country in the medal ranking system and an increase in sport participation." For Grix it is even the other way around, that the focus on competition discourages people from doing sport (Haut 2014, 43).

The conclusion of a case study on the public funding of sport in Brazil from 2004 to 2011 is that the country witnessed "a decade of promoting elite sport as a priority at the expense of other sports dimensions. ... Our hypothesis is that the privileges granted to elite sport will continue to negatively influence the development of educational and participation sport" (Castro et al. 2015, 14). A case study on the Netherlands comes to similar results: "In the distribution and destination of the rising public sport budget substantially more money was allocated to elite sport" (Waardenburg and van Bottenburg 2013, 471).

While the effect of Olympic success on sporting participation is controversial, inspiring the youth ("sporting legacy") is usually an important argument in Olympic bidding campaigns. However, studies examining the trickle-down phenomenon suggest that the effects of such events on host populations' activity levels are negligible. According to Weed "no reliable evidence was available to indicate that any Games staged to date had raised sport participation in the host community" (Weed 2009, 7). However, Potwarka and Leatherdale argue in their work on trickle-down effects that "researchers should consider more localized participation data among particular sub-populations of host residents" (Potwarka and Leatherdale 2015, 3). While both authors did not find in their work on trickle-down effects at the Vancouver 2010 Winter Olympics any statistically significant changes in Canada or the hosting province of British Columbia (BC), they identified increased sporting activities among female youth living in two of the three regions that housed Vancouver 2010 Olympic venues. Potwarka and Leatherdale call this an "epicenter effect." They conclude in their study that "Targeted and contextual approaches to understanding trickle-down effects may reveal evidence of impact among particular sub-populations rather than concluding such effects do not exist more generally" (Potwarka and Leatherdale 2015, 12).

More important than the supposed "trickle-down effect" might be that "today sport as a cultural institution is a significant contributor to the vitality, vibrancy and international profile of a nation" (Green 2007, 921–922). I will argue in this chapter that nationalism and gaining soft power in world affairs are the main drivers for the desire of countries to aim for sporting success at the Olympics.

The Olympic Games, as "the biggest show on television" (Billings 2008), is the perfect platform for countries since the event consists of competitions between nation-states. This is similar to continental and global championships such as the UEFA European Championship and the FIFA World Cup, but different to other sporting events such as the UEFA Champions League or the Tour de France where teams consist of athletes from different countries. A major difference to all the other mentioned sporting events is that the Olympic Games consist of not all, but many sports, and not just a single sport such as football, cycling, etc. This means that a "true" champion of all the nations can be identified.

For Bairner, "the most powerful form of national performance today may be seen in sport" (Bairner 2015, 375). Why is there the desire to outperform other countries at the Olympics? According to Krüger this is related to the fact that modern nations are products of bloody wars of the nineteenth and twentieth centuries:

> The practice and concept of competitive sport were ennobled by the Olympic spirit in the last decade of the nineteenth century, and offered a convincing alternative for expressing national enthusiasm and aggression

without war. The losers of athletic competitions just "surrender," but are not killed or captured like in wars. One major reason for the global success of competitive sports is that in fact their nonviolent nature was compared very favorably to the horrors of warfare. Competitive sports are able to satisfy the same elementary feelings and needs of humans, such as love and hate, being together and fighting against each other ...

(Krüger 2015, 525)

For the former US ambassador to Finland, Derek Shearer, "Sport in our globalized era is a force for good – for increased international understanding, peaceful competition, and promotion of global citizenship" (Shearer 2014, 57).

The IOC also emphasizes the international spirit of the Olympic Games. Whereas at the FIFA World Cup, the largest mega sporting event apart from the Olympics, only 32 national teams can participate, the Olympics is a sporting event for athletes from all nation-states, and a true global event. Like at the FIFA World Cup, athletes need to qualify for Olympic events, but the IOC also gives in some individual sports Wild Cards to underachieving nations to make sure all countries are represented. It brings people from all over the world together – at the opening and closing ceremonies, in the Olympic village, and at the competitions.

However, while the Olympics might contribute to internationalism, they are in reality mainly a national contestation. Since 1908, nation-states are the only legitimate unit in the Olympic Games. Before 1908 it was not the citizenship but the club membership that was the main criteria for eligibility. For example, there were cases of Swiss members in the German team because they belonged to German clubs (Horne and Whannel 2012, 90).

Citizenship as the main criteria for eligibility to compete at the Games also means that stateless people cannot be athletes at the Olympics. There are about 10 million stateless people in the world today ("Nowhere to Call Home" 2014). Apart from stateless people, the case of illegal immigrants in Israel shows that there are other examples of athletes who cannot compete in the Olympics. Asylum seekers with their families who entered Israel illegally dominate youth running competitions in Israel. These athletes are usually from African countries such as Ethiopia (Kalifa 2015). While they win many championships in Israel, they cannot participate in any international event due to their legal status: they cannot represent Israel in international competitions, since they are not citizens of that country. Israel officially wants to deport illegal immigrants who entered the country, from the government's point of view, solely for economic reasons. The athletes also can not represent their home country on the international level because they are not participating in the respective national qualification events; if they would do so, this would require a voluntary departure from Israel, with no way back. Plans of the IOC for a refugee team in Rio 2016 might also improve the situation for stateless athletes.

The IOC claims in its Olympic Charter that it wants to contribute to building a peaceful and better world. Certainly there are some internationalist rituals at the Games such as the Olympic oath-taking ceremony, the Olympic flag that represents the five continents of the world and the Olympic hymn. For D'Agati, "the Olympics is not a source of nationalism. The Olympics offer only a stage through which a national identity is performed or displayed" (D'Agati 2011, 7). However, the Games are dominated by national symbols. It starts with the Opening Ceremony when the athletes enter the stadium behind their national flag with their national team: "National flags, teams, uniforms, anthems at the victory ceremonies, and the 'unofficial' medal tables in the media – all contribute to an image of the Olympic Games as a symbolic contest between nations" (Horne and Whannel 2012, 109). How serious is such a symbolic contest between countries? Bairner raises the question: "Does sport enflame political nationalism or does it, as one Scottish nationalist argued, simply produce what he called ninety-minute patriots but presumably could also be described as eighty-minute patriots, eighteen hole patriots, nine inning patriots and so on?" (Bairner 2015, 377).

Nationalism is defined as a concept that can have a cultural as well as a political character. The cultural dimension focuses on shared identities based on common language, religion, and traditions, "although nations exhibit various levels of cultural heterogeneity" (Heywood 2013, 109). An example for the cultural dimension of nationalism at the Olympics are the Mongolian athletes in the opening and closing ceremonies: "The flag bearer is quadrennial adorned in native Mongol attire and serves as a constant reminder of that state's ancient past" (D'Agati 2011, 76).

However, the political dimension of nationalism, sovereignty, is more important to understand why countries so heavily invest into Olympic success. Sovereignty has an internal as well as an external component. It is about power within the state as well in the international order (Heywood 2013, 58).

I will link the following four dimensions of political nationalism with the aim of nations to be successful at the Olympics: First, sporting success is a tool of legitimacy for nation-states. Second, sporting success can unify divided nation-states. Third, sport has become a tool for nations to achieve statehood. Finally, winning medals at the Olympic Games can increase the political weight of a country on the international level. Figure 4.2 summarizes the drivers for nationalism at the Olympics, which will be elaborated in detail below.

I will discuss the four dimensions in detail: First, that Olympic success is used as a tool for legitimacy. This does apply to all countries, those who win medals at the Games as well as those who have no or low chances to win medals and cannot prove their importance in the medal count but seek legitimacy solely from their participation. According to Kang et al.:

Sport offers a particularly robust resource for postcolonial or smaller countries that lack historical or other contemporary sources of national recognition. When a country lacks sources for global recognition, such as economy, science, and technology, sport often assumes the burden of inventing the nation-state on the global stage.

(Kang et al. 2015, 100)

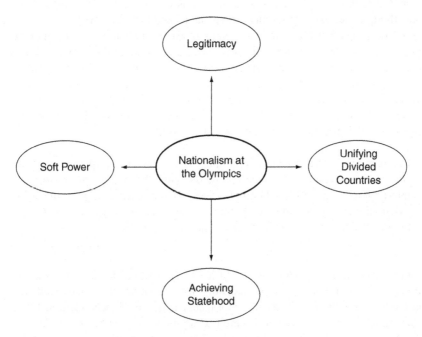

Figure 4.2 Drivers for Nationalism at the Olympics.

One example of a country that seeks legitimacy with its participation at the Games is Stanton's case study "Syria and the Olympics: National Identity on an International Stage." Syria participated in all Olympic Summer Games since 1948, except for 1956 when the country boycotted the Games to protest foreign involvement in the Suez Crisis (Syria has never sent athletes to the Winter Games). Syria has won only three Olympic medals: A Syrian-American who lived in the United States won the first one, a silver medal, in 1984. The country won a gold medal in 1996, and a bronze medal in 2004. Sending small contingents of athletes to each Games without taking home many medals is described by Stanton as a "typical path for a country of its size and resources": "The primary achievement for Syria as for other newly independent states was not medalling in the Olympics, nor even fielding a sizeable cohort, but participating" (Stanton 2014, 6).

The same argument applies to Lebanon, another country studied by Stanton. In 1947, one year after Lebanon achieved full independence, Gabriel Gemayel founded the country's National Olympic Committee (NOC). While the country's medal count has been small, Stanton argues that Lebanon's participation in the Olympics was an important part of a broader effort to develop Lebanese interest and participation in sports, as well as to enhance Lebanon's position among its neighbors and within the international community. Joining the Olympic community provided Lebanon with an international identity centered on sport, human development, and peace – all positive postwar goals, which likely helped make Olympic membership so uncontroversial (Stanton 2012, 2019).

Stanton argues that for countries such as Syria and Lebanon, participation at the Olympics is one of the signs of statehood to gain recognition from the global community of sovereign states. The concept "signs of statehood" has a domestic and an international dimension: On the domestic level, signs of statehood are a functional and universally recognized currency and identity building, like a national anthem. On the international level, acceptance for membership in the United Nations is the most important sign of statehood.

> Membership in the Olympic community by no means compares to United Nations membership – but it should be recognized as a second- or third-tier international sign of statehood. For new states, particularly in the mid-twentieth century, joining the Olympic community seems to have been high on the checklist of "what we do now that we are a state."
>
> (Stanton 2014, 5)

Examples are the many countries of Africa that affiliated themselves to international sports organizations immediately after gaining their independence (Simiyu Njororai 2010, 445). Zambia, for instance, became independent in 1964. In the same year, the National Olympic Committee of Zambia (NOCZ) was formed: "At the Tokyo Olympic Games in 1964, Northern Rhodesia entered the Games as a colony of Britain but it marched out at the closing ceremony as Zambia, a newly independent nation" (Banda 2010, 244). While during colonial times certain sports were mainly expatriate sports, they became more inclusive in the independent, postcolonial societies, and participation in those events at the Olympics was seen as a success, even if no medals were won.

Houlihan and Zheng also discuss the motives of small countries to participate in the Olympics. They argue that the Olympics give small states many highly visible opportunities on an international stage. They share a formal symbolic equality of status with the major (sports) powers most evident in the opening and closing ceremonies. In international sport, there is the "one nation – one vote principle." Finally, the IOC provides small states with development funding from the resources of the Olympic Solidarity program (Houlihan and Zheng 2014, 9).

Not all small countries prove their legitimacy at the Olympics through participation only. There are also small and poor countries that are able to win medals at the Olympics (how they manage to achieve this is discussed later in this book). An example is the small island country of Cuba: "Like all socialist states, from its inception Cuba has relied heavily on the symbolic capital of its sporting prowess, most especially its athletes' international successes, to legitimate the state's presence in the global community of states" (Carter 2008, 200). According to Carter, Cuba is an example of

> the use of sport to support revolutionary claims of state legitimacy and the importance of state control over the infrastructure and practices of sport …

Cuban health care is renowned worldwide with lower death rates per birth than many major United States cities. Its education system is widely regarded as excellent with basic indicators among the highest in the world. Cuban sport, especially its track and field, baseball, and boxing, is also recognized as world-class.

(Carter 2008, 195–196)

(However, Carter is also referring to the joke that the three successes of the Cuban revolution are health, education, and sport but the three failings are breakfast, lunch, and dinner.)

After World War II, Germany and Japan – who were banned from the 1948 Olympics in London – put a lot of emphasis into Olympic success: "These examples show how governments have used the Olympics to legitimize themselves within the International Community, and arguably internally to their own people" (D'Agati 2011, 5). However, not only developed countries that have caused global wars are in need of proving their legitimacy at the Olympics. Nowadays, all nation-states are witnessing external threats by cultural and economic globalization:

51 of the world's 100 largest economies are corporations; only 49 of them are countries. General Motors is broadly equivalent, in this sense, to Denmark; Wal-Mart is roughly the same size as Poland; and Exxon Mobil has the same economic weight as South Africa.

(Heywood 2013, 74)

State power is not only undermined by the power of transnational corporations but also by the limited ability to solve global problems such as climate change on the national level; furthermore, the growing importance of supranational and intergovernmental political organizations such as the European Union (EU) and the World Trade Organization (WTO) have reduced the capacities of the nation-state as well. Seeking legitimacy is something that applies to all countries – from weak states that need to prove that they are able to maintain domestic order, to highly developed countries such as EU Member States who have lost some of their sovereignty to the European Union. Sporting success proves to the domestic population that the nation-state is still capable of solving problems, and contributes to trust in the government.

However, many nation-states are not only under threat from the outside but also from within the state. My second argument is that Olympic success can unify divided nation-states. This might hardly apply to ethnically relatively homogeneous nation-states such as northern European countries like Denmark, Sweden, and Norway where people speak the same language and have state churches (but even in those kind of countries Olympic success can integrate, for example, nationals with an immigration background). Other countries are more diverse: "In Kenya, one can argue that the success in middle and distance running has enhanced feelings of national unity despite the presence of major societal divisions based on class, wealth, ethnicity and language, and along regional and political lines" (Simiyu Njororai 2012, 199). Another example is Canada, a country where people speak mostly English, but in the province of Quebec many speak French. In Belgium there are the Dutch-speaking Flemish and the French speaking Walloons. Spain is a multinational federation: Catalonia, Galicia, the Basque Country, and Andalusia are recognized in Spain as four historic nations (Bickerton and Gagnon 2011, 367–391). For multinational states sports and the Olympic Games are an opportunity to develop a common identity. Consequently, Spain puts a lot of effort in the success of team sports that consist of people from different regions of the country. Spain has won medals at Olympic Games in team sports such as basketball (three times), field hockey (five times), handball (four times), soccer (three times), and water polo (three times).

Lebanon, a multi religious country with 18 state recognized sects, is using sport as an instrument to bring people of different backgrounds together. Lebanon's Olympic teams have broadly reflected the country's religious diversity, with both Christians and Muslims represented on all teams (with the exception of Games in which only one Lebanese athlete competed) (Stanton 2012, 2116).

Canada is another example demonstrating the instrumental use of sport to promote a common identity. For example, in a speech in 1968, Prime Minister Pierre Trudeau argued that sport "could serve as a powerful force for national unity" (Green 2007, 931). Particularly, an Olympic gold medal in the most popular Canadian sport, ice hockey, makes the people in the country happy and contributes to unite the country. This might also influence important political decisions such as the 1995 referendum in Quebec, which resulted in a close decision against Quebec's separation from Canada.

As an expression of unity and to strengthen awareness of a specifically Canadian national identity, Canadian Olympic teams have used the maple leaf emblem since the Olympic Games in 1908, 56 years before the official proclamation in 1964 as Canada's national symbol. On February 15, 1965, the red and white maple leaf flag became the official flag of Canada. The new Canadian flag replaced symbols of British influence in Canadian cultural affairs such as the Union Jack, the national flag of the United Kingdom that has also been part of the Canadian flag, by introducing an emblem of one united body represented by an indigenous symbol. According to Barney and Heine:

> The international visibility of the Olympic spectacle served firmly to position the maple leaf emblem as a dominant signifier of Canadian national identity at home and abroad.... The design sought to overcome connotations of ethnicity, religion and well-imbedded imperial arguments, each of which at one time or another had been implied by the various editions of Canadian flags prior to 1964.
>
> (Barney and Heine 2014, 14)

However, the example of Yugoslavia shows the limits of using the Olympics for ethnic conflict resolution. Yugoslavia was a successful sporting nation that won 87 medals at the Olympic Games, and hosted the Winter Olympics in 1984 in Sarajevo. Despite being a successful sporting nation, there was a rise of nationalism within Yugoslavia in the 1980s. After the Yugoslavia wars in the 1990s, the country split into seven parts: Bosnia and Herzegovina, Croatia, Kosovo, Macedonia, Montenegro, Serbia, and Slovenia. Croatia's third place at the 1998 FIFA World Cup "demonstrated football's role in nation-building" and a "triumph for an ethnic-nation-state" (Hunter 2003, 409–425).

To avoid a similar fate to Yugoslavia's, there are examples of countries that are even competing at the Olymics during civil wars. Syria, for example, competed in the London 2012 Olympics, after the Civil War had already started in 2011. Ten Syrians competed at the London Games, a cohort proudly described by the government as "the country's biggest team since the 1980 Moscow Games." This was considered by the al-Assad government as a sign of its ability "to maintain 'normal' priorities despite the conflict" (Stanton 2014, 10). However, the Syrian athletes who competed received their funding directly from the IOC, rather than through Syria's NOC. The International Olympic Committee wanted to ensure that the athletes were not considered part of the al-Assad government (Stanton 2014, 11).

Lebanon is a similar example. The country was facing a civil war from 1975 until 1990. However, the small Mediterranean nation-state fielded the largest team during the heart of its civil war years, sending 22 athletes to Los Angeles in Summer 1984, and 21 to Seoul in Summer 1988. Since the war ended, the Olympic team numbers have declined. According to Stanton, "Sports provided a key link to the international community at a time when many Lebanese felt disconnected from the outside world" (Stanton 2012, 2115).

It is questionable whether Syria's participation at the 2012 Olympics can contribute to hold the country together, and it remains to be seen whether the country continues to participate as one entity at the Olympics or whether it will fall into different nation-states such as Yugoslavia. Still, the participation of new nation-states at the Olympics has become an important part of their nation building. This leads to my next argument, that the Olympics are used as a tool for nations to achieve statehood.

Coming back to the case of Spain: In Catalonia there is a strong movement to split from Spain, with sport being a major tool for the region to become a separate nation-state. Catalonia has its own National Olympic Committee (NOC). However, the IOC does not recognize it. Kosovo, which declared independence from Serbia in 2008, was for a period of time another unrecognized national Olympic committee before being recognized by the IOC in December 2014. This means that Kosovo, a nation that is not recognized as a nation-state by the United Nations (while the UN recognized all the other six nations from former Yugoslavia) will be able to participate in the 2016 Summer Olympics in Rio. The second most important sport governing body in the world apart from the IOC, FIFA (Fédération Internationale de Football Association), has granted Kosovo some kind of recognition even before the IOC. Since 2014, Kosovo has been allowed to play international friendlies, but the country is not allowed to play its national anthem before the match, or to wear national colors. In the first two years (2014–2016), Kosovo is also not allowed to play against countries from former Yugoslavia.

The IOC has more members than the United Nations. In the 2012 Summer Olympics in London, 204 National Olympic Committees participated whereas the United Nations had only 193 Member States by mid-2014. Palestine is one of the nations that has so far not been recognized by the UN, but has been recognized by the IOC. The IOC recognized it in 1995. The Olympic Games offer Palestine a platform for gaining recognition from the international community for its desire for national self-determination and a two-state solution in the Israeli–Palestinian conflict. Palestine has been a UN-observer since 2012, another step toward its recognition as a nation-state.

Due to the "state-centric view of world politics" (Ryan 2005, 137–154) it is likely that the number of nations seeking recognition as a nation-state and using sports as a "language of nationalist self-expression" (Morgan 1999, 50–67) will increase in the future.

The world has witnessed a significant growth of nation-states. From its 51 founding members in 1945, the United Nations has almost quadrupled the number of members to 193 in 2014, with South Sudan being the most recent recognized UN state in 2011. The last main wave of state creation happened after the dissolution of Yugoslavia and the Soviet Union, and the world consists of far more nations than nation-states. Today, the Kurds are the largest ethnic group without their own state. The Kurdish population is spread over four countries (Iran, Iraq, Syria, and Turkey) (Ryan 2005, 137–154). There are about 36 million Kurds living in the region with about half of them in Turkey (Danziger 2012, 116). Like Catalonia, Kurdistan has an unrecognized National Olympic Committee. As the Football Federation (KFF) president Safin Kanabi was quoted, "We want to serve our nation and use sports to get everything for our nation" (Dorsey 2015).

In Scotland, an independence referendum took place in September 2014. This was one of the reasons for the Scottish Olympic Committee to not allow Scottish football players to play on the team UK men's football team at the London 2012 Summer Olympics. However, there won't be a Scottish team at the Rio 2016 Olympics since a narrow majority of the Scottish population decided to remain in the United Kingdom. However, there will also be no Great Britain soccer team in Rio 2016 as there was in the 2012 Games (the last time a British soccer side entered the Games before London was in 1960). This applies to the men's as well as to the women's soccer event. FIFA required full agreement between England, Scotland, Wales, and Northern Ireland. However, there were concerns particularly from the Scottish and Welsh football association: "The other home nations had feared a united British team could risk their independence within FIFA and insisted that entering a team at London 2012 was a one-off due to it being a home Games" (Smith 2015).

It is one of the particularities of international sport that England, Scotland, Wales, and Northern Ireland are in FIFA and other international sporting federations such as rugby as separate entities, while the International Olympic Committee requires a united team Great Britain at the Olympic Games. A counter-example is Monaco. Monaco is a member of many international organizations, including the United Nations. While the IOC has recognized Monaco's National Olympic Committee and the city-state has been participating in the Olympic Games since 1920 (being the country with the most appearances that never won any medal), FIFA does not recognize the microstate of less than 40,000 inhabitants. Monaco's only professional football club, AS Monaco, plays in the French league (Menary 2007, 112).

Sometimes countries are organized in different continental sporting associations. For example, in 2005 Australia's soccer team moved from the Oceania Football Federation (OFF) to the Asian Football Federation (AFC), but a similar move was rejected by the Olympic Council of Asia in 2007, making it impossible for Australia to participate in the Asian Games, a kind of continental version of the Olympic Games that is recognized by the IOC. Australia's move within the world of soccer was motivated by having more competitive games and having better chances to qualify for the FIFA World Cup, since Asia has four guaranteed spots at the FIFA World Cup while the winner of the Oceania region is not automatically qualified and faces a play-off match against a South American or Asian country (Menary 2007, 4, 6). Kazakhstan is a similar example: It switched in soccer from Asia (AFC) to Europe (UEFA) in 2004, but in the Olympics it is still an Asian country that is participating in the Asian Games as it did successfully in Incheon, South Korea, in 2014 when it ranked 4th in the medal table.

I agree with Menary that there is "arbitrariness of international status" in sport and there are no clear standards or requirements for achieving recognition (Menary 2007). While the special status of England, Scotland, Wales, and Northern Ireland can be explained historically (they belonged from the beginning to most international sporting federations), there is no rationale of still allowing them to compete by their own while Catalonia, for example, is denied to do so. Menary gives in his book *Outcasts: The Lands that FIFA Forgot* another example of FIFA's arbitrariness: The different treatment of the nations of Zanzibar and New Caledonia. According to the FIFA statute, associations are recognized that are "an independent state recognized by the international community." Zanzibar is an African island that is part of Tanzania while New Caledonia is French territory located in the southwest Pacific Ocean east of Australia. "The African island's situation bears many similarities with New Caledonia. Neither territory is in the United Nations (UN) but both are members of one of the six regional confederations that provide FIFA with its membership" (Menary 2007, 1). However, "international community" is a vague term that leaves space for different interpretations. New Caledonia was admitted to FIFA in 2004, while Zanzibar was not a member as of October 2015.

When the IOC recognized Kosovo in 2014, the Serbian Sports Minister Vanja Udovicic attacked the IOC's decision as a "precedent" that could have "serious consequences for the global system of sports" ("IOC Grants Full Olympic

Recognition to Kosovo" 2014). However, Kosovo's recognition was by no means a precedent. Disputes about the recognition of National Olympic Committees are as old as the Olympic movement. For example, at the 1908 Games in London there was a conflict about the participation of the nations of the Austro-Hungarian Empire. Austria, Bohemia, and Hungary were allowed to represent different nations. However, the participation of those athletes serving in the army of the Empire was restricted:

> A special verdict forbade their participation in the national team; they were forbidden to compete in international events as Hungarians until 1908. Just before the London Games, this restriction was relieved for individual athletes, but Hungarian fencers, who were also soldiers of the Monarchy, were still not allowed to participate in the team events.
>
> (Onyestyák 2013, 762)

Finland participated in every edition of the Summer and Winter Olympic Games since 1908, despite not gaining its independence from the Russian Empire until 1917. The national identity of the Finnish people, who were under Swedish rule for centuries before the Russian Empire, was built through sports, and particularly remarkable successes of Finish athletes at the Olympic Games: "Finnish athletes were amongst the first to take international sport seriously. The new field of sport offered an ideal platform for the development of cultural values and the formation of national identity" (Koski and Lämsä 2015, 16).

Apart from Kosovo, there are other examples of nations who received recognition by the IOC but not the UN, such as Palestine. The IOC recognizes all 193 UN member states of the UN, the last one was South Sudan, becoming the 206th IOC member in August 2015.

At the beginning of 2015, the IOC had 12 more members than the UN, with Kosovo the 205th national Olympic committee being recognized. Table 4.1 lists the 13 nations with National Olympic Committees that were recognized by the IOC but did not succeed in becoming members of the United Nations. A majority of the non-UN but IOC members are small nations, five of them have less than 100,000 inhabitants. Another five (Chinese Taipei, Hong Kong, Kosovo, Palestine, Puerto Rico) of the 13 nations have more than one million inhabitants, Chinese Taipei (Taiwan) being the largest one of them with a population of about 23 million.

Taiwan's participation under the name Republic of China (ROC) in the Olympics was the reason for China's boycott of the Olympics until the 1980 Winter Olympics in Lake Placid. China demanded from the IOC and international sporting federations a one-China policy. In 1979 an agreement was found that allowed both China (People's Republic of China, PRC) and Taiwan (ROC) to participate in the Olympics:

> Finally, the name "Chinese Taipei" made it sound as though Taiwan was a province of China. The new IOC chairman Juan Antonio Samaranch presented

Table 4.1 IOC Members That Are Not Recognized by the United Nations

National Olympic Committee (NOC)	IOC Member Since	Population Size (2014)
Aruba	1986	110,663
American Samoa	1987	54,517
Bermuda	1936	69,839
British Virgin Islands	1982	32,680
Cayman Islands	1976	54,914
Chinese Taipei	1960	23,359,928
Cook Islands	1986	10,134
Guam	1986	161,001
Hong Kong	1951	7,112,688
Kosovo	2014	1,859,203
Palestine	1995	4,420,495
Puerto Rico	1948	3,620,897
Virgin Islands	1967	104,170

Source: Own elaboration. Population figures adapted from "The World Factbook," *Central Intelligence Agency*, www.cia.gov/library/publications/the-world-factbook/rankorder/2119rank.html?countryname=Argentina&countrycode=ar&regionCode=soa&rank=33#ar.

the formula to Taiwan and pleaded with them to accept it, promising that the Olympics would always treat Taiwan as an equal and with respect. In the end, Taipei agreed only because it would otherwise lose out completely.

(Cha 2009, 101)

Taiwan boycotted the 1980 Olympic Games, but since 1984 both countries – China and Taiwan – have participated in all Olympic Games. After China's return to the Olympics, only 23 small states continued to officially acknowledge Taiwan. South Korea continued to align with Taiwan until 1992 before closing the South Korean embassy in Taipei and opening one in Beijing. Taiwan tries to develop its national identity "under the shadow of the powerful PRC," while at the same time there is mistrust of South Korea in the country since 1992. Nevertheless taekwondo, a sport invented in Korea,

continued to gain support in Taiwan as the most successful sport to bring global recognition to Taiwan in the international athletics scene. Taekwondo gave the first ever gold medal to Taiwan at the Olympics in the 2004 Athens Games, and has since brought a total of seven Olympic medals to the country.

(Kang et al. 2015, 103)

Apart from participating and winning medals at the Olympics, Taiwan has also recently been successful in bidding for international sporting events, another milestone in attempts to use sports diplomacy for its international recognition. It hosted the 2009 Deaflympics, the 2009 World Games, and won in 2011 its bid to the International University Sports Federation (FISU) to host the 2017 World University Games. For Lee and Li "it is a landmark that Taipei won its bid to host the highest level sporting event ever in Taiwanese history, an event that is second in size only to the Olympics (and which is known as the Junior Olympics)" (Lee and Li 2015, 1053). They conclude in their research on Taiwan's successful bid that the experience of having hosted international sporting events, having existing facilities and venues, and having tacit consent and support from China were all important contributing factors to Taiwan's success. The latter was the most important factor, since Chinese authorities believed in the past that Taiwan was likely to use international mega sporting events to promote the image of "Two Chinas" or "One China and One Taiwan." However, this changed after a more Beijing-friendly party gained power in 2008 (Lee and Li 2015, 1044–1056).

Hong Kong is a former British colony that returned to China's sovereignty in 1997. Hong Kong started to participate in the National Games of China immediately after 1997 rather than in the Commonwealth Games, while continuing to participate in the Olympics as its own entity. Under the "One Country, Two Systems" principle, Hong Kong enjoys a high degree of autonomy in all areas, among them sport, except for diplomacy and defense. Similar to the case of Taiwan, the official name of Hong Kong at the Olympics is "Hong Kong, China." Hong Kong delegations can use the regional flag but the national anthem of the People's Republic of China has to be played in medal ceremonies. Hong Kong has so far won three Olympic medals, two of them after 1997 with the Chinese anthem played at the medal ceremony. According to Zheng's case study on sport in Hong Kong, "Hong Kong has evolved from a sporting desert to a region that has achieved some sporting breakthroughs in the last two decades" (Zheng 2015, 2). The highlight was hosting the equestrian events of the 2008 Beijing Olympic Games and Paralympic Games. However, "the relatively 'honeymoon relationship' between the sports community in Hong Kong and that in Mainland China may be threatened by an increased degree of 'Mainlandphobia' within civil society in Hong Kong" (Zheng 2015, 14).

Puerto Rico is a US territory. Residents of the island have been American citizens since 1917 and have served in the US military. However, residents cannot vote for president or senate, and have only one nonvoting delegate in the House of Representatives. While Puerto Rico has its own National Olympic Committee, "from a constitutional perspective, Puerto Rico belongs to the United States. The federal government has almost absolute power over Puerto Rico, but has delegated to Puerto Rico about the same authority over local matters that the states possess" (Pierluisi 2015). At the Summer Olympics, Puerto Rico has won eight medals, six of them in boxing. Different to other nations that have a recognized NOC, Puerto Rico is not aiming for independence. In 2012, Puerto Rican voters rejected territorial status and expressed a preference for statehood. Congress responded by authorizing a federally sponsored referendum that might be held in 2017 (Pierluisi 2015).

When the IOC recognized Kosovo, it argued that Kosovo met the sports and technical requirements for acceptance, including the definition of a "country" in the Olympic Charter as "an independent state recognized by the international community." The IOC said Kosovo's national Olympic body, which was set up in

1992, has more than 30 affiliated national sports federations, including 13 from Olympic sports. Six of those are full members of international federations (archery, judo, sailing, table tennis, and modern pentathlon). However, apart from the lack of recognition by the United Nations, there are important countries such as the United Nations Security Council members Russia and China, which have not recognized Kosovo. By the end of 2014, 110 countries had recognized Kosovo, including 23 of the 28 EU Member States, and 24 of NATO's 28 members ("IOC Grants Full Olympic Recognition to Kosovo" 2014; Dorsey 2015).

In the long term, the number of IOC members might further grow. There are between 3,000 and 5,000 national communities and 575 potential nation-states (Ryan 2005, 137–154). "Some scholars predict that the current reorganization of states based on nationality identities will produce more than 50 new states and that nation-based conflicts might remain the major cause of violence and instability" (Danziger 2012, 126). Related to sports, Menary notes that:

> in places where identity is slowly starting to mean less and less, in an age of globalization where satellite TV is watering down local sports in favor of global brands, some peoples are trying to keep alive an identity that is being lost ...
>
> (Menary 2007, 188)

Table 4.2 lists 15 unrecognized National Olympic Committees I was able to identify by mid-2014 (there might be even more). Usually, athletes from these unrecognized NOCs compete for other countries at the Olympics. For example,

Table 4.2 Unrecognized National Olympic Committees

Unrecognized NOCs	Population Size
Abkhazia	240,705
Anguilla	16,086
Catalonia	7,518,903
Faroe Islands (recognized Paralympic Committee)	49,709
Gibraltar	29,185
Kurdistan	28,000,000
Macau	597,914
Montserrat	5,215
New Caledonia	267,840
Niue	1,611
Northern Cyprus	265,100 (2006)
Northern Mariana Islands	51,483
Somaliland	3,500,000
South Ossetia	51,547
Turks and Caicos	49,070

Source: Own elaboration. Population figures adapted from "The World Factbook," *Central Intelligence Agency*, www.cia.gov/library/publications/the-world-factbook/rankorder/2119rank.html?countryname=Argentina&countrycode=ar&regionCode=soa&rank=33#ar.

athletes from Catalonia compete for Spain; athletes from Kosovo competed before Kosovo's IOC recognition usually for Albania since people of Albanian descent largely populate Kosovo. Transnistrians have represented several countries since 1992, mostly Moldova. Abkhaz-born competitors have represented Georgia, Russia, and Ukraine. In 2012, the first Turkish-Cypriot athlete competed at the Olympics, representing Turkey (Heijmans 2014).

Most unrecognized NOCs have, different to the recent success cases of Palestine and Kosovo, low chances of getting recognized by the IOC in the near future, given their low support in the international community. While Kosovo, as noted above, was recognized by more than half of all countries (110) before being recognized by the IOC, South Ossetia and Abkhazia, for example, are only recognized by Russia, Nicaragua, Venezuela, and Nauru. The Turkish Republic of Northern Cyprus is recognized internationally only by one country, which is (not surprisingly) Turkey (Heijmans 2014).

There are examples of associations and international sporting events formed as a platform for nations that are not recognized by the IOC or any of the international sport governing bodies recognized by the International Olympic Committee. Examples are the Viva World Cup organized by the New Federation Board, and the ConIFA World Football Cup organized by ConIFA. Both organizations organize alternative soccer World Cups for teams that represent nations, dependencies, unrecognized states, minorities, stateless peoples, regions, and micro-nations not affiliated to FIFA. Organizations such as the New Federation Board and ConIFA operate outside the jurisdiction of the IOC and its international sporting federations. Apart from the lack of global recognition, members also do not receive the development money that other members from IOC and the international federations such as FIFA usually receive. According to Menary umbrella federations such as ConIFA and New Federation Board "act as a waiting room" for places either trying to get into FIFA as well as those like Occitania or Sápmi (more commonly, but pejoratively, known as Lapland) for whom football served as a vehicle to project their unique identity and for whom membership in FIFA would be impossible (Menary 2007). However, unrecognized nations need to take into consideration that playing matches against politically controversial opponents such as the Turkish Republic of Northern Cyprus might imperil their own position with respect to official football authorities.

Moving to my fourth point, the power perspective, which explains why Olympic success has become a policy priority around the globe. The 1936 "Nazi Games" in Germany were an extreme example of a country showcasing its power to the world:

> The Berlin Games remain the most memorable and by far the worst example of using the Olympics for an ethnical or racial stage and also of using the Olympics as an opportunity for reinventing a national identity. Since the Nazi Games, the Olympic Movement and many states have condemned using the Olympics for such practices, but in fact the practice has continued unabated.
>
> (D'Agati 2011, 6)

While the 1936 Games served to prove supposed supremacy of the Aryan race, during the Cold War, countries tried to prove the superiority of one political and economic system over another. Sport became a substitute for actual warfare, and according to D'Agati, the Olympics became a new battleground for Cold War politics that allowed the participating nations to compete against each other in an acceptable manner: "Sports, from as early as 1952 and through 1992, were one of a few arenas for direct competition between the two superpowers, which had already rejected the use of actual warfare to settle the irreconcilable differences between them" (D'Agati 2013, 7).

Particularly for the Soviet Union Olympic success was "a metaphor for the greatness of the Soviet state" (D'Agati 2013, 5). While one of the most famous Olympic Cold War stories is the "miracle on ice" when the Soviet ice hockey team was defeated in the 1980 Winter Olympics by the underdogs at that time, the United States, the Soviet Union outnumbered the United States at the Lake Placid Games by 22:12 in the total medal count and 10:6 in the gold medal ranking. "While the US-versus-USSR hockey tournament was an unexpected success for the United States, it is impossible to suggest that the Soviet Union lost anything more than a symbolic victory in Lake Placid" (D'Agati 2013, 104).

According to Carter, "Sport was the only arena in which the Soviet bloc was able to demonstrate superiority over the world's industrialized capitalist nations" (Carter 2008, 200). For example, at the 1976 Olympic Games on North American soil in Montreal, the Soviet Union finished first and the GDR second. Particularly the performance of East Germany was remarkable, given the small population size of just 16 million. The country won 90 medals at the 1976 Summer Games: "Montreal cemented the GDR's position as the world's leading sports nation, an unofficial title that granted the country international and domestic respect that it lacked in many other areas" (McDougall 2013, 841). At the Winter Olympic Games 1980 in Lake Placid, the GDR athletes gained more medals than any other team. "The GDR was by far the most successful younger brother in the socialist or communist family behind the Iron Curtain. The East German athletes were so successful that they gradually threatened the sporting dominance of big brother Soviet Union" (Krüger et al. 2015, 53). For the GDR, "Sports was a way to justify the state" (Johnson 2008). GDR athletes were referred to as "diplomats in track suits" (Krüger et al. 2015, 19).

However, the world has changed, and for the first time there are more democratic than non-democratic countries. In the last four decades, the number of countries in the world where the public can elect its representatives has more than tripled: As Table 4.3 shows, there were 39 electoral democracies in 1974, 76 in 1990, and 125 in 2014, the latter representing almost two-thirds (64%) of all countries in the world. The explosion in transitions to democracy occurred in the aftermath of the fall of the Berlin Wall in 1989. This is also called the third wave of democratization.

The first wave lasted from 1826 to 1926, and was then reversed in part by the rise of fascism and authoritarianism in the 1920s and 1930s; the second

Table 4.3 Electoral Democracies in the World

Year	Number of Electoral Democracies	Total Number of Countries	Total Percentage of Electoral Democracies
2014	125	195	64
2000	120	192	62.5
1990	76	165	46
1974	39	142	27.5

Source: Adapted from Freedom House, http://freedomhouse.org/.

Note
As defined by Freedom House, an "electoral democracy" should satisfy the following criteria: A multiparty, competitive political system; universal adult suffrage for all citizens; regularly contested elections paired with ballot security, ballot secrecy, absence of voter fraud, and results reflective of the will of the public; substantial public access of major political parties to the electorate, through media and open political campaigning.

wave came after the Second World War and was reversed in the 1960s and 1970s; the third wave was initiated in Portugal in 1974 and reached explosive levels after 1989.

(Mair 2011, 111)

Democracies are less likely to be at war with each other – this is called the "democratic peace" theory (Kinsella et al. 2012, 123–124). However, choosing similar models of free markets and liberal democracies does not mean that countries have become equal: "Although their rights and responsibilities as laid out in international law may be identical, their political weight in world affairs varies dramatically" (Heywood 2013, 58). Sport offers an arena to compete with each other in a "global sporting arms race" (Bingham and Shibli 2008) to gain international prestige by means other than expansionist nationalism. One could argue that the world has changed from the "Cold War" to "The New Gold War" (the latter is a headline from an article in the *Wall Street Journal*) (Johnson 2008).

Whereas one might criticize the new "gold war" from different angles, for example by arguing that financial resources could be better used for other societal needs, this kind of "war" is certainly better than a real war where opponents meet on the battlefield instead of on the sports field. While modern sports might sometimes cause tensions between countries, they also contribute, according to Krüger, to the spread of secularism and equality in the world:

Islamism and Islamic terrorism are not least motivated by a fundamental challenge from Western culture and civilization that is regarded as faithless and sinful. No doubt, modern sport is part of the powerful tradition of that Western culture and civilization.

(Krüger 2015, 518)

Nye has invented the term "soft power." According to Nye "power means the ability to influence the behavior of others to get the outcomes one wants" (Nye 2004, 1). He differentiates between military, economic, and soft power, and defines the latter as a country's

> ability to get what you want through attraction rather than coercion or payments ... When you can get others to admire your ideals and to want what you want, you do not have to spend as much on sticks and carrots to move them in your direction. Seduction is always more effective than coercion.
>
> (Nye 2004, Preface)

Sport is a popular tool for gaining soft power because little else attracts the masses as much as sport. Organizing mega sporting events and investing in elite sport successes can be for countries a "vehicle to global recognition" and to achieve geopolitical goals (Cornelissen 2010, 3008–3025). According to Grix:

> Sport is clearly part of a soft power strategy and hosting sports mega-events – especially the Olympics – is clearly considered by states to provide a major contribution in the process of improving their nation's image, profiling and showcasing themselves globally and attracting others through inbound tourism, increased trade and a growing sense of national pride through the often experienced, but under-researched feel-good factor that accompanies major sport events.
>
> (Grix 2013, 15–25)

For the former US ambassador to Finland, Shearer, "sport can change a country's brand" (Shearer 2014, 53). When it comes to the Olympics, they can, according to D'Agati, be seen "as a vehicle for identity formation and reformation on a scale unmatched in any mere domestic manifestation" (D'Agati 2011, 184).

According to Nye, the soft power of a country rests primarily on three resources: its culture (in places where it is attractive to others), its political values (when it lives up to them at home and abroad), and its foreign policies (when they are seen as legitimate and having moral authority). Sport fits mainly with the first resource, culture. Nye points out that within culture there is also "popular culture, which focuses on mass entertainment" (Nye 2004, 10). Sport certainly serves mass entertainment purposes. Other examples are movies, music, television, technology, and universities, sources that have particularly contributed to the soft power of the United States: "Much of American soft power has been produced by Hollywood, Harvard, Microsoft, and Michael Jordan" (Nye 2004, 17). Michael Jordan is a former professional basketball player in the National Basketball Association (NBA) and is considered to be one of the best players of all time. He is known across the whole world.

Nye also links the second category of soft power, political values, with the sports sector:

Even popular sports can play a role in communicating values. An America is created that is neither military hegemon nor corporate leviathan – a looser place, less rigid and more free, where anyone who works hard shooting a ball or handling a puck can become famous and (yes) rich. And the numbers are large. National Basketball games are broadcast to 750 million households in 212 countries and 42 languages. Major league baseball games flow to 224 countries in 11 languages. The National Football League's Super Bowl attracted an estimated 800 million viewers in 2003. The number of sports viewers rivals the 7.3 billion viewers worldwide who went to see American movies in 2002.

(Nye 2004, 47)

For the former US ambassador to Finland, Shearer, "in a globalized world, sport is a vital part of almost every country's soft power" (Shearer 2014, 56). An example is an aid program led by outstanding Chinese coaches to promote table tennis, the most popular sport in China, in Africa (Chen et al. 2015, 2). Nye agrees that

Soft power is available to all countries, and many invest in ways to use soft-power resources to "punch above their weight" in international politics.... Even if they do not have the overall power resources to match the largest countries, smaller or less powerful countries still can present challenges greater than their military size would imply.

(Nye 2004, 89)

An example given by Nye is Norway, which "has developed a voice and presence out of proportion to its modest size and resources." Norway is, according to Nye, "a force for peace in the world: Conflict mediation, allocation of significant funds to foreign aid; and its frequent participation in peacekeeping forces." The case of Norway is an excellent example of how the sports sector helps a country to "punch above its weight" in global affairs: The Olympics Winter Games ranking is led by Norway, and being ranked 11th in the overall ranking of the total number of medals ever won at Summer as well as Winter Games is also a remarkable achievement for a country of about five million people. According to Nye, "Soft power includes shaping others' perceptions" (Nye 2004, 115). Norway's sporting success helped the country to create a favorable image in public opinion in other countries.

Ernst & Young tried to operationalize the soft power concept by developing a respective index. The number of Olympic medals a country has won is included in the Soft Power Index. Soft power is defined as the ability of a country to influence other states without hard power, defined as threats or payoffs. There are three variables: global integrity, global integration, and the global image of a country. The three variables are comprised of different indicators. The number of Olympic medals a country won at the Olympics is one of the indicators for the global image of a country, apart from the export of media goods, the popularity of its language, the number of its citizens who are global icons and the number of its companies that are globally admired (Ernst & Young 2015).

When I interviewed Nye, he was skeptical about the soft power index. He argued indexes are "problematic" because they are based on resources. "But an increase of resources does not necessarily lead to an increase in the outcome, because soft power depends on the recipient." For example, the Summer Olympics in 2008 were very successful for China. Apart from a Chinese city (Beijing) being the host, China won more gold medals than any other country at the event. However, the crackdown on human rights activists after the event, and the jailing of Nobel Peace Laureate Liu Xiaobo (and his famous empty chair at the Oslo ceremony) significantly affected China's attractiveness, and were examples of how some of the soft power gains can be lost in just a brief period of time (Nye in discussion with the author).

Another example is Russia's soft power success at the Sochi Winter Olympics 2014. Apart from hosting the event, Russia won the medal ranking at the 2014 Sochi Winter Olympics. The last time Russia won the winter medal ranking was in 1994 when the Winter Olympics took place in Lillehammer, Norway. Returning 20 years later to 1st position in the medal ranking goes along with the Russian narrative around its home Games, branding a new image of its greatness to the domestic population as well as the global audience (Müller 2011, 2091). Russia only hosted the Olympic Games once before, in 1980, when the Summer Games in Moscow were boycotted by a US-led bloc of more than 50 countries. According to Ostapenko:

> thus the Sochi Games may be not only the first winter Olympics ever held in Russia but also a huge international "comeback opportunity" to present a stronger, better, more glamorous Russia as well as to re-position the country's image globally.
>
> (Ostapenko 2010, 60)

Müller agrees, and argues that the Sochi 2014 Winter Olympics were characterized by "a nationalist narrative which frames the Olympic Games not primarily as a stimulus for economic development and global competitiveness but as a contribution to Russian greatness" (Müller 2011, 2091). For Persson and Petersson, the Winter Games in Sochi in 2014

> are discursively constructed as a manifestation of Russia's return to great power status. In official Russian discourse, there is an encounter between the Russian great power myth and the myth of Olympism, both of which are employed to strengthen the status of Russia and of President Putin personally.
>
> (Persson and Petersson 2014, 192)

However, Russia's uses of hard power in Crimea lead to a loss of its soft power gains (Nye 2014). For the former US ambassador to Finland, Shearer, "a potential problem with hosting a mega sports event in today's globalized media environment is that the host country cannot control the message received" (Shearer 2014, 55).

Another example is New Zealand, a small country with only 4.5 million people, that has the ambition to "punch above its weight" in global sports and international affairs. With so far 100 Olympic medals won, sport has certainly made a major contribution to put New Zealand "on the map" (Sam 2015, 5). However with its politcally controversial decision to compete in the country's main sport, rugby, against South Africa during the time of Apartheid, it lost sympathy all over the world, and even caused a boycott of African countries of the 1976 Montreal Summer Olympics.

Nye argues that we are living in a unipolar world when it comes to military power whereas on economic and other issues the world is much more multipolar (Nye 2004, 2). However, if it comes to sport, the United States has consistently been an Olympic superpower, only its main competitors have changed. That's why Morgan calls the Olympics a platform for a "discourse of dominant nations" (Morgan 1999, 50–67). The first US rivalry was with the United Kingdom. "During the Cold War, America's primary competitor in soft-power resources was the Soviet Union, which engaged in a broad campaign to convince the rest of the world of the attractiveness of its communist system" (Nye 2004, 73). Investments into Olympic sporting success became part of this competition over the supremacy of communism, and accordingly capitalism. Since the end of the Cold War, China has become the new rival to the United States, reflecting the struggle for title of the leading economic power in the world ("NBS Summer Seminar" 2012).

Dyreson writes in his book *Crafting Patriotism for Global Dominance: America at the Olympics* that beginning with the first modern Olympic Games in 1896 in Athens,

> the United States launched a concerted effort to make the Olympics into referendums on national prowess. Though other nations have certainly used the Olympics to fuel nationalistic uprisings, the United States has been crafting patriotism for longer and with greater vigor than any other polity.
>
> (Dyreson 2009, 2)

The Olympics have been the perfect stage for the United States, because the global sport of soccer and the FIFA World Cup were for a long time not popular in the country, while at the same time popular domestic sports such as American football and baseball failed to spread globally. Also, Nye notes that the country's general disadvantage for using sport as a soft power tool is that "soccer, Europe's primary sport, is far more popular globally than American football or baseball" (Nye 2004, 76). Hence, the United States had to look to other sports and events for international competitions.

Apart from putting much emphasis in sporting success at the Olympics, the United States has also hosted the Games eight times, more than any other country in the world. According to Dyreson, Olympic sports garnered "enormous prestige around the world" for the United States, and the federal government tried to Americanize the world through sport "by promoting American Olympic teams as international advertisements for American way of life," particularly by globalizing "the cult of consumption" and the "desire to sell expensive sporting equipment to the rest of the world" (Dyreson 2009, 157). Starting from the 1920s and 1930s "swimming fit neatly into the folds of American sporting nationalism" (Dyreson 2009, 162). American companies could sell expensive pools and equipment to the global leisure class, while American athletes were dominating the swimming competitions at the Summer Games. A recent trend at the Olympics is "Californication." While this term is usually used to describe the influence of the "golden state" on American culture, California is often even able to influence global developments:

> California incubated mountain-biking, snowboarding, triathlon and beach volleyball, as it has incubated so many other cultural movements since the middle of the twentieth century, from surfing and Hollywood cinema to personal computers and the "summer of love." Beneath the alleged globalization of the Olympics rests an architecture of Americanization.
>
> (Dyreson 2009, 174)

For other countries, the promotion of Olympic success is a tool to emerge on the global stage. According to a case study on the public funding of sport in Brazil from 2004 to 2011:

> although educational sport is a clearly identified priority in the Federal Constitution, and participation sport was prioritized in government planning during the years we have analyzed, the federal government opted to execute a budget that prioritized elite sport and, more specifically, the promotion of a specific sporting event, that is, the 2007 Pan and Para Pan Games.
>
> (Castro et al. 2015, 11)

The rationale was that investments in sport should not only have an impact on the internal developments, as in the case of educational or participation sport. They also should increase the visibility of the country on the global scene: "Investments in sports must have an impact on Brazil's status on a global level, and many people believe that this can be achieved through the development of elite sport" (Castro et al. 2015, 13).

According to Tan and Houlihan, for China, sporting success has been both a barometer of domestic modernization and changing international status. There is

> the country's need for international respect and affirmation as a world power and the desire to distance itself from the "century of humiliation" that dated from the middle of the nineteenth century, and the desire to lose the label of the "sick man of East Asia."

There has been a "change in sports diplomacy objectives, from the 'friendship first, contest second' concern of the 1970s to the contemporary concern with demonstrating China's modernization and rapid economic progress through topping the Olympic and Paralympic medals tables and hosting sports mega-events" (Tan and Houlihan 2012, 134).

Apart from the struggle for global hegemony, the Olympics are a platform for regional rivalries such as the one between Australia and New Zealand, as well as the struggle for regional hegemony such as in Latin America between Venezuela and Brazil.

For some countries the concept of soft power is related to a very basic goal of every state: Security: "Survival is the fundamental element of security. It entails the very existence of the state, such that other states do not conquer it and that internal forces do not destroy it" (Danziger 2012, 123). One example is that of Qatar that invests in sporting success for reasons of national security. According to Dorsey:

> soft power is a key Qatari defense and security strategy based on the realization that it will never have the military strength to defend itself irrespective of what hardware it acquires or the number of foreigners it recruits to populate its armed forces.
>
> ("The Turbulent World of Middle East Soccer" 2014)

Qatar is a tiny country with a population of 2,040,000 people, among them only 11% Qatari nationals. Qatar has borders with Saudi Arabia, and is in the neighborhood of Iran. The land area of Iran is about 150 times that of Qatar, and Saudi Arabia is approximately 200 times larger than Qatar. Saudi Arabia's population is about 15 times larger than Qatar's; Iran's population is almost 40 times larger than Qatar's. In the past, Qatar was under Bahraini (1783–1868), Ottoman (1871–1916), and British (1916–1971) rule. Qatar wants to maintain its independence that it gained from the United Kingdom in 1971. A bad example is the Gulf War (1990–1991) when Iraq invaded and annexed Kuwait, another tiny and sparsely populated Gulf country. To avoid a similar fate, Qatar has hosted a US military base with about 10,000 servicemen since 2003. The United States will continue to operate and maintain troops at Qatar's Al Udeid Air Base through at least 2024, following the signing of a 10-year Defense Cooperation Agreement in December 2013. The pact also involves training Qatari forces (Khatri 2013). With 11,800 personnel, Qatar's armed forces are the second smallest in the Middle East (Blanchard 2014, 5). By comparison, the Saudi Arabian army has about 150,000 and the Iranian army has about 700,000 servicemen (Reiche 2014, 12).

However, Qatar is an example that "even the best advertising cannot sell an unpopular product" (Nye 2004, 110) and for the limits to use sport as a successful soft power tool. After the FIFA 2022 World Cup was awarded to the country, the abuse of migrant workers in Qatar became a widely discussed issue in the global media. In my article "Investing in Sporting Success as a Domestic and

Foreign Policy Tool: The Case of Qatar" I argue that there is the need for significant political changes in Qatar to successfully use sport as a policy tool for gaining soft power. This fits with what Nye writes on China, the main competitor of the United States in the most recent Olympic history, that "the soft power of Asian countries is likely to increase in the future, but at this stage they lag in soft-power resources behind the United States and Europe ... Domestic policies and values sets limits" (Nye 2004, 89).

Part I

General Olympic Success Factors

In the following four chapters I discuss general factors explaining success and failure of countries at the Olympic Games. Chapters 5, 6, and 7 discuss the importance of the macro variables wealth, population size, and geography of countries for their success and failure at the Olympics. The fourth general characteristic I discuss in Chapter 8, ideology, has become more of a historic than a contemporary explanation since the end of the Cold War and the fall of the Berlin Wall in 1989 (see for a summary of my Olympic success factor model Figure 1.1).

5 Wealth

Many studies on Olympic success emphasize the importance of the socio-economic conditions of a country. While as a general rule countries with a higher gross domestic product (GDP) tend to be more successful than poor countries, there are also outliers defined as countries with low GDP who perform well and countries with high GDP who underperform. The explanatory power of the wealth variable differs also from the type of Olympic Games (Summer/Winter) and particularly among sports.

Emphasizing the importance of the GDP is a popular argument since the first academic papers on Olympic success were written. Novikov and Maximenko, for example, concluded in their work, "The analysis shows that the amount of per capita national income exerts the strongest influence on Olympic achievements of the given countries" (Novikov and Maximenko 1972, 34). The authors argued that the influence of the socio-economic development of a country is more significant than the population size:

> The influence of the above-mentioned factors on the level of sports achievements differ. As far as the quantitative influence of the first factor is concerned, it is 3.72 times higher than that of the second. Thus, the successes of countries at the Olympic Games depend to a considerably larger degree on the socio-economic living conditions of the population than on the number of inhabitants of the given countries.
>
> (Novikov and Maximenko 1972, 39)

For the importance of the socio-economic development the authors gave the reason that it "conditions possibilities regarding the training of Olympic teams, the number and quality of sports facilities, apparatus and sports equipment, the level of the science of sport, and the introduction of its achievements into practice, etc." (Novikov and Maximenko 1972, 39).

According to another early work on Olympic success that was written in the 1970s by Kiviaho and Mäkelä:

> Economic development and population are understandable factors in absolute Olympic success because of their implications for sport training. If

sporting talent is distributed evenly among populations, those nations which are population-rich have naturally better possibilities, especially if they have the economic resources to exploit the advantages which a large population provided.

(Kiviaho and Mäkelä 1978, 15–16)

Rathke and Woitek also argued that the effect of population is only positive for relatively rich countries: "This observation might help to explain the mixed outcome in the literature concerning population effects" (Rathke and Woitek 2008, 533).

When analyzing the medal count of the Summer Olympic Games in Seoul 1988 and in Barcelona 1992, Den Butter and Van der Tak concluded that the medals won correlated strongly with income as well as with more general welfare indicators. However,

> Money income is the major determinant for the relative performance in sports indeed and that other aspects of the quality of life, which are included in the multidimensional indicators of human welfare, play a minor role only in the "production" of Olympic winners.
>
> (Den Butter and Van Der Tak 1995, 34)

When analyzing the outcome of the Summer and Winter Olympic Games from 1952 until 2000, Johnson and Ali found that "Nations that won at least one Summer medal average over fifty percent higher GDP per capita of non-medal nations" (Johnson and Ali 2000, 5).

Several other studies confirmed the importance of GDP for Olympic success: Bernard and Busse, for instance, concluded, "Real GDP is the best single predictor of a country's Olympic performance" (Bernard and Busse 2004, 413). They argued that the statistical significance of GDP per capita indicates "that two countries with the same GDP will win approximately the same number of medals, even if one is more populous with lower per capita income and the other is smaller with higher per capita GDP" (Bernard and Busse 2004, 415). However, Bernard and Busse also noted that the former Soviet Union and Eastern European countries are examples of the deviation from the correlation of GDP and Olympic success.

Bian used for his work on Olympic success data from the Summer Olympic Games in 1988, 1992, 1996, and 2000. His results were "consistent with previous studies on national Olympic performance ... the richer a country is, the more Olympic medals it will likely win" (Bian 2005, 43).

Lui and Suen investigated the determinants of the number of medals won by a country in the 14 Olympic Summer Games between the 1952 and the 2004 Olympic Games. They also included in their analysis data from the Pan-American Games from 1951 to 1999. The paper concluded, "Population and income have a substantial effect on the number of medals won" (Lui and Suen 2008, 15). According to the authors, the level of income in a country is an important factor in determining the number of medals won "because income affects the demand for sports as well as the technology used to produce world class athletes" (Lui and Suen 2008, 2).

Rathke and Woitek covered in their work the period from the 1952 Summer Olympic Games in Helsinki to the 2004 Summer Games in Athens, and included 131 countries in the analysis. They concluded that their research "reproduces the results from the literature: GDP is a good predictor of success for both output measures (medal shares and point shares)" (Rathke and Woitek 2008, 534).

Success in Olympics and other major international competitions is, according to Sotiriadou and Shilbury, "closely related, in the long term, to the amount of resources that countries invest in the promotion of excellence in sport." There is "a linear relationship between money spent on developing elite athletes and total medals won, with an approximate estimate of $37 million per gold medal" (Sotiriadou and Shilbury 2009, 139).

Van Tuyckom and Jöreskog examined the probability of success in the 1984 and 2004 Summer Olympics. They concluded that "rich, socially well-developed, and big countries still have considerable advantages when it comes to international (Olympic) sports" (Van Tuyckom and Jöreskog 2012, 200). As the authors explain, economic development matters because it allows countries to invest more in elite sports.

The conclusion of the study by Tcha and Pershin was that "A country wins medals in a more diversified range of sports if its wealth increases or if it is a socialist country" (Tcha and Pershin 2003, 231).

An interesting argument from the literature on the role of GDP for Olympic success is that the number of participants of a country depends on its wealth and can be therefore considered as part of the explanation that the wealth of a country matters, because countries with more participants are more successful. According to the work of Kuper and Sterken, "The data clearly reveal that national medal success is dependent on participation.... A one-percentage point increase in participation leads almost to a homogeneous increase in medal success" (Kuper and Sterken 2003, 10). Moosa and Smith confirmed the results of Kuper and Sterken in their case study on the Sydney 2000 Summer Games. Their analysis showed that:

> only two variables are robust: the number of athletes and expenditure on health. Further empirical analysis showed that these two variables are independently important and cannot be deleted from a model designed to explain Olympic success.... While the number of athletes and expenditure on health may be a reflection of the size of the economy and the resources available for sport, it is possible to show that these two variables are important in their own right, and that a model that does not include them is misspecified.
>
> (Moosa and Smith 2004, 299)

Referring to Maguire and Pearton (Maguire and Pearton 2000, 759–769), who group the performance of nation-states in sport in core countries, semi-peripheral countries, and peripheral countries, Simiyu Njororai notes, "the typology hides the unique successes in selected sports. For example, not all economically peripheral countries are also peripheral in some sports and vice versa for core countries" (Simiyu Njororai 2010, 447–448). Simiyu Njororai refers to the achievements of Kenyan runners that are in stark contrast to Kenya's economic and social infrastructure, where it ranks poorly in nearly every social and economic category (e.g. life expectancy, per capital income, and child mortality).

What makes the research from Johnson and Ali interesting is that the authors differentiated in their analysis between the type of Games (Summer or Winter) and the athletic events. They concluded that GDP per capita is more important for the Winter Olympics than for the Summer Olympics. Furthermore, "There might be an advantage to high income nations in events which rely on equipment or expensive facilities" (Johnson and Ali 2000, 19). To test for differences, the authors differentiated between three categories of sports: "Labor-intensive events" in the Summer Games (wrestling, judo, the marathon, and 10,000 meter run) as well as in the Winter Games (cross-country, Nordic skiing), "capital-intensive events" at the Summer Games (equestrian, modern pentathlon, sailing) as well as the Winter Games (luge, bobsleigh, ski jumping), all of which require expensive infrastructure; finally as a third type in each season, team-based sports such as handball and ice hockey. The results of this differentiated approach were that:

> income per capita weighed most heavily in favor of competitors in capital-intensive events, but was insignificant in team events. Population size was significant and positive in all summer events, but with much larger relative impact in labor-intensive and particularly team events ...
>
> (Johnson and Ali 2000, 20)

Forrest said in an interview that there are four sports "where there is virtually no chance that anyone from a poor country can win a medal – equestrian, sailing, cycling and swimming." He gives the example that there is only one swimming pool for every six million people in Ethiopia. Wrestling, judo, weightlifting, and gymnastics, he says, tend to be the best sports for developing nations (Anderson 2012).

According to an article in the *New York Times*, the Olympic sport that recently showed the least competitive balance is badminton. Nearly 85% of the medals in the last Olympics Games 2000, 2004, 2008, and 2012 have been shared by China, Indonesia, and South Korea. Interestingly, of the four sports with the least competitive balance (badminton, table tennis, rhythmic gymnastics, and beach volleyball), only one of them is dominated by a nation ranked in the top 20 of GDP per capita (Silver 2012).

Emrich et al., in their examination of the determinants of Olympic success on the Summer Games of 1996, 2000, 2004, and 2008, as well as on the Winter Olympics of 1998, 2002, 2006, and 2010, came to similar results as Forrest and Johnson and Ali. They concluded that the strong influence of GDP per capita in the case of the Winter Olympics reflects a strong dependence on specific and costly sports facilities in winter sports. Such specific and costly sports facilities are only accessible to a relatively small proportion of the population, which explains why population size per se does not matter in winter sports. In contrast, only a small number of the sports practiced at the Summer Olympics require access to specific sports facilities, implying that a large proportion of a countries population can do summer sports at low costs.

(Emrich et al. 2012, 1896)

De Bosscher et al. argue that:

there might be a minimum level of absolute funding required for an elite sporting system to start delivering results.... A minimum threshold starting point might be the €34m spent by Denmark as it is a tipping point for achieving a market share of more than 0.5% and the delivery of performance as expected ...

(De Bosscher et al. 2015, 358)

While the study by De Bosscher et al. has a broad empirical basis, all 15 investigated cases are developed countries. It is questionable whether the €34 million spent by Denmark can be transferred to the context of developing and middle-income countries.

Tables 5.1 and 5.2 show examples for one sport where the wealth of the country matters (equestrian, Table 5.1) as well as for one sport where Olympic success cannot be linked with the GDP of the respective country (marathon, Table 5.2). Table 5.1 proves that equestrian is an example of a capital-intensive event at the Olympics that is dominated by wealthy countries. Out of the 419 Olympic medals, 329 (78.5%) in equestrian were won by wealthy countries with a GDP above US\$30,000; if one also includes in the group of wealthy countries nation-states with a GDP above US\$20,000, the percentage increases to 86.2% (361 out of 419 of Olympic medals).

Equestrian is not only a sport of wealthy countries; even within wealthy countries it is mainly practiced by the upper class of society. An exception is Sweden, with 42 medals after Germany (60) and the United States (49), the most successful equestrian nation-state at the Olympic Games, as Table 5.1 shows. In Sweden, equestrian sports is a "folk sport":

The idea that many people should have the opportunity to learn riding and that horse riding in riding schools should be open to many has remained. Today, governmental subsidies make it less expensive to horse ride in Sweden than in some other countries.

(Hellborg and Hedenborg 2015, 249)

One of the reasons for the affordability of equestrian sport in Sweden is that the riding schools own most horses while membership in the schools is not expensive.

Table 5.1 Equestrian Medals and Per Capita GDP of Country and Population Size

Country	GDP Per Capita (US$)	Population Size	Equestrian Medals Won
Norway	55,400	5,147,792	1
Switzerland	54,800	8,061,516	23
United States	52,800	318,892,103	49
Netherlands	43,300	16,877,351	26
Canada	43,100	34,834,841	6
Australia	43,000	22,507,617	11
Austria	42,600	8,223,062	3
Ireland	41,300	4,832,765	1
Sweden	40,900	9,723,809	42
Germany	39,500	80,996,685	60
Belgium	37,800	10,449,361	13
Denmark	37,800	5,569,077	6
Great Britain	37,300	63,742,977	32
Japan	37,100	127,103,388	1
France	35,700	66,259,012	39
Saudi Arabia	31,300	27,345,986	2
New Zealand	30,400	4,401,916	10
Spain	30,100	47,737,941	4
Italy	29,600	61,680,122	23
Portugal	22,900	10,813,834	3
Poland	21,100	38,346,279	6
Hungary	19,800	9,919,128	1
Chile	19,100	17,363,894	2
Argentina	18,600	43,024,374	1
Mexico	15,600	120,286,655	7
Romania	14,400	21,729,871	2
Bulgaria	14,400	6,924,716	1
Brazil	12,100	202,656,788	3
West Germany	N/A	N/A	25
Soviet Union	N/A	N/A	15
Czechoslovakia	N/A	N/A	1
TOTAL			419

Source: Adapted from "The World Factbook," *Central Intelligence Agency*, www.cia.gov/library/publications/the-world-factbook/rankorder/2119rank.html?countryname=Argentina&countrycode=ar&regionCode=soa&rank=33#ar. "Olympic Sports Equestrianism," *Sports Reference*, www.sports-reference.com/olympics/sports/EQU/.

No country with a current per capita GDP below US$12,000 has ever won an Olympic medal in equestrian, while in marathon, a labor-intensive event at the Olympics, there are seven countries with a per capita GDP below US$12,000, as Table 5.2 shows. Two of them – Kenya and Ethiopia – belong to the most successful countries in the marathon competition at the Olympics. Their GDP is even below US$2,000. Kenya won 10, and Ethiopia nine Olympic marathon medals. Apart from Japan, which also won nine medals, only the United States was more successful, winning 12 medals at the Olympics.

Table 5.2 Marathon Medal-Winning Countries at the Olympics

Country	GDP Per Capita (US$)	Population	Marathon Medals Won
Norway	55,400	5,147,792	1
United States	52,800	318,892,103	12
Netherlands	43,300	16,877,351	1
Australia	43,000	22,507,617	1
Ireland	41,300	4,832,765	1
Sweden	40,900	9,723,809	2
Germany	39,500	80,996,685	1
Belgium	37,800	10,449,361	3
United Kingdom	37,300	63,742,977	5
Japan	37,100	127,103,388	9
Finland	35,900	5,268,799	5
France	35,700	66,259,012	4
South Korea	33,200	49,039,986	2
New Zealand	30,400	4,401,916	3
Italy	29,600	61,680,122	4
Greece	23,600	10,775,557	2
Portugal	22,900	10,813,834	3
Estonia	22,400	1,257,921	1
Hungary	19,800	9,919,128	1
Chile	19,100	17,363,894	1
Argentina	18,600	43,024,374	3
Russia	18,100	142,470,272	2
Romania	14,400	21,729,871	2
Brazil	12,100	202,656,788	1
South Africa	11,500	48,375,645	4
China	9,800	1,355,692,576	1
Morocco	5,500	32,987,206	2
Djibouti	2,700	810,179	1
Kenya	1,800	45,010,056	10
Uganda	1,500	35,918,915	1
Ethiopia	1,300	96,633,458	9
GDR	N/A	N/A	3
Czechoslovakia	N/A	N/A	1
Soviet Union	N/A	N/A	1
Yugoslavia	N/A	N/A	1
TOTAL			104

Sources: Adapted from "The World Factbook," *Central Intelligence Agency*, www.cia.gov/library/publications/the-world-factbook/rankorder/2119rank.html?countryname=Argentina&countrycode=ar&regionCode=soa&rank=33#ar. "Olympic Medal Winners: Every One since 1896 as Open Data," *Guardian*, June 25, 2012, www.theguardian.com/sport/datablog/2012/jun/25/olympic-medal-winner-list-data#data. "London 2012 Athletics, Marathon Women Final," *Olympic.org*, www.olympic.org/olympic-results/london-2012/athletics/marathon-w.

From the 53 African countries that were participating in the London 2012 Summer Olympics, 39 nation-states have never won gold at the Olympics, and 27 of those have never won any kind of medal. In her article "Rarely a Gold Medal for African Nations," Powell explains the underachievement of African countries with lack of investment, corruption, poor planning, and bad facilities:

> The famous Kinshasa stadium in the Democratic Republic of the Congo that saw Muhammad Ali and George Foreman "Rumble in the Jungle" is now a home for families who live in decrepit conditions. The middle of the stadium, where the two greats went toe-to-toe, is now, literally, a toilet.
>
> (Powell 2012)

While this proves the importance of wealth and shows that wealthier countries are more likely to have Olympic success than poor nation-states, Table 5.3 shows that there also outliers: Kenya and Ethiopia, for example, are poor African countries, but are still successful at the Olympics. They have won far more Olympic medals than wealthier countries such as Saudi Arabia.

While the data shows that the wealth of a country is beneficial in certain sports such as equestrian, it does not explain (1) why the countries with a high GDP listed in Table 5.1 are successful in equestrian, while others with a similar high GDP as well (such as Hong Kong, Israel, Kuwait, Singapore, Taiwan, and Qatar – all of them countries with a per capita GDP in 2013 above US$35,000) have never won a single medal in equestrian, and (2) how certain poor countries such as Kenya and Ethiopia were able to write Olympic success stories. This shows that without including other variables in the analysis, wealth has only a limited explanatory power to explain Olympic success.

Table 5.3 Outliers: Unsuccessful Wealthy and Successful Poor Olympic Nation-States

Country	GDP Per Capita (US$)	Population Size	Olympic Medals Won
Qatar	102,100	2,123,160	4
Singapore	62,400	5,567,301	4
Hong Kong	52,700	7,112,688	3
Kuwait	42,100	2,742711	2
Saudi Arabia	31,300	27,345,986	3
United Arab Emirates	29,900	5,628,805	1
Bahrain	29,800	1,314,089	1
Jamaica	9,000	2,930,050	65
Kenya	1,800	45,010,056	86
Ethiopia	1,300	96,633,458	45

Sources: Adapted from "Olympic Medals Overall Medals," *Olympic.it*, www.olympic.it/english/mdeal/id_overall.htm. "The World Factbook Country Comparison," *Central Intelligence Agency*, www.cia.gov/library/publications/the-world-factbook/rankorder/2119rank.html?countryname=Argentina&countrycode=ar&regionCode=soa&rank=33#ar.

6 Population Size

In one of the first academic articles on Olympic success, Kiviaho and Mäkelä argued that "if sporting talent is distributed evenly among populations, those nations which are population-rich have naturally better possibilities, especially if they have the economic resources to exploit the advantages which a large population provided" (Kiviaho and Mäkelä 1978, 15–16). While the importance of the economic strength of a country for Olympic success was discussed in the previous section, this chapter focuses on the explanatory power of population size. Does the population size of a country really matter for Olympic success? A larger population increases the group of potential athletes, but is there also a correlation between population size, potential athletes, and Olympic success? Do large countries win more medals than small countries? The answers to these questions seem to be clear when looking at the enormous Olympic success of the 1st and 3rd most populated countries in the world, China and the United States. However, there are plenty of counterexamples, such as the poor Olympic performance of the second most populated country in the world, India, which I will discuss in this section. However, what is evident is the disadvantage of the smallest countries in the world when it comes to Olympic success, and that population size matters more for success at the Summer than at the Winter Olympics.

Houlihan and Zheng made a case study on the importance of the population size for the 2012 Summer Olympics. They focused in their work on the sporting success of small states, defined as countries with a population below 10 million people. Their research is relevant, since the vast majority of states that take part at the Olympic Games are small states. According to Houlihan and Zheng, the median population size of the 204 countries that participated in the London 2012 Olympic Games was just over 6.6 million, and almost one-quarter (47) had a population of less than one million. Taking London 2012 as an example, they identified a

> pattern of marginal presence and negligible success ... Those countries with a population below 1 m accounted for just three Olympic medals in 2012, and the 102 countries with the smallest population accounted for just 11% (106) of the 962 medals won. The total number of athletes competing in

London was approximately 10,800 with over half that number coming from just 17 countries.

(Houlihan and Zheng 2014, 1)

The findings of Houlihan and Zheng are confirmed by a previous work of Johnson and Ali. They found out that "nations that won at least one Summer medal average five times the population of non-medal nations" (Johnson and Ali 2000, 5).

Because of the difficulties of small countries to win medals at the Olympic Games, the smallest National Olympic Committees in the European Olympic Committee decided in 1981 to create a special event, the "Games of Small States of Europe" (GSSE). The GSSE are designed for European countries with less than one million inhabitants. The GSSE were developed in accordance with the rules of the Olympic Charter and of the international federations. The first GSSE took place in 1995 in San Marino. Apart from San Marino, there are seven other GSSE founding member states: Andorra, Cyprus, Iceland, Lichtenstein, Luxembourg, Malta, and Monaco. Montenegro joined the GSSE in 2009. In 2013, the 15th edition of the Games took place in Luxembourg (Games of Small States of Europe 2015).

While the work of Houlihan and Zheng and Johnson and Ali showed that small countries win fewer medals than larger nation-states, this does not mean that there is a correlation between the population size and the medals a country wins.

Bernard and Busse developed a model to predict Olympic success, based on the Olympic Summer Games results from 1960 until 1996. Giving the example of China, India, Indonesia, and Bangladesh which counted for 43% of the global population but won only 6% of total medals in 1996, the authors give three reasons why the medals won at the Olympics are not proportional to the population size of a country:

> First, countries cannot send athletes in proportion to their populations for each event, for example, in team competitions, where each country has at most one entry. Second, in medal counts, teams events count as one medal even though a country must provide a number of athletes. Finally, the number of athletes from each country is determined by the IOC in negotiation with the country's Olympic committee. As a result, not all the Olympic caliber athletes from a large country are able to participate.
>
> (Bernard and Busse 2004, 413)

Den Butter and Van der Tak argue similar to Bernard and Busse:

> A country with two times as many inhabitants as another country is not expected to win two times as many Olympic medals. Or in the economists' jargon: the "production" of Olympic medals is apparently subject to diseconomies of scale with respect to population. This may partly be caused

by the fact that each country is only allowed to delegate a limited number of participants per sporting event.

(Den Butter and Van Der Tak 1995, 31).

Different authors agree that while population size might matter to a certain extent at the Summer Games, it is less relevant for the Winter Olympics. Johnson and Ali conclude in their work "small nations outperform their larger competitors at the Winter Games, while the reverse is definitely true at the Summer Games" (Johnson and Ali 2000, 20). According to Pfau, "Population may be less important because skills for winter sports are specialized to colder regions of the world, particularly Scandinavia, which tend to have smaller populations" (Pfau 2006, 10).

The arguments of Johnson and Ali and Pfau were confirmed by Emrich *et al.* who focused in their work on the Summer Games of 1996, 2000, 2004, and 2008, as well as on the Winter Olympics of 1998, 2002, 2006, and 2010. They conclude that while population size is significant in the case of the four Summer Olympics, it is never significant in the cases of the Winter Olympics. They argue that winter sports' specific and costly sports facilities are only accessible to a relatively small proportion of the population, which explains why the population size per se does not matter in winter sports. "In contrast, only a small number of the sports practiced at the Summer Olympics require access to specific sports facilities, implying that a large proportion of a countries population can do summer sports at low costs" (Emrich *et al.* 2012, 1896).

Tables 6.1, 6.2, and 6.3 give examples from three continents about the correlation between population size and the number of medals won at the Summer Olympic Games. Table 6.1 is on the performance of African countries and shows that the 7th most populated African country, Kenya, has won 3.74 times more medals than the most populated African country, Nigeria, despite the fact that Nigeria has a population 3.94 times that of Kenya. Ethiopia, Egypt, and South Africa have also won more medals than Nigeria.

Table 6.1 Performance of African Countries at the Olympics

Country	Population Size	Number of Summer Olympic Medals Won
Nigeria	177,155,754	23
Ethiopia	96,633,458	45
Egypt	86,895,099	26
Democratic Republic of the Congo	77,433,744	0
Tanzania	49,639,138	2
South Africa	48,010,056	86
Kenya	45,010,056	86
Algeria	38,813,722	15

Sources: Adapted from "Olympic Medals," *Olympic.it*, www.olympic.it/english/mdeal/id_summer. htm. "The World Factbook Country Comparison," *Central Intelligence Agency*, www.cia.gov/ library/publications/the-world-factbook/rankorder/2119rank.html?countryname=Argentina&country code=ar&regionCode=soa&rank=33#ar.

Table 6.2 is on the performance of Asian countries at the Olympics. While the population sizes of China and India are gigantic – both above one billion people, with China slightly more populated – a significant gap exists in the Olympic performances of both countries. China has won 18.2 times more Olympic medals. This is particularly remarkable if one takes into consideration that India started participating in the Olympics in 1900, while China's Olympic path started much later in 1952, with the next participation of the country not until 1984. While Japan's success is not surprising, given the economic strength of the country, even Indonesia has won one more medal at the Summer Olympic Games in spite of having 4.87 times fewer inhabitants than India.

Similar to Africa (Table 6.2), in Latin America it is not the most populated country that has won the most Olympic medals. Cuba ranks only 10th in population

Table 6.2 Performance of Asian Countries at the Olympics

Country	Population Size	Number of Summer Olympic Medals Won
China	1,355,692,576	473
India	1,236,344,631	26
Indonesia	253,609,643	27
Pakistan	196,174,380	10
Bangladesh	166,280,712	0
Japan	127,103,388	398
Philippines	107,688,231	9
Vietnam	93,421,835	2

Sources: Adapted from "Olympic Medals," *Olympic.it*, www.olympic.it/english/mdeal/id_summer. htm. "The World Factbook Country Comparison," *Central Intelligence Agency*, www.cia.gov/ library/publications/the-world-factbook/rankorder/2119rank.html?countryname=Argentina&country code=ar&regionCode=soa&rank=33#ar.

Table 6.3 Performance of Latin American Countries at the Olympics

Country	Population Size	Number of Summer Olympic Medals Won
Brazil	202,656,788	109
Mexico	120,286,655	62
Colombia	46,245,297	19
Argentina	43,024,374	70
Peru	30,147,935	4
Venezuela	28,868,486	12
Chile	17,363,894	13
Ecuador	15,654,411	2
Cuba	11,047,251	208

Sources: Adapted from "Olympic Medals," *Olympic.it*, www.olympic.it/english/medal/id_summer. htm. "The World Factbook Country Comparison," *Central Intelligence Agency*, www.cia.gov/ library/publications/the-world-factbook/rankorder/2119rank.html?countryname=Argentina&country code=ar&regionCode=soa&rank=33#ar.

among Latin American countries (Table 6.3 does not list Guatemala that has more inhabitants), but it is by far the most successful Olympic nation-state. Brazil has a population size 18.34 times larger than Cuba but the Caribbean island has won 1.9 times more medals. Mexico, the second most populated country in Latin America, has 10.9 times more inhabitants than Cuba, but Cuba has won 3.4 more medals in the history of the Summer Olympics.

7 Geography

To what extent does the geography of a country influence its Olympic success? The main explanatory power of this independent variable is to differentiate between success at the Summer and at the Winter Games. Not surprisingly, "Geographical and climate conditions matter more for sporting success in Winter Olympics" (Emrich et al. 2012, 1896) and "colder nations outperform warmer ones" (Johnson and Ali 2000, 20). For example, no African nation has ever won a medal at the Winter Olympics.

The Summer Olympics is a much larger event, and has a longer history than the Winter Games. The modern Olympic Summer Games started in 1896 in Athens, while the first Winter Games took place 28 years later in Chamonix, France, in 1924. Table 7.1 compares the size of the events and shows significant differences: Whereas in London 2012 the number of participating National Olympic Committees was 204, only 88 countries participated in Sochi. This means that a majority of all countries in the world do not participate in the Winter Olympic Games. There are 28 different sports at the Summer Olympics and seven sports at the Winter Olympics. There were 98 events in Sochi compared with 302 in London 2012. Whereas the Sochi Games had less than 3,000 participants, there were more than 10,000 in London. While in the history of the Olympics only 45 nation-states have won a medal at the Winter Games, 129 countries have won a medal at the Summer Games. In Sochi 2014, 26 countries won a medal, but two years earlier in London,

Table 7.1 Summer Olympics 2012 and Winter Olympics 2014 in Comparison

	Sochi 2014	*London 2012*
Countries (NOC)	88	204
Participants	2,800	10,568
Events	98	302
Medal-winning countries	26	85

Sources: Adapted from "Factsheet, London 2012 Facts and Figures," *International Olympic Committee*, November 2012, www.olympic.org/Documents/Reference_document6s_Factsheets/London_2012_Facts_and_Figures-eng.pdf. "Factsheet, Sochi 2014 Facts and Figures," *International Olympic Committee*, February 2015, www.olympic.org/Documents/Games_Sochi_2014/Sochi_2014_Facts_and_Figures-eng.pdf.

85 nation-states were successful in reaching the podium at least once ("Olympic – Overall Medals by Country" 2014).

There is an enormous geographic concentration of winter sport medals: Among the 26 countries that won medals in Sochi, 19 are located in Europe: Austria, Belarus, Croatia, Czech Republic, Finland, France, Germany, Great Britain, Italy, Latvia, Netherlands, Norway, Poland, Russia, Slovakia, Slovenia, Sweden, Switzerland, and Ukraine; four of the medal-winning countries are from Asia (China, Japan, Kazakhstan, South Korea); two are from the Americas (both from North America: the United States and Canada) and one is from Oceania (Australia) ("Olympic Medal Count – 2014 Sochi Winter Olympics" 2014).

Even if a country has favorable geographic conditions for winter sports, it still might not be able to provide the costly infrastructure needed for capital-intensive sports such as luge, bobsleigh, and ski jumping. This concurs with Andreff's econometric testing that covered all Winter Olympics from 1964 up to 2010. He concluded about the significance of snow coverage for Olympic success:

> Snow coverage surprisingly does not appear as a significant determinant of Winter Olympics medal wins.... Some countries with high snow coverage do not perform that well at Winter Games such as Tajikistan and Kyrgyzstan. It is not enough for a country to have snow, if it does not have enough ski resorts and winter sports facilities to train potential medal winners.
>
> (Andreff 2013, 334–335)

An example of a country with snow but without skiing resorts is Bolivia. Bolivia has no lack of mountains or snow, but the country has not participated in any Winter Olympics since 1992, after occasionally participating earlier. The country's highest mountain is the snowcapped Nevado Sajama at an altitude of 6,542 m. The country has only one ski resort, located on the mountain Chacaltaya. Its size had to be reduced to a tiny stretch of 180 meters, after more than 80% of the glacier has melted in the last 20 years (Romero 2007; BBC News 2009). While this specific case is related to climate change, the general lack of winter sport facilities in the country has more to do with economic than geographic causes.

While Bolivia, a country with mountains and snow, has left the winter sport arena, Qatar, a Middle Eastern nation-state without any snow and mountains, is in the process of entering the world of winter sports. The Qatar Winter Sports Committee was established in the desert country in 2014, and is promoting three sports: ice hockey, ice-skating, and ice curling. According to a statement by the Qatar Winter Sports Committee in early 2015:

> Our first focus is finding and discovering talent among the Qataris players, even in all the winter sports. We have more than 20 players officially registered under the youth team (Qatar Ice Hockey National Team) and more than 197 under the minor team.
>
> (Qatar Winter Sport Committee n.d.)

I visited the ice rink of the Qatar Winter Sports Committee in January 2015. It is located in the "Villaggio" shopping mall in Doha. I also saw other ice rinks in other shopping malls, but they did not have the original hockey size like the one in "Villaggio." The World Curling Federation (WCF) accepted the Qatar Curling Federation to conditional Member Association in October 2014. As a conditional Member, Qatar will be supported in its development activities through access to WCF staff and programs. In a press release of the WCF, Rashed Al-Sulaiti, President of Qatar Curling Federation, is quoted as follows:

> We are delighted to have been accepted as conditional members of the World Curling Federation. We have already put in place plans to establish the sport of curling and will be working hard over the coming months to ensure the sport continues to develop in Qatar.
>
> (World Curling Federation 2014)

While countries without favorable winter sport conditions are mainly focusing on indoor sports such as curling, hockey, and skating, the example of Dubai shows that even outdoor winter sports such as skiing can be promoted in a country without snow and mountains. Ski Dubai is the first indoors ski resort in the Middle East. It consists of 22,500 square meters covered with snow all year round. Like in Qatar, Ski Dubai is part of a shopping mall, the Mall of the Emirates (Ski Dubai n.d.).

While Qatar and the United Arab Emirates have not yet won any medals at the Winter Games, the examples show that for some winter sports favorable geographic conditions are not needed, only the resources to establish the necessary infrastructure. Another example is the Netherlands. Vaalserberg ("Mount of Vaals") is the highest "mountain" of the country. It is a hill with a height of 322.7 meters. While this limits the opportunities for the Netherlands in skiing, the country is the most successful skating nation at the Winter Olympics. For instance, the Netherlands won in four speed skating events in Sochi all of the available gold, silver, and bronze medals. The country leads the all-time Winter Olympics speed skating ranking, having won one-fifth (105 out of 527) of all speed skating medals in the history of the Games (Mallon 2014a).

Whereas the geography of a country might only have limited explanatory power for the overall performance of a country at the Summer Olympics, it certainly matters for certain types of sport. For example, small countries with a large population density lack space for sports such as golf. Lebanon is one such example: the country consists of only $10,452 \text{ km}^2$. In 2014, 437 people were living on average on one square kilometer. This explains why the country has only one golf course and does not have any world-class athlete in that sport.

Another example is limited water sport opportunities for land-locked countries. Table 7.2 shows that the top 12 ranked Olympic medal-winning countries in sailing have access to the sea. Austria, ranked 13th, is a country known for its large lakes. The same applies to Switzerland, the second best ranked country without access to the sea at position 24. This shows that without access to the sea or in exceptional cases the availability of large lakes such as in Austria and

Switzerland, success in sailing is not possible. The three countries that lead the Olympic sailing ranking (Great Britain, United States, Norway) are also economically strong countries. The importance of the wealth of a country, particularly in costly sports such as sailing, was discussed previously. At the same time, sailing has the most competitive balance with only 29% of the medals captured by its top three nations, and 27 other nations winning at least one medal during the last four Olympic Summer Games 2000–2012 (Silver 2012).

Table 7.2 All-Time Olympic Sailing Medal Ranking

Country	Gold	Silver	Bronze	Combined	Landlocked Y/N
Great Britain	26	18	11	55	NO
United States	19	23	17	59	NO
Norway	17	11	3	31	NO
Spain	13	5	1	19	NO
Denmark	12	9	7	28	NO
France	11	9	12	32	NO
Sweden	10	12	13	35	NO
Australia	10	5	8	17	NO
New Zealand	8	5	5	18	NO
Brazil	6	3	8	17	NO
Netherlands	5	8	7	20	NO
USSR	4	5	3	12	NO
Austria	3	4	0	7	YES
Italy	3	3	8	14	NO
Greece	3	2	2	7	NO
Germany	2	4	4	10	NO
Belgium	2	4	3	9	NO
Finland	2	2	7	11	NO
Federal Republic of Germany (1950)	2	2	3	7	NO
German Democratic Republic (1955)	2	2	2	6	NO
China, PR	2	2	1	5	NO
Ukraine	1	2	2	5	NO
Equipe Unifiée Allemande	1	1	1	3	NO
Switzerland	1	1	1	3	YES
Poland	1	0	3	4	NO
Israel	1	0	2	3	NO
Bahamas	1	0	1	2	NO
Hong Kong	1	0	0	1	NO
Argentina	0	4	5	9	NO
Canada	0	3	6	9	NO
Portugal	0	2	2	4	NO
Japan	0	1	1	2	NO
Russia	0	1	1	2	NO
Slovenia	0	1	1	2	NO

8 Ideology

There is compelling evidence that countries with a socialist/communist ideology have performed better at the Olympics than nation-states with free market economies (I am using the terms socialist/communist as synonyms and do not substantially differentiate between them). While the world has changed since the fall of the Berlin Wall in November 1989, and there are not many countries left that do not follow a capitalistic development model, "Ideology" is an important factor to explain Olympic success in the past, particularly in the era of the Cold War.

According to D'Agati who has written a book about what he calls the "Soviet-American surrogate war," "the contest of ideologies ... accentuated the entire Olympic Movement by attaching a deeper, more symbolic, and intrinsically more competitive spirit to its quadrennial events" (D'Agati 2013, 1).

Novikov and Maximenko already concluded in their work in the early 1970s that "The achievements of socialist countries at the Olympic Games are markedly higher in comparison with the sports success of capitalist countries" (Novikov and Maximenko 1972, 38–39). Three decades later, Kuper and Sterken came as well to the conclusion that socialist countries have more success in medal counts. Their research covered Olympic success in the Summer Games from 1896 until 2000 and included those 118 countries that had won at least one medal in that period of time. What Kuper and Sterken discovered about the Summer Olympics was confirmed in Andreff's econometric testing that covered all Winter Olympics from 1964 up to 2010. He noticed that "being a centrally planned economy with some sort of communist regime was an advantage to win Winter Olympics medals until 1988" (Andreff 2013, 326).

According to Bernard and Busse, "The forced mobilization of resources by governments clearly can also play a role in medal totals. On average, the Soviet Union and Eastern Bloc countries had medal shares more than 3 percentage points higher than predicted by their GDP" (Bernard and Busse 2004, 413).

Why did communist countries put so much emphasis on Olympic success? The Hungarian Communist Party stated immediately after World War II and before the 1948 Summer Olympics that "the success of Hungarian athletes in the London Games would increase our reputation, reinforce the faith in the Hungarian restoration, and would reinforce the acknowledgement of our sport-power."

According to Onyestyák, "the requirement of outstanding international sporting results required the use of large sums of money to support elite sport and to create adequate institutions and facilities for sport" (Onyestyák 2013, 766).

According to Carter's case study on Cuba, "Like all socialist states, from its inception Cuba has relied heavily on the symbolic capital of its sporting prowess, most especially its athletes' international successes, to legitimate the state's presence in the global community of states" (Carter 2008, 200). Apart from Cuba, the most striking example is the GDR, which used to be the "world's leading sports nation, an unofficial title that granted the country international and domestic respect that it lacked in many other areas" (McDougall 2013, 841). For the GDR, "Sports was a way to justify the state" (Johnson 2008).

Tables 8.1 and 8.2 show the performance of the German Democratic Republic and Cuba at the Olympics. Cuba belongs to the first generation of countries that participated in the Olympics. It missed the first modern Games in 1896 but started participating in the Olympics in Paris in 1900. Being an island country in the Caribbean, Cuba has focused on the Summer Olympics, while the GDR participated in the Winter as well as Summer Games and was successful at both of them. Both countries achieved their Olympic success with a relatively small population base of about 11 (Cuba) and 16 million people (GDR). What is interesting is that out of the 208 Olympic medals Cuba won between 1900 and 2012, only 12 were won before the revolution (that lasted from 1953 until 1959). Another interesting observation about Cuba is that it remained successful after the end of the Cold War that led to the loss of its main ally, the Soviet Union.

The GDR's rank in the top 10 of the all-time Olympic medal ranking is remarkable because the country participated only in six Winter and five Summer Olympics over a period of 20 years, from 1968 until 1988. The reason for the lower number of Summer Olympic appearances is that the country joined the Soviet Union-led boycott of the 1984 Games in Los Angeles. The GDR was in the top five of the medal count at all Summer Games. As Table 8.1 shows, the GDR was always one of the two most successful countries in the medal rankings apart from its first Winter Games appearance in 1968 in Grenoble.

Table 8.2 shows Cuba's performance at the Summer Olympics after the revolution. After boycotting the Olympics in 1984 and 1988, the country had its most successful Olympic appearance at the first Games following the end of the Cold War. In 1992 in Barcelona, Cuba won 31 medals and achieved 5th position in both the AP and IOC medal count. While the number of medals won decreased from 31 in 1992 to 14 in London in 2012, and the position in the medal count declined to the 16th in IOC standings and 17th in AP position, this is still a remarkable achievement, given that 76 countries in the world have a larger population size compared with Cuba and the country is, according to the CIA World Factbook, globally ranked at 131 when it comes to its per capita GDP. What makes the case of Cuba particularly interesting is the fact that it won 72.1% of all its Olympic medals (150 out of 208) after the end of the Cold War, while at the same time the performance of most other former allies of the Soviet Union declined.

Table 8.1 The German Democratic Republic at the Olympic Games

German Democratic Republic	Gold	Silver	Bronze	Combined	IOC Ranking	AP Ranking
1968 Mexico City	9	9	7	25	5	4
1972 Munich	20	23	23	66	4	4
1976 Montreal	40	25	25	90	2	3
1980 Moscow	47	37	42	126	2	2
1984 Los Angeles*	–	–	–	–	–	–
1988 Seoul	37	35	30	102	2	2
Summer Games TOTALS	**153**	**129**	**127**	**409**	**9**	**11**
1968 Grenoble	1	2	2	5	10	7
1972 Sapporo	4	3	7	14	2	2
1976 Innsbruck	7	5	7	19	2	2
1980 Lake Placid	9	7	7	23	2	1
1984 Sarajevo	9	9	6	24	1	2
1988 Calgary	9	10	6	25	2	2
Winter Games TOTALS	**39**	**36**	**35**	**110**	**12**	**11**
All Time TOTALS	**192**	**165**	**162**	**519**	**9**	**10**

Source: Adapted from "A Map of Olympic Medals," *New York Times*, August 4, 2008, www.nytimes.com/interactive/2008/08/04/sports/olympics/20080804_MEDALCOUNT_MAP.html?_r=1&. "A Map of Winter Olympic Medals," *New York Times*, http://2010games.nytimes.com/medals/map.html.

Note
* Did not participate.

One could argue that communist countries were successful in sports because they were using the capitalistic principle of materialistic incentives. Athletes enjoyed "Privileges not enjoyed by the average citizen, by having access to a lifestyle unmatched except by the Communist party elite" (Moosa and Smith 2004, 291). Onyestyák writes in her case study on Hungary that "being a top athlete signified a distinctive status, security, provisioning, a chance to travel abroad and a chance to import western goods illegally" (Onyestyák 2013, 767). Another argument is that there were "dehumanizing effects on athletes of Soviet and East German systems of elite development" (Green 2007, 945) and in communist states occurred "longevity, structural organization, explicit and systematic cheating and the abuse of minors" (Dimeo 2013, 200). Krüger et al. write in their book on *German Sports, Doping, and Politics* that one important explanation for the East German success at the Olympic Games is systematic doping by the GDR government: While there was also doping in the Federal Republic of Germany and other Western countries, "the difference was that neither state officials nor politicians nor sports officials had ordered anybody to dope" (Krüger et al. 2015, 44). In the GDR, there was "Staatsdoping" – doping organized by the state. Krüger et al. provide the example of GDR swimming:

When GDR coach Rolf Gläser was asked about the unusually deep voices of the female swimmers of the GDR, he gave the following cynical answer:

Table 8.2 Cuba at the Olympic Games

Cuba	Gold	Silver	Bronze	Combined	IOC Ranking	AP Ranking
1960 Rome	0	0	0	0	–	–
1964 Tokyo	0	1	0	1	30	31
1968 Mexico City	0	4	0	4	31	25
1972 Munich	3	1	4	8	14	16
1976 Montreal	6	4	3	13	8	10
1980 Moscow	8	7	5	20	4	8
1984 USA*	–	–	–	–	–	–
1988 Seoul*	–	–	–	–	–	–
1992 Barcelona	14	6	11	31	5	5
1886 Atlanta	9	8	8	25	8	9
2000 Sydney	11	11	7	29	9	8
2004 Athens	9	7	11	27	11	11
2008 Beijing	2	11	11	24	28	12
2012 London	5	3	6	14	16	17
TOTALS	**72**	**67**	**69**	**208**	**18**	**21**

Sources: Adapted from "A Map of Olympic Medals," *New York Times*, August 4, 2008. www.nytimes. com/interactive/2008/08/04/sports/olympics/20080804_MEDALCOUNT_MAP.html?_r=1&. "London 2012 Olympics Medal Tracker Overall," *ESPN Summer Olympics*, http://espn.go.com/olympics/summer/2012/medals.

Note
* Did not participate.

"They are not here to sing." Everybody knew that the deep voices were the result of long-term doping with anabolic steroids.

(Krüger et al. 2015, 84)

While (capitalistic) incentives and doping might be factors necessary to mention, it is certainly not sufficient to explain communistic Olympic success. For Rathke and Woitek, "A possible explanation for this finding could be that communist countries have been more successful than market economies in providing women equal access to sporting activities" (Rathke and Woitek 2008, 533).

Other authors bring forward the argument that the early institutionalization of the promotion of elite sport gave Soviet bloc countries a comparative advantage for some decades. According to Houlihan and Zheng, outside the communist countries of the 1950s to the 1980s, there was little evidence of a widespread systematic government-funded approach to elite sport development: "In the 1960s and 1970s, it would have been rare to find outside the communist group of countries a central government department with sport among its portfolio of responsibilities" (Houlihan and Zheng 2013, 344).

However, the advantage of communist countries decreased over time. Van Tuyckom and Jöreskog examined the connection between political, social, and economic welfare characteristics and the probability of success in the 1984 and 2004 Summer Olympics. They concluded that "Political development is significant in

1984 but this effect disappears in 2004" (Van Tuyckom and Jöreskog 2012, 197). Andreff concluded in his work that communist countries had an advantage in winning Olympic medals only until 1988 (Andreff 2013, 326). Since then, two developments have diminished the advantage of communist countries: The first development is that the Cold War has ended and not many communist countries are left. Sporting success did not save the GDR in 1989/1990 when the reunification of Germany happened, and since then many Eastern European countries have transformed toward liberal, Western style democracies. However, the few communist countries that are left such as Cuba and China (with the latter maybe being better described as a socialist market economy) are still doing very well at the Olympics.

The second development is that many countries have adopted major elements of the elite sport policies of communist countries. According to Van Tuyckom and Jöreskog:

> this is probably due to the general globalization and liberalization process that has occurred since the early 1980's which narrowed the "political gap" between countries. There is a great deal of evidence that in the 1980's communist countries performed better because economies with central planning allowed for more specialization. Also, more national resources were dedicated to training and supporting athletes in economies with central planning than in market-based economies.... However, since the breakdown of the Eastern European communist systems, things have changed, and in the last decade market-based economies have also further specialized in sports.
>
> (Van Tuyckom and Jöreskog 2012, 198)

Bergsgard gives the example of Australia and Canada who "certainly picked up ideas about how to organize high performance sport from the communist bloc countries during the 1960s and 1970s" (Bergsgard et al. 2007, 194).

Kuper and Sterken give an additional explanation by referring to the fact that the character of the once pure amateur Olympics has changed by integrating professional sports more with the Games since 1988 (Kuper and Sterken 2003, 10). Since then it is common that athletes from professional Western leagues such as the NBA and the NHL participate in the Olympics.

While the superior performance of communist nation-states during the Cold War is obvious, the questions remain of (1) why were some non-communistic countries also very successful at the Olympics and (2) why were there also deviations in the performance of the communistic countries? Why, for example, were East Germany and Cuba able to outperform not only capitalistic but also other communist countries? How were countries with free market economies such as Norway and West Germany able to successfully compete with their socialist competitors? This goes back to the central question of this book of the conditions for success and failure of countries at the Olympics. Cuba and the GDR are examples for pioneering countries in implementing crucial elements of the success recipe that I call in the next section the WISE formula.

Part II

Specific Olympic Success Factors

After discussing the importance of four macro variables in Chapters 5–8, I discuss the policy level and introduce in Chapters 9, 10, 11, and 12 the WISE formula, WISE standing for the promotion of women in sport (W, Chapter 9), the institutionalization of the support of Olympic sports (I, Chapter 10), the strategic specialization on medal-promising sports (S, Chapter 11) and the ability to early adopt new trends in elite sport policies and be a pioneer in promoting sports newly added to the Olympic program (E, Chapter 12). Chapters 13 and 14 discuss two other policies, the naturalization of foreign-born athletes (Chapter 13), and hosting the Olympic Games to benefit from the home advantage (Chapter 14). Different from the policies summarized in the WISE formula in Chapters 9–12, these approaches are not accessible for all countries, and are therefore discussed separately. While in some cases the naturalization of foreign-born athletes and hosting the Olympic Games contribute to Olympic success, these explanations for success and failure at the Games apply to only a limited number of countries and are therefore not included in the WISE formula (see for a summary of my Olympic success factor model Figure 1.1).

9 Promotion of Women (W)

Focusing solely on men in elite sport is not sufficient: Without the promotion of female elite sport, a country cannot excel at the Olympics. A piece of evidence for this assumption is a study by Berdahl et al. based on the results of the Summer Olympics 2012 in London and the Winter Olympics 2014 in Sochi. The study proved that gender equality enhances national performance at the Olympics. According to the authors, their study provides the first evidence that "higher levels of gender equality in a country predict significantly greater success at winning Olympic medals for both its female and male athletes." They conclude that "gender equality is a win–win that allows members of both genders to realize their true potential" (Berdahl et al. 2015, 1).

Berdahl et al. investigated the correlation between the medals a country won at the Olympics and each country's gender gap score, a composite measure of economic, political, health, and educational equality between the sexes. The data was based on the World Economic Forum Global Gender Gap Report. They concluded that a country's gender gap score significantly predicted Olympic medals won by women and men. When splitting each country's gender gap score into each of its four components (economic, political, health, and educational equality between the sexes), it was revealed that educational equality best predicted Olympic medals for women and for men. "These findings contradict the common belief that access to opportunities is a zero-sum game in which gains for women inevitably result in losses for men" (Berdahl et al. 2015, 2).

One example of a country that has demonstrated success due to its investments in female athletes is China. At the 2004 Athens Summer Games, China won two-thirds of its medals in women's competitions (39 out of 63) (Johnson 2008). In its entire Summer Olympic history until London 2012, 2,076 athletes competed for China, 1,015 of them men and 1,061 women. The percentage of 51.1% is one of the highest women's participation rates among all countries in the world. Only East Timor (60%), Bhutan (57.9%), and Saint Kitts and Nevis (52.9%), three mini nation-states with East Timor the most populated with about 1.2 million people, have higher rates than China (Mallon 2015b). I will give more information on China's systematic promotion of female sporting success at the Olympic Games in the chapter on specialization, discussing the case of women's weightlifting.

Contrary examples are the countries listed in Table 9.1. They represent the National Olympic Committees with the lowest all-time female participation in the Summer Games. Six of the nine countries listed in the table are from Asia, three of them (Kuwait, Qatar, Saudi Arabia) belong to the wealthy Gulf Cooperation Council (GCC), a trade bloc comprised of the six Arab states of the Persian Gulf (Bahrain, Kuwait, Oman, Qatar, Saudi Arabia, and the United Arab Emirates).

What makes the numbers in Table 9.1 even more dramatic is the fact that most of those countries only recently started to participate in the Olympic Games. Qatar, for example, participated in the Olympics for the first time in 1984 in Los Angeles. Traditional Olympic powerhouses like the United States (25.4%), Germany (26.3%), and Great Britain (27.3%) have much higher women's participation rates than Qatar. However, these rates would be even higher if only the period of time would be counted since Qatar participated in the Olympic Games (since 1984). The United States, Germany, and Great Britain competed in the Olympics from the very beginning in 1896, but in those times the Games had only a few women's events, as Table 9.2 shows (Mallon 2015b).

According to Pfister, "women's chances of participating and competing in elite sports depend to a large extent on their cultural and religious backgrounds" (Pfister 2010, 2928). Six of the nine countries listed in Table 9.1 are Muslim-majority countries: Afghanistan, Iraq, Kuwait, Saudi Arabia, Pakistan, and Qatar. Pfister concluded in her work on "Muslim Women and Olympic Games: Barriers and Opportunities":

> Whereas male athletes were more or less socially accepted in most Islamic countries, women participating in sports competitions were a contradiction in terms for most of their rulers and (religious) leaders, as well as for the largest part of the population.... Muslim women were tiny minorities at the Olympics – if they were present at all.
>
> (Pfister 2010, 2929)

Table 9.1 Countries with Fewest Number of Women Athletes at the Summer Olympic Games

NOC	Total	Men	Women	Percentage
Saudi Arabia	142	140	2	1.4
Kuwait	192	189	3	1.6
Pakistan	354	346	8	2.3
Afghanistan	100	97	3	3.0
Monaco	64	62	2	3.1
Iraq	174	168	6	3.4
Qatar	108	104	4	3.7
Botswana	52	50	2	3.8
British Virgin Islands	23	22	1	4.3

Source: Adapted from Mallon (2015b).

Up to 1980, among Muslim-majority countries, only women from secular countries, i.e. Turkey, Indonesia and pre-revolutionary Iran, were given the opportunity to compete in elite sports and the Olympics. Turkey is the most successful country with a majority Muslim population at the Olympic Games. The second strongest "sports power" among Islamic countries is Iran. While men won a vast majority of the Turkish medals, in the case of Iran only men won the 60 medals the country was able to win in its Summer Olympics appearances until 2012 (the country participated in some Winter Olympics but never won a medal). If Iranian women would have won another 60 medals, Iran would be ranked much higher in the all-time Olympic medal ranking (precise rank depended on number of gold medals won) and would have won more medals at the Olympic Games than for example Greece or New Zealand that are considered relatively successful sporting nations.

At regional Games such as the Pan-Arab and the Asian Games, Mediterranean Arab countries such as Syria were among the most successful Arab countries in the medals tables because they fielded female as well as male athletes (Stanton 2014, 7). However, even relatively progressive Arab countries such as Lebanon only recently started including women in their Olympic squads. Lebanon competed in all the Olympic Games since 1948 (apart from 1956, 1994, and 1998) and sent more than 160 athletes, but over 90% have been men. Lebanon's Olympic team did not include women until 1972 (Stanton 2012, 2116).

The number of female Muslim Olympians increased slowly while the number of all-male teams dropped to 33 in Barcelona (1992), 28 in Atlanta (1996), and nine in Sydney (2000). The overall percentage of female athletes at the 2008 Summer Games in Beijing was 42%; the percentage of women among the athletes from Islamic countries, by contrast, was only 25% (Pfister 2010, 2930).

Tables 9.2 and 9.3 show how women's participation has increased at the Summer and Winter Games. Women accounted for 44.2% of the participants at the 2012 Summer Games in London, compared with 23% at the Games in 1984 in Los Angeles, 13.2% at the 1964 Games in Tokyo, 4.4% in 1924 and 2.2% in 1900 (both Games took place in Paris). The total number of female participants at the Summer Olympics increased from just 22 in 1900 in Paris to 4,676 in 2012 in London. The number more than doubled since 1988 in Seoul when 2,194 women competed in the Games. While women competed in all 26 sports, the number of female events was still slightly below half of all the events (46.4%), in spite of the fact that there are also two events – rhythmic gymnastics and synchronized swimming – that are solely for women. (At the 2014 swimming World Championship in Kasan, Russia, there was for the first time a mixed-gender competition in synchronized swimming.)

At the Winter Games, the participation of women in 2014 in Sochi was slightly lower than at the Summer Games: 40.3% compared with 44.2% in London. However, this is still a remarkable number, given that in 1980 only 21.7%, and in 1994 only 30% of all Winter Olympic Games participants were women. At the first Winter Olympic Games in 1924, only 4.3% of all participants were women. One of the reasons for the significant increase of female

Table 9.2 Women's Participation in the Summer Olympic Games

Year	Sports	Women's Events*	Total Events	% of Women's Events	Women Participants	% of Women Participants
1900	2	2	95	2.1	22	2.2
1904	1	3	91	3.3	5	0.9
1908	2	4	110	3.6	6	0.9
1912	2	5	102	4.9	48	2.0
1920	2	8	154	5.2	63	2.4
1924	3	10	126	7.9	135	4.4
1928	4	14	109	12.8	277	9.6
1932	3	14	117	12.0	126	9.0
1936	4	15	129	11.6	331	8.3
1948	5	19	136	14.0	390	9.5
1952	6	25	149	16.8	519	10.5
1956	6	26	151	17.2	376	13.3
1960	6	29	150	19.3	611	11.4
1964	7	33	163	20.2	678	13.2
1968	7	39	172	22.7	781	14.2
1972	8	43	195	22.1	1,059	14.6
1976	11	49	198	24.7	1,260	20.7
1980	12	50	203	24.6	1,115	21.5
1984	14	62	221	28.1	1,566	23.0
1988	17	72	237	30.4	1,194	26.1
1992	19	86	257	33.5	2,704	28.8
1996	21	97	271	35.8	3,512	34.0
2000	25	120	300	40.0	4,069	38.2
2004	26	125	301	41.5	4,329	40.7
2008	26	127	302	42.1	4,637	42.4
2012	26	140	302	46.4	4,676	44.2

Source: Adapted from "Factsheet Women in the Olympic Movement," *International Olympic Committee*, May 2014, www.olympic.org/Documents/Reference_documents_Factsheets/Women_in_Olympic_Movement.pdf.

Note
* Including mixed events.

Table 9.3 Women's Participation in the Olympic Winter Games

Year	Sports	Women's Events*	Total Events	% of Women's Events	Women Participants	% of Women Participants
1924	1	2	16	12.5	11	4.3
1928	1	2	14	14.3	26	5.6
1932	1	2	14	14.3	21	8.3
1936	2	3	17	17.6	80	8.3
1948	2	5	22	22.7	77	11.5
1952	2	6	22	27.3	109	15.7
1956	2	7	24	29.2	134	17.0
1960	2	11	27	40.7	144	21.5
1964	3	14	34	41.2	199	18.3
1968	3	14	35	40.0	211	18.2
1972	3	14	35	40.0	211	18.2
1976	3	15	37	40.5	231	20.6
1980	3	15	38	39.5	232	21.7
1984	3	16	39	41.0	274	21.5
1988	3	19	46	41.3	301	21.2
1992	4	26	57	45.6	488	27.1
1994	4	28	61	45.9	522	30.0
1998	6	32	68	47.1	787	36.2
2002	7	37	78	47.4	886	36.9
2006	7	40	84	47.6	960	38.2

Source: Adapted from "Factsheet Women in the Olympic Movement," *International Olympic Committee*, May 2014, www.olympic.org/Documents/Reference_documents_Factsheets/Women_in_Olympic_Movement.pdf.

Note
* Including mixed events.

participants is the addition of events for women at the Games: Ski jumping was the last sport added to the program, making its Olympic debut in Sochi in 2014 (International Olympic Committee 2014a). Nordic combined (a sport in which athletes compete in cross-country skiing and ski jumping) remains the only winter discipline in which women don't compete ("Women's Ski Jumping Has Arrived ... But There's Still a Hill to Climb" 2014).

Three delegations (Saudi Arabia, Qatar, and Kuwait) consisted of "men only" teams at the Beijing Games in 2008. The Beijing Games were the first Games in which Oman and the United Arab Emirates (UAE) sent women to compete. At the 2012 London Summer Olympics, Qatar, Saudi Arabia, and Brunei included women in their Olympic squad for the first time (Reiche 2014, 6).

One hundred years after the first Olympic Games, Lida Fariman from Iran was the first Muslim woman to carry the flag of her country, at the 1996 Olympic Games in Atlanta. Not only is the participation of Muslim women low, but the same is also true of the success rate. It was not until 1984 that a Muslim woman won an Olympic gold medal (the Moroccan hurdler Nawal El Moutawakel). According to Pfister's data on the 2008 Summer Olympics, only six out of 381 medals for women were won by women from Islamic countries, which "clearly points to the marginalization of this group in elite sport" (Pfister 2010, 2933).

Pfister argues that:

> Women from Islamic countries do not fail because they are less talented or possess less will power and commitment but because they have to struggle with obstacles and limitations, ranging from the lack of training facilities and financial support to conflicts with families or attacks from Islamists.
>
> (Pfister 2010, 2933)

According to Pfister, progress for women and women's sport depends to a high degree on the support of governments and rulers. However, even in countries with ample resources and the will to modernize, women face major cultural obstacles. This applies, for example, to Qatar, a country that recently started to heavily invest in the sport sector.

The Qatar Olympic Committee initiated a study on women's participation in sports and physical activities: "The study found that just 15% of Qatari women ages 15 and older regularly participated in sports" (Qatar National Development Strategy 2011–2016, 197).

In his analysis on barriers to female sports participation in Qatar that is based on a case study of the Georgetown University Qatar women's basketball team operating in the mixed-gender environment of Education City, Harkness concluded that "families who do not support sports-related activity for women serve as a major barrier to participation" as well as "the belief that women should not engage in heavy physical activity in front of men" (Harkness 2012, 2168). "It is thought that males who witness females involved in bodily motion will interpret these behaviors as sexual and be unable to control their lustful urges" (Harkness 2012, 2170).

The coach of the national female soccer team told me in January 2014 when I conducted interviews in Doha for a paper on Qatar that she visited a local girl's school and invited 30 girls to practice with the national team after watching an internal tournament. However, only one out of the 30 girls got approval from her family to play football in public (Reiche 2014, 6).

Apart from domestic cultural restrictions, there are also external barriers to the participation of Muslim women at the Olympics, particularly dress codes by International Sport Federations (ISFs) that are responsible for the rules of sports. An example is FIFA's decision to ban the hijab in 2007 for safety concerns, before lifting the ban in 2014 – a process that is analyzed by McLaughlin and Torres in their article "A Veil of Separation: Intersubjectivity, Olympism, and FIFA's Hijab Saga" (McLaughlin and Torres 2014).

FIFA's ban particularly affected the Iranian national women soccer team. In June 2011, the Iranian team attempted to play a qualifying game for the 2012 Olympics against Jordan in Amman, using the hijab. The Bahraini FIFA official overseeing the game did not allow the Iranian players to wear their hijabs. In turn, the Iranian coach decided to forfeit the game. Therefore, FIFA awarded Jordan with a 3–0 victory. Iran also forfeited the remaining three games of the second round of the Asian Football Confederation's qualifying tournament for the 2012 Olympics and therefore did not qualify for the London Games.

For McLaughlin and Torres the ban of the hijab is a contradiction of the intention of the Olympic Movement to be inclusive. They are referring to the IOC's fourth fundamental principle: "The practice of sport is a human right. Every individual must have the possibility of practicing sports, without discrimination of any kind." McLaughlin and Torres also quote Pierre de Coubertin, the founder of the Olympic movement, that "world peace depends upon the celebration of human diversity and not the eradication of it" (McLaughlin and Torres 2014, 367).

There are huge differences in dress codes among International Sport Federations (ISFs). Whereas some ISFs, such as shooting, have no restrictions and allow women to be covered, in beach volleyball, for example, female players have to use shorts of a maximum length of 1.18 inches above the knee, and sleeved or sleeveless tops. McLaughlin and Torres argue, "When guided by Olympism, the ISFs should not make policy restrictions regarding what women wear unless they have strong and compelling evidence that safety or fair play are compromised" (McLaughlin and Torres 2014, 368).

FIFA finally lifted the hijab ban in 2014, citing the lack of medical literature about injuries resulting from wearing headscarves in football matches.

Certainly, sports such as shooting which allow women to cover their bodies are more accepted in Muslim countries than other sports such as beach volleyball that are practiced in a bikini. However, the fact that many Olympic federations recently allowed Muslim women to wear the hijab during competitions and the trend toward the production and marketing of sports clothes that are adapted to Islamic requirements (such as the burkini and the hijood), might increase the female participation from Arab countries.

If countries do not promote female sports, this might become an even larger obstacle for Olympic success in the future: Not only has the number of women's events and participants at the Games increased. The strict separation of men's and women's events might gradually disappear and mixed-gender teams might become a new trend. At the Youth Olympics in Nanjing 2014, the president of the International Olympic Committee, Thomas Bach, said he hoped that all of the mixed-gender events in Nanjing would serve as a test for men and women competing on the same teams in more sports at the Olympics: "This is one of my darling subjects. They are a great opportunity to develop women's sports in smaller countries" (Zaccardi 2014).

Equestrian sport is one of the few sports where women and men compete against each other. In equestrian sports, there are three disciplines on the Olympic program: dressage, jumping, and eventing. When equestrian sports became part of the regular program of the Olympic Games in 1912, only men were allowed in these sports. However, regulations changed over time and women were allowed to participate in dressage in 1952, show jumping in 1956, and eventing in 1964. Women were banned from participating in the Olympic eventing until the 1964 Games because it was considered as too dangerous for them. Furthermore, "Questions like 'how would men be able to concentrate on horse riding with so many young and beautiful women in the stables?' were frequently asked in the press" (Hellborg and Hedenborg 2015, 251). Such questions are not asked anymore, and today, in addition to equestrian, badminton and tennis also have mixed-gender events in the Summer Olympics.

Two events in figure skating, pairs and ice dancing, have been mixed-gender competitions at the Winter Olympics for many decades before mixed biathlon and luge relays were added to the program in Sochi in 2014. For the next Winter Games in Pyeongchang in 2018, mixed doubles in curling as well as the mixed-gender country-versus-country Alpine event were added to the program (Belson 2015).

10 Institutionalization (I)

Creating administrative capacities for the promotion of Olympic success has become a standard in those countries aiming for medals at the Games. Driving forces for this development were the Soviet bloc countries: "The GDR regime had installed a consistent system of supporting top-level sports starting in the late 1950s" (Krüger et al. 2015, 19). The institutionalization of the promotion of elite sport gave countries like the GDR a comparative advantage for some decades. According to Houlihan and Zheng, outside the communist countries of the 1950s to the 1980s, there was little evidence of a widespread systematic government-funded approach to elite sport development:

> In the 1960s and 1970s, it would have been rare to find outside the communist group of countries a central government department with sport among its portfolio of responsibilities. However, by the turn of the century most countries that aspired to Olympic success had acknowledged elite sport as a function of government and had allocated responsibility to a government department or governmental agency.
>
> (Houlihan and Zheng 2013, 344)

One of the pioneers in the institutionalization of elite sport development among the Soviet bloc countries was Cuba, a country that is the most successful Latin American nation-state at the Olympics in spite of competing with neighboring countries with much larger population bases and stronger economies such as Argentina, Brazil, and Mexico. Two years after the revolution, the new government created in 1961 the Instituto Nacional de Deportes, Educación Física y Recreación (INDER) as the main actor to develop elite sport athletes. According to Carter, sporting facilities and opportunities were not readily available to the majority of the Cuban populace before 1959: "INDER has methodically constructed sport facilities throughout the country to provide a venue for all aspiring athletes" (Carter 2008, 201). There were nearly 10,000 venues built by 1990. In addition, INDER has developed programs to identify likely talent for development into world-class athletes.

Different from other former communist countries, Cuba also remained strong at the Olympics after the fall of the Berlin Wall in 1989. However, given that 80–85%

of Cuba's external trade was with the Soviet-led economic bloc, the country's economy struggled, and significant adjustments in its institutional framework were necessary to maintain its sporting successes. According to Carter, Cuba started "exploiting the capitalist system to extend their socialist national agenda" (Carter 2008, 205). In 1993, officials of the national sporting authority INDER decreed that each sport had to become economically viable. INDER officials created a state-owned corporation, CubaDeportes, S.A., "whose purpose was to turn Cuba's prolific sports enterprises into profit-making enterprises in the global market" (Carter 2008, 204). Carter describes in his case study the capitalist transformation of the Cuban sports industry: CubaDeportes entered into various agreements with sporting goods companies to supply Cuba's elite athletes with their equipment and travel costs. For example, the German company Adidas took on the entire sponsorship of all Cuban national teams in 2001.

Apart from such sponsorships, the exportation of Cuban expertise has become another important income generator: Athletes are competing in foreign leagues and coaches working for a variety of foreign sports programs at the Olympic and professional level. For example, there were between 5,000 and 10,000 sports personnel working in Venezuela alone in 2006, with another estimated 3,500 in Mexico. In exchange, countries are delivering economic goods to Cuba (such as Venezuela that is delivering oil to Cuba). Athletes and coaches have to give 80% of any salary earned to CubaDeportes, and retain the remaining percentage after their costs of living overseas were subtracted. According to Carter, "Cuba's sports programs now operate self-sufficiently – that is, solely on each program's hard currency earnings from these labor exports and its joint venture sponsorships" (Carter 2008, 209). In return, INDER announced that effective March 2007, any Olympic or World Championship medalist would receive a monthly pension for life (Carter 2008, 210).

The Soviet Union actively promoted its sport model to allied countries. During the 1960s and 1970s, the USSR developed sports relations with more than 30 African nations. Sports specialists were studying in the Moscow State Higher Institute of Physical Education. The USSR also provided African countries with material aid, sports equipment, literature, organized sports exhibitions, and constructed sports facilities. An example of the USSR's relations with African countries is the bilateral agreement with Ethiopia that was signed after the revolution of 1976, and the establishment of a Marxist state in that country. A sports commission was established known as the Commission for Physical Education and Sport.

> The Commission determined the sports policies, which were presented to the government for final approval; established sports clubs and organizations as government and public bodies; planned and executed sport on a national and international level; represented the country at international sports conferences; organized a national system of sport, and drafted the sporting calendar.
>
> (Chappell and Seifu 2000, 38)

Ethiopia is one of the most successful African countries at the Olympics and has won, including the London 2012 Games, 45 medals (all in athletics), despite widespread poverty and a very low per capita GDP below US$1,500.

China was also inspired by the USSR. However, the East Asian country took the system even further:

> China had inherited the Soviet sports structure, with its professional coaches, sports medicine and science, major sports clubs sponsored and financed by the armed and security forces, sports ranking system, residential boarding schools, etc. Whereas the Soviet Union had 46 sports boarding schools in 1990, and East Germany 20, China had 150. Whereas the USSR had 15,000 professional coaches, China had 18,173 in 1991. It is revealed that full-time athletes in China spend an average 7–8 hours a day on sports training.
>
> (Riordan and Jones 1999, 168)

According to Tan and Houlihan, China's adoption of the Soviet model of elite sport development is more complex to explain "through acceptance and utilization of elements of market commercialism, such as the soliciting of sponsorship income, the promotion of an internal money-based transfer system and the marketing of intangible commercial rights" (Tan and Houlihan 2012, 147). Material rewards have also become an important element in motivating Chinese athletes to achieve excellent performance (Tan and Houlihan 2012, 139).

Dennis and Grix analyze in their book *Sport under Communism: Behind the East German Miracle* the institutional history of the Olympic success of the GDR. They conclude that much of what characterizes elite sport development in modern-day democracies such as Australia, Britain, and Canada can be traced to the model developed in the German Democratic Republic (GDR): "A hands-on government approach that fosters a professional sporting environment, in which youth talent development, top-class facilities, high-quality coaching and the latest sports science combine to create Olympic success" (McDougall 2013, 842).

The *Wall Street Journal* wrote in an article on the introduction of elite sport schools in Germany: "After years of distancing itself from East Germany's controversial sports legacy, Germany is rebuilding a network of Communist-style sport schools" (Johnson 2008). The newspaper considered this as an example that Germany is "slowly adopting central sports planning from East Germany." The German Olympic Council (DOSB) argued that to improve at the Olympic Games, "we need elite sport schools." The decision to revive athlete schools came after Germany finished 6th in the overall medal ranking at the Athens 2004 Games, a relatively low rank for the country that is ranked 3rd in the all-time IOC Olympic medal rankings, and 4th in the AP rankings. In 1992, Germany had the third highest medal count, in 1996 the fifth highest. In 2008, there were already 39 elite sport schools in Germany, "20 old Communist-era schools in the former East Germany and 19 new ones in the West" (Johnson 2008). These schools receive twice the level of support than normal high schools get.

Apart from the elite schools, another legacy from the GDR is the Institute for Research and Development of Sports Equipment (Institut für Forschung und Entwicklung von Sportgeräten, FES) that was already founded in 1963. The official treaty of German unification guaranteed the continued existence of basic institutions that led to the GDR sporting success, among them the FES that still works on developing sports equipment for German elite athletes to make them more competitive at the international level, particularly at the Olympic Games. There are about 50 people working in the East Berlin headquarter of the FES, half of them engineers. Their main responsibility is developing innovative equipment in the sports of canoeing, rowing, cycling, sailing, sledge, bobsleigh, ice-skating, and skeleton. In addition, there are also subtasks for the sports of triathlon, skiing, swimming, and shooting. According to the FES director, "with the help of FES sport equipment a multitude of medals were won at world championships and Olympic Games" (Institut für Forschung und Entwicklung von Sportgeräten 2015). The German newspaper *Frankfurter Allgemeine Zeitung* (FAZ) called the institute in an article about its 50th anniversary in 2013 a "medal factory" and described how technological innovations developed by FES have to be kept secret until the Olympic Games begin, keeping competitors from copying them. Hackers from China and other countries such as Italy have tried several times to access the FES computer network. Other countries such as France and Great Britain are starting to adopt the FES model by establishing similar institutional capacities (Reinsch 2013, 28).

While elite schools and institutions like the FES are examples of how the East German elite sport system was maintained in the reunified Germany, some GDR sports structures were already transferred to the West during the Cold War. "Step by step, the West German sports concept came close to that of the GDR, whereas the official and ideological rhetoric of politicians as well as officials asserted the contrary" (Krüger et al. 2015, 97). For example, in the run-up to the Olympic Games in 1972 in Munich, West Germany started to employ full-time national coaches and sports officials, founded the German Sports Aid Foundation, established elite sports centers, formed A, B, and C squads, and developed the competition "Youth Training for Olympia": "Many elements were based on the institutions and methods of the GDR, which seemed distinctly superior to West Germany regarding its preparation for the Olympic Games in Munich" (Krüger et al. 2015, 59). Krüger et al. conclude in their book on German sports, "step by step, the West German concept of free, autonomous sport changed to a system of state-sponsored sport similar to that in the GDR – minus the political and ideological context" (Krüger et al. 2015, 199).

After the end of the Cold War, East German top-level sporting expertise became an "export hit":

> The knowledge and skills of GDR coaches were much sought after by former rivals in many countries. Some found jobs in Austria or in other German-speaking countries, where the language barrier did not apply. The

rise of China as a sporting world power can also be associated with the work of former experts from the GDR.

(Krüger et al. 2015, 147)

Bergsgard and his co-authors agree that the East German legacy remains influential:

Australia and Canada certainly picked up ideas about how to organize high performance sport from the communist bloc countries during the 1960s and 1970s. Since then Australia, and especially the Australian Institute of Sport (AIS), has been a powerful model for many other countries.

(Bergsgard et al. 2007, 194)

Sotiriadou and Shilbury refer to the AIS as "a medal factory": "AIS plays a vital role in the preparation of teams for major competitions and provides financial help, as well as access to first-class facilities and services" (Sotiriadou and Shilbury 2009, 146). AIS is also responsible for a systematic talent identification system that selects and develops the athletes.

The establishment of the Australian Institute of Sport (AIS) in 1981, and of the Australian Sports Commission (ASC) in 1985 as well as the increasing federal support for elite sport during the 1980s, were the result of the poor performance of the Australian team at the 1976 Montreal Olympic Games which acted, according to Green,

as a symbolic reminder of the country's "failure" on the international stage.... The establishment of the AIS and the ASC in the 1980s was a clear indication of the federal government's primary concern and of its determination that Australia would return to glory.

(Green 2007, 926)

The institutionalization of Australian elite sport was based on the "recognition that Australian sport could not match the successes of communist nations without adopting the organizational strategies and the more professional and scientific approach to 'producing' athletes that had underscored the success of the Eastern Bloc athletes" (Green 2007, 927). "The expectation is that by providing the optimum training facilities, coaching and science expertise, and international competition through targeted grants and scholarships, there is a greater probability that world-class Australian performers will follow" (Green 2007, 942).

New Zealand set up a similar institutional framework for the promotion of elite sport as Australia, but to do so it needed 20 more years and the failure at the 2000 Olympic Games, when the country only won one gold and three bronze medals and was ranked 46th in the IOC medal count. This failure was very sensitive for the country, since the Games were held in Sydney and the host Australia, New Zealand's biggest sporting rival, won 58 medals and was the 4th most successful country in the gold medal count. New Zealand's government established a new central sport agency, Sport and Recreation New Zealand (SPARC). SPARC changed its name in 2012 to Sport New Zealand (Sport NZ) and created a separate subsidiary responsible for elite sport called High Performance Sport New Zealand (HPSNZ). According to the chief executive of Sport NZ "nothing had changed – just the brand" (Sam 2015, 8). HPSNZ is responsible for developing and supporting the country's elite athletes, and developing a network of world-class training facilities (Sport and Recreation New Zealand, SPARC).

Canada was also an early adopter of the Eastern-bloc system. According to Green, "The state presence is so great that Canada is sometimes referred to as the GDR of the Commonwealth" (Green 2007, 943). Like in the case of Australia, disappointments at the Olympics were the starting point for the institutionalization of Canadian elite sport: "Canadian defeats in international competitions and the country's political need for nationally unifying symbols are important historical explanations of this early institutionalization of elite sport" (Bergsgard et al. 2007, 196). In addition, the federal government wanted to ensure that Canada would have a "best ever" performance in 1988 when the country hosted the Olympic Winter Games for the first time (Green 2007, 931).

According to Green's comparative study on Australia, Canada, and the United Kingdom:

> It is clear in all three countries the state agencies (primarily, the ASC, Sport Canada and UK Sport) have been fundamental in the process of specifying, constructing and upholding, through resource control and dependency, the pattern of values and beliefs supportive of elite achievement.
>
> (Green 2007, 945)

While Australia first learned from the GDR and other communist bloc countries for the establishment of the ASC, it later inspired others and was the blueprint for the institutionalization of elite sport policies in several countries. One example is Trinidad and Tobago, which used the Australian sport system as model, when the Sports Company of Trinidad and Tobago (SporTT) was established in 2004. The small twin island country with a population of about 1.2 million people has had remarkable success in the history of the Summer Olympics, winning 18 medals as of London 2012. While most medals were won in athletics, the country also had success in swimming and weightlifting (McCree 2009, 461–476; Sam and Jackson 2015, 1–9).

Again, like in Canada and Australia, traumatic events led to the establishment of an elite sport institution in Norway, particularly Norway's poor performance at the 1984 Summer Olympics in Los Angeles, and disappointing results at the 1988 Winter Games in Calgary in which the leading winter sport nation failed to win a single gold medal. In addition, the IOC decision in 1988 that Lillehammer would host the 1994 Winter Games was another driver for setting up Olympia-toppen (OT) in 1988. According to Augestad et al., "OT in Norway has been termed 'DDR-light', referring to the centralized and highly scientific and systematic elite sport regime of the former German Democratic Republic, excluding of course the extensive use of doping, which characterized that regime" (Augestad et al. 2006, 304).

OT is, according to Augestad et al., highly centralized and similar to the elite sport systems in other nations. Common characteristics are administrative head-quarters, close links to the education system, a specific training center for elite sport, and close links with sport medical/sciences facilities. There is a strong belief that scientific methods can improve performance. An example Augestad et al. give is a project aimed at improving the gliding effect of cross-country skis. OT spent several million Norwegian crowns for this project (Augestad et al. 2006, 293–313).

According to Ronglan's study on elite sport policies in Scandinavian countries, the centralization of elite sport support in Denmark, Norway, and Sweden is a response to increasing demands at the international stage and can be traced back to the 1980s.

> Until the 1980s, no organizational unit had any sole responsibility for elite sport in neither of the Scandinavian countries. The general rule was that the same associations that promoted youth and mass sport also had the main responsibility for elite sports within their domain.
>
> (Ronglan 2014, 7)

Team Denmark (TD) was established as a new elite sport body in Denmark in 1985, and Olympiatoppen (OL) was established in Norway between 1988 and 1989. In Sweden, contrary to Denmark and Norway, no specific elite sport body has been established. However, the Swedish Olympic Committee (SOC) has been professionalized and expanded:

> Its way of supporting elite sport has become quite similar to TD and OLT: offering expertise and support to federations, teams and athletes and intervening in performance processes (but only in Olympic sports). This way, the three nations today seem quite similar concerning the ways targeted elite sport bodies.
>
> (Ronglan 2014, 8–9)

The example of Sweden shows that there are not always governmental national sports agencies to promote the elite sport sector. Some countries (in addition to Sweden, for example Germany) give their national governing bodies (NGB, like Swedish Olympic Committee, SOC, and German Olympic Sports Confederation, DOSB) autonomy, "but with a certain degree of governmental control, such as formal objectives and transparent measurement instruments to evaluate NGB funding criteria" (De Bosscher et al. 2015, 360).

After the Olympic Games in 1984 in Los Angeles, the Israeli government created an elite sport unit as a division of the Ministry of Education. The task of the unit was to promote Israeli elite sport athletes and improve the country's performance at the Games. The decision for the new elite sport unit was made after Israel once again won no medals at the Olympic Games in 1984, despite sending the largest team in Israeli history to Los Angeles (33 athletes in 11 events). Israel had participated in all Summer Olympic Games since 1952 (apart from 1980, when the country boycotted the Moscow Games). The new administrative support for Israeli athletes paid off: after a rank of fourth in sailing in 1988, Israel won its first Olympic medals in 1992 in Barcelona. Although Israel missed the podium in London in 2012, it won at least one medal at all other Summer Olympic Games between 1992 and 2008. In Barcelona 1992 and Athens 2004, Israel even won two medals at each Games. Apart from the improved performance at the Summer Games, Israel has also been able to send athletes to the Winter Games since the Winter Olympics in Lillehammer in 1994 (Alperovich 2008, 237–240).

Japan, host of the 1964 Summer Games, is a latecomer concerning the institutionalization of its elite sport promotion. The Japan Institute of Sports Sciences (JISS) was inaugurated in 2001: "It is a centralized institute with the primary aim to support and develop athletes of medal-winning potential" (Yamamoto 2012, 290). The inauguration of JISS can be explained with Japan's disappointing performance at the 1996 Atlanta Summer Games, when Japan only won 14 medals and ended up 23rd in the IOC's medal count. This resulted in a policy process aiming to improve Japan's chances at the Olympics.

Countries who are institutionalizing their elite sport promotion need to be patient:

> Setting up elaborate, complex and integrated systems for co-ordination, organization and governance takes time and experience and cannot be considered a quick fix for achieving sporting success.... This is less about money in and more about doing things right and doing the right things.
>
> (De Bosscher et al. 2015, 369)

It has become a global trend to finance elite sport institutions with revenue from public lotteries. The advantage of channeling lottery money into sports is that gambling revenue is independent from state budget upturns and downturns. While the trend of establishing lotteries for sport promotion mainly occurs in developed countries, there are also examples such as China that introduced a lottery to subsidize its elite sport system.

One of the pioneers of the lottery funding system was Sweden. The Swedish government set up in 1934 "Svenska Spel," a state-controlled gambling institution, and decided to allocate the revenues of Svenska Spel to sport (Fahlén and Stenling 2015, 3).

In Switzerland, since 1938 a quarter of the profits of the "Société du Sport-Toto," an association set up by the Cantons to run sports betting, support Swiss sports. While these funds were mostly used to build sports facilities in municipalities, they today support Swiss elite sport and mainly go to the Swiss Olympic team, but also to the National Football Association and the Swiss Ice Hockey League (Chappelet 2010, 106).

Another pioneer was Norway that established a state gaming corporation in 1946. In Canada and Germany, lotteries that include sport as beneficiary were established in the 1970s in connection with the Munich and Montreal Olympics in 1972 and 1976. In the United Kingdom, the National Lottery was established in 1994 and is now the primary source of funding for elite sport development (Bergsgard et al. 2007, 256). Only 40% of the elite sport funding comes from the state budget in the UK, while the rest comes from the lottery (Anderson 2012). In Italy, lotteries (Totocalcio, Totogol, Totosei) also became the main source of funding for Italian high-performance sport (Digel 2005).

In the Netherlands, the largest portion of the income of the national sports governing associations comes, apart from membership fees, from lottery money. Since the introduction of the first lottery in 1960 and the second in 1975, the net profits have been divided among sport organizations (receiving three-quarters) and charity organizations (receiving one-quarter). "The fact that sport organizations receive the lottery money without interference of national government makes them more independent" (Waardenburg and van Bottenburg 2013, 470).

In Chile, a law was passed in 1975 to allow betting on the results of the weekly soccer games played in the domestic professional league. For many years, this was the main source of public funding for sport facilities (Bravo and Silva 2014, 140). Japan established in 2002 a soccer lottery (known as "toto") with the objective of generating revenue that "top-level athletes can be developed to perform on the world stage, and a rich sports environment can be established" (Yamamoto 2012, 280).

While in many countries lotteries support elite sport, the extent of support is quite varied, and not everywhere are lotteries as significant a source as in the UK. In Portugal, sport is promoted by lottery money, but the same funds also compete with other sectors such as tourism, social security, education, health, and youth work "with sport having no objective advantage in this situation" (Fernandes et al. 2011, 141).

Apart from lotteries, there are other instititutions that promote elite sport succes in some countries. In Germany (that also uses lottery money for the promotion of elite sport success), the military plays a key role: About half of all German summer Olympic medal winners and even more than half of all German medal-winning athletes at the Winter Games are employed by the German army ("Bundeswehr") (Haut 2014, 46). In Russia, the military is also of high importance for elite sport success (Digel 2005).

In the United States, there is a unique structure of the elite sport promotion: Different to most other countries, the US government has never directly funded the United States Olympic Committee (USOC) (Binns 2009). The promotion of Olympic sports is in the United States a decentralized program which is largely independent of the government (D'Agati 2011, 71). However, "Even in the USA, where elite athletes are nurtured through the college system, the prominent role of state-funded universities suggests that American exceptionalism is more evident in organizational structure than in independence from state resources" (Houlihan and Zheng 2013, 340). In the United States sport is tightly linked to public education, different from countries such as Germany where traditional sports clubs are the backbone of the elite sport system: Athletes develop in junior and high schools, and the best of them receive college athletic scholarships. While the US government does not directly subsidize Olympic sports, it gives tax-free status to the US Olympic Committee, and also to university sports programs (Johnson 2008). Whereas some of the most famous US universities are private (such as Harvard, MIT, Stanford), there are also plenty of public universities such as the universities of Berkeley, Los Angeles, Virginia, and Michigan, that have ambitious, publicly funded sports programs, with some of their coaches often being the highest paid public servants in that state.

Now that elite sport institutions have been established all over the world, a new trend is that sport is promoted in specific government departments. One of the pioneers was South Korea with the establishment of a "Ministry of Sports" in 1983 (Won and Hong 2015, 143). In the Netherlands in 1994 for the first time a state secretary of sport was appointed and the term "sport" appeared in the name of a Dutch ministry (Waardenburg and van Bottenburg 2013, 470). One year later in 1995, Brazil established a "Special Ministry for Sports." In the United Kingdom, "Sport" is featured in the title of a government department (the Department for Culture, Media and Sport, DCMS) since the inception of the Labour government in 1997, reflecting a trend toward central government control of this policy sector since the mid-1990s: "Sport policy has witnessed unprecedented government intervention in both elite and grass-roots sport policy" (Grix and Carmichael 2012, 74). Like in the UK, sport is included in a ministerial title in Japan. The Ministry of Education, Culture, Sports, Science and Technology (MEXT) "is striving to promote sport through increasing sport opportunities for children, promoting sport activities in line with the life stages, improving community sport environments, and enhancing international competitiveness of athletes" (Ministry of Education, Culture, Sports, Science and Technology 2015).

The growth of state involvement in sport can also be seen as an example of the expansion of the welfare state in developed countries:

> The development of modern welfare states is characterized by a stepwise expansion of government responsibilities, from the basic and state defining tasks of defense and policing via core welfare state issues, for example social security, to what could be considered to be secondary welfare state issues like leisure policy.
>
> (Bergsgard et al. 2007, 7)

In their case study on sport policy in Sweden, Fahlén and Stenling state "together with progressive policies for education, healthcare, housing and the labor market, policy for leisure and sport was given a prominent position in the public domain of the welfare society in the making" (Fahlén and Stenling 2015, 4).

However, sport has also been institutionalized in governments beyond the major sporting powers. Singapore established a sports ministry in 2000 (Houlihan and

Zheng 2014, 9). In Venezuela, the Ministry of Sports was created in 2008, with two vice ministries, one of them responsible for high performance sport and the other one responsible for physical activity (López de D'Amico 2012, 146). In Iran, the Ministry of Sport and Youth was established in 2011 (Dousti et al. 2013, 151–158, 155). In Chile, a Ministry of Sport was established in 2013. Since the 1990s the focus of the Chilean government has gradually shifted toward elite sports. The National Institute of Sport (Instituto Nacional de Deportes, IND) was established in 2001 and is, among others, responsible for supporting professional sports. IND is located in the capital city of Santiago, but also has representations in the 15 regions of the country. IND established a national system of tournaments and competitions to identify medal prospects and talents, and IND awards monthly stipends to athletes who have reached a minimum standard of athletic performance (Bravo and Silva 2014, 129–142).

While institutionalization might be necessary for elite sport success, it does not automatically lead to Olympic medals. It all depends on how the respective institution functions. A negative example is Lebanon. Nassif and Amara analyze the structure of the Lebanese national sport system. The Ministry of Youth and Sports (MYS) and the Youth and Sports Committee in the Lebanese Parliament were both formed in 2000. While there is no official distribution of powers according to religious affiliations inside the national sport system, sport remains informally structured according to political and religious allegiances. For Nassif and Amara, it is evident that confessionalism is strongly spread in various sports institutions in the country. Around 80% of federations are still managed by presidents and general secretaries from the same community.

> The fact that a sport is dominated by one religious community reduces significantly the number of people interested in it. Generally, athletes, referees and trainers are more prone to choose a sport which is managed by people of their own community.
>
> (Nassif and Amara 2015, 7)

The government's funding system for the sport sector is also based on political rather than performance criteria.

11 Specialization (S)

Focusing on specific medal-promising sports is today one of the most common strategies countries are choosing to win medals. Those countries that fail to do so are left behind in the Olympic medal race.

One of the first countries that specialized in specific sports to maximize its Olympic success was the German Democratic Republic (GDR): Dennis and Grix write in their book *Sport under Communism: Behind the East German Miracle* that the GDR government had already adopted in 1969 a high-performance directive which focused attention and money on specific Olympic sports. All sports were classified in two groups: Sports 1 and Sports 2. Only those sports grouped in Sports 1 would get governmental support. The authors conclude that much of what characterizes elite sport development in modern-day democracies such as Australia, Britain, and Canada can be traced to the model developed in the GDR (McDougall 2013, 843).

A first victim of the 1969 high-performance directive was the sport of ice hockey. The GDR national ice hockey team qualified for the first time in 1968 for the Winter Olympic Games. After GDR lost six out of seven matches at the Games in Grenoble, France, including the game against West Germany, and ended up on the last position in group A, the government classified ice hockey as one of the "Sports 2" sports that do not deserve government support. An effect was that the GDR ice hockey league was reduced from eight clubs in the 1967/1968 season ahead of the 1968 Winter Olympics to two clubs starting in 1970. From 1970 onwards, the GDR ice hockey championship was played with only two teams. The duel between Dynamo Weißwasser and Dynamo Berlin lasted until the German reunification in 1990. The rational of this decision was that ice hockey would be not likely to win an Olympic medal for the GDR, that the sport withdraws athletes from individual sports where single athletes can win numerous medals, and that ice hockey absorbs costly resources (ice rinks, expensive equipment) which could be better used for more medal-promising sports (Farkas 2015).

Other examples for sports that were not promoted in the GDR are basketball, equestrian, field hockey, and tennis. Interestingly, even 25 years after the German reunification, athletes in the German national teams in these sports are still predominantly from the West. In the highest field hockey men and women leagues, there is not even one team from East Germany (Armbrecht 2015).

Is the degree of specialization dependent on how developed a country is? Tcha and Pershin examined the economics of the Olympics to identify patterns of specialization or the concept of comparative advantage. They investigated three consecutive Summer Olympic games: Seoul (in 1988), Barcelona (in 1992), and Atlanta (in 1996). They concluded that countries in the high-income group spread their medal collection over various sports, while those in the low-income group concentrated on select sports only. Middle-income specialized less than low-income countries, collecting medals from more diversified sports. But compared to high-income countries, this group of countries diversified less (Tcha and Pershin 2003, 216–239).

However, specialization is, according to research from Houlihan and Zheng on the Olympics and elite sport policy, not only a strategy by low-income countries but also by major sports powers and medium powers that have developed a competitive advantage in a relatively narrow range of sports by identifying one or more niche sports in the Olympic program and concentrating resources in the respective disciplines. Based on an analysis of the summer Olympic Games between 1992 and 2012, Houlihan and Zheng conclude:

> Even sports powers are often reliant on a small number of sports/events for a significant proportion of their medals.... Almost all the most successful countries rely heavily on a limited number of sports for a significant proportion of their medals with most obtaining well over half their gold medals and around half of all their medals from just three sports.
>
> (Houlihan and Zheng 2013, 338–355)

Houlihan and Zheng give examples for competitive advantages of countries: Australia in swimming, Cuba in boxing, China in table tennis, Germany in canoeing and rowing, Great Britain in cycling and sailing, South Korea in archery, and the United States in swimming and athletics. For medium sports powers, the degree of reliance on a small number of sports disciplines is even more distinct: Ethiopia has won its medals in only one discipline (athletics), but Azerbaijan (wrestling, boxing), South Africa (swimming, athletics), and Iran (wrestling, weightlifting) are also heavily reliant on two sports for a majority of their medals, with Iran winning 54 out of 60 medals in wrestling and weightlifting. According to Houlihan and Zheng, "In seeking to maximize the medal return on public investment in elite Olympic sport it makes sense for countries to pursue a strategy of reinforcing historic advantages and seeking out sports where competition is relatively weak" (Houlihan and Zheng 2013, 345). However, the effect of specialization is "that it is increasingly difficult for other countries to achieve Olympic success" (Houlihan and Zheng 2013, 352).

Only few countries are able to win medals in a variety of sports. An example is the United States that has won medals in 14 out of the 15 sports that were in the Olympic program in Sochi 2014: Alpine skiing, biathlon, bobsledding, cross-country skiing, curling, figure skating, freestyle skiing, ice hockey, luge, Nordic combined, short-track speed skating, skeleton, ski jumping, snowboarding, and speed skating. Only in biathlon, a sport that is very popular in European winter sport nations such as Germany and Norway, the United States has failed to win any medal in the history of the Winter Games. However, winning medals in 14 out of 15 Winter Olympic sports makes the United States the nation that has won medals in the most sports at the Winter Games. Many winter Olympic sports are dominated by the United States: for example, the United States has 48 Olympic figure skating medals, the most won by a single nation. However, according to Mallon's data, one could argue the Soviet Union was even more successful than the United States at the Winter Games. The country won medals in only 10 of the 15 current sports, but freestyle, short-track, skeleton, and snowboarding were sports that were not yet in the Olympic program when the Soviet Union still existed. "So one can say that the former Soviet Union is the only nation to have won Winter Olympic medals in every sport on the Olympic Program available to them" (Mallon 2014a).

The Soviet Union was successful in all sports at the Winter Olympics, and while it invested significant resources into the development of the only team sport in the Winter Games, ice hockey, the country did not invest in all team sports, and often displayed "a tradition of avoiding competition where they could not succeed" (D'Agati 2013, 111). This tradition is especially apparent in the Summer Games team sport of field hockey. Prior to the 1980 Summer Olympics in Moscow, no Soviet men's or women's national field hockey team ever participated in the Olympics. While both teams were able to win bronze medals at the home Games in 1980, the achievement happened in the absence of field hockey powerhouses such as West Germany, which joined its ally the United States in boycotting the Moscow Games. Apart from 1980 and 1988, there was no other Soviet field hockey appearance at the Olympics:

> Field hockey was never a sport of interest in the Soviet Union, so there was no history for the sport to grow out of.… Field hockey was part of a crowded field of sports at the Summer Olympics. Repeated dominance in many other sports in the Summer Olympics meant one additional team spot held less value in the eyes of Soviet sports bureaucrats.
>
> (D'Agati 2013, 173)

After the dissolution of the Soviet Union in 1991, Russia was not able to be more successful than the Soviet Union in field hockey. Russia has never qualified for any field hockey event at the Summer Olympics.

More common than the holistic approach of the United States (and of the Soviet Union at the Winter Olympics) is to specialize in the most promising sports. Even among developed countries that are considered to be sporting powerhouses, there are some countries that owe more than a third of their medals to a single sport. Examples are Australia (37.6% of all medals in swimming), listed in the all time top 10 rankings of the Olympic Summer Games, and Austria (35.2% of all medals in alpine skiing), in the top 10 of the Winter Games (Heijmans 2015a).

According to OlympStats, 41 countries have only won medals in a single sport in the history of the Olympic Games. Whereas a majority of these cases (27) have only won a single Olympic medal, Ethiopia's long-distance runners have won a total of 45 Olympic medals. Liechtenstein has won all its nine medals in alpine skiing, Costa Rica all its four medals in swimming. Namibia's four medals in 100 and 200 meters running were all silver medals won by Frank Fredericks. Liechtenstein's medals were all won by members of two different families, the Wenzels and the Frommelts (Mallon 2014e).

Whereas the above-mentioned countries have won all medals in a single sport, there are some other countries that have a very high percentage of medals won in a single sport. Kenya, the most successful long-distance-running nation apart from Ethiopia, has won 79 out of its 86 Olympic medals in athletics. The remaining seven medals were won in boxing. Jamaica, a powerhouse in sprinting, has won 66 out of its 67 Olympic medals in athletics and a single medal in track cycling. Zimbabwe won seven out of its eight Olympic medals in swimming. Morocco won 19 out of 22, and Bahamas 10 out of 12 medals in athletics. A unique case is Pakistan that won eight out of its 10 Olympic medals in a team sport, field hockey, which is very popular in the Islamic Republic (Heijmans 2015a).

The tendency of small states to specialize in one or two sports makes them vulnerable to potential decisions by the IOC to remove certain sports from the Olympic program. Houlihan and Zheng give the example of the potential removal of wrestling from the Olympic schedule which would be a major problem for the future medal prospects of Azerbaijan, Georgia, and Iran: Azerbaijan won seven of its 10 medals, and Georgia all but one of its seven medals in that sport at the London 2012 Olympics (Houlihan and Zheng 2014, 4). Iran has won 38 out of its 60 all-time Olympic medals in wrestling.

Specialization in only a few sports can have different reasons: First of all, it can be linked to a country's historic advantage in a respective sport: "Taking each country in turn the emergence of public policy for sport is related to the history of sport in the countries over the last one hundred years or so" (Bergsgard et al. 2007, 16). An example is the case of Hungary that won 83 of its 476 Summer Olympic medals (17.43%) in fencing prior to London 2012, making fencing the most successful single sport in the Hungarian Olympic history. "From 1908 until 1964, a Hungarian fencer always won the sabre gold medal at the Olympics, with the exception of 1920 when Hungary was not invited after the First World War" (Onyestyák 2013, 762).

Given the difficulties in competing with countries that are historically strong in a sport (path dependency), other nations have decided to focus on new sports that were recently added to the Olympic program (the latter is discussed in more detail in the next section on early learning). An example of new sport specialization is South Korea. While being ranked fifth in the London 2012 and 13th in the Sochi 2014 medal tables (both according to the IOC's "gold first" approach), the country was a latecomer when it comes to Olympic success: "Since the period of modernization of Korea, Korean sport has grown dramatically in a relatively short period of time" (Won and Hong 2015, 148). South Korea won its first Olympic gold medal at the 1976 Montreal Summer Olympics and its first Winter Olympics medals ever in Albertville in 1992.

At the Winter Olympics, South Korea has successfully focused on short-track. Whereas speed skating has been part of the Olympic program since 1960, short-track belongs to the Winter Games program since just 1992. It is very difficult to compete with the Netherlands in speed skating: In Sochi 2014, it won 23 out of 36 available medals (64%), although South Korea did manage to win two speed skating medals. Skating is very popular and receives a lot of support from government and private sponsors. However, as a relatively new winter sport nation, South Korea has decided to focus on short-track speed skating, and has so far been very successful with this strategy. It won 21 of the 48 gold medals in short-track since it became a medal sport at the 1992 Games ("South Korea, Netherlands Ink Skating Accord" 2014).

According to Won and Hong, approximately 80% of the total medals won by Korean athletes came in those sports sponsored by the top business conglomerates such as Samsung, LG, and Hyundai. They focus on certain non-professional sports in which there are potentials to win Olympic medals. This private funding goes back to a public initiative in the early 1980s when the government asked businesses to be involved in the promotion of elite sports, promising them in return to be eligible to benefit from a tax refund (Won and Hong 2015, 145).

Tables 11.1, 11.2, and 11.3 give examples for the historic advantage of countries in sports at the Summer Olympics (archery, swimming) as well as one sport

Table 11.1 Olympic Swimming Medal-Winning Countries

Country	Gold	Silver	Bronze	Total
United States	232	162	126	520
Australia	57	63	63	183
East Germany	38	32	22	92
Germany	14	25	35	74
Japan	20	24	29	73
Great Britain	16	25	32	73
Hungary	26	24	18	68
Soviet Union	12	21	26	59
Netherlands	20	18	19	57
Canada	7	14	22	43
France	8	13	19	40
China	12	17	8	37
Sweden	8	14	13	35
West Germany	3	5	14	22
Russia	5	7	7	19
TOTAL	**478**	**464**	**453**	**1,395**

Source: Adapted from "Olympic Sports United States Swimming," *Sports Reference*, www.sports-reference.com/olympics/countries/USA/summer/SW1/. "Olympic Sports Swimming," *Olympic.it*, www.olympic.it/english/event/id_20.

Table 11.2 Medal-Winning Countries in Archery at the Olympics

Country	Gold	Silver	Bronze	Total
South Korea	19	9	6	34
United States	14	9	8	31
France	7	10	7	24
Belgium	11	7	3	21
Great Britain	2	2	5	9
China	1	6	2	9
Italy	2	2	3	7
Soviet Union	1	3	3	7
Japan	0	3	2	5
Finland	1	1	2	4
Ukraine	1	1	2	4
Australia	1	0	1	2
Netherlands	1	0	1	2
Sweden	0	2	0	2
Mexico	0	1	1	2
Chinese Taipei	0	1	1	2
Germany	0	1	1	2
Poland	0	1	1	2
Unified Team	0	0	2	2
Spain	1	0	0	1
Indonesia	0	1	0	1
Russia	0	0	1	1
TOTALS	**62**	**60**	**52**	**174**

Source: Adapted from Sport Reference, "Olympic Sports, Archery," www.sports.reference.com/olympic/sports/ARC/. Olympic, "Olympic Sports, Archery," www.olympic.it/english/event/id_35.

Table 11.3 Olympic Luge Medal-Winning Countries

Country	Gold	Silver	Bronze	Total
Germany	17	11	8	36
East Germany	13	8	8	29
Austria	5	7	7	19
Italy	7	4	6	17
West Germany	1	4	5	10
Soviet Union	1	2	3	6
United States	0	2	3	5
Latvia	0	1	3	4
Russia	0	3	0	3
TOTALS	**46**	**46**	**44**	**129**

Source: "Olympic Sports Luge," *Sports Reference*, www.sports-reference.com/olympics/sports/LUG/.

at the Winter Games (luge). Table 11.1 shows that in the all-time Olympic swimming ranking, the United States has won by far the most medals. The United States (37%) and Australia (13%) have won more than half (703) of all 1,395 swimming medals in the history of the Olympics. The Australian swimming medals account for about 40% of all Australian medals at the Summer Olympics, and about 38% of the entire Olympic medals of the country (including the 2014 Sochi Games, Australia only won 12 medals at Winter Games).

Table 11.2 shows that archery, a sport mainly present at the Summer Olympics since 1972 (after also being in the program at some of the very first Olympic Games), is dominated by only four countries: South Korea, the United States, France, and Belgium won 110 out of 174 archery Olympic medals, almost two-thirds (63.22%) of all Olympic archery medals ever.

Table 11.3 shows how Germany is dominating the winter sport of luge. About 58% of all medals in luge were won by different German teams (East Germany, West Germany, and the reunified Germany). If one includes Austria, about three-quarters (73%) of all Olympic luge medals have been won by German-speaking countries. Since the Italian luge team is usually recruited from South Tyrol, a majority German-speaking province of Italy, Olympic medal winning in luge is nearly an entire ethnic German domain, with only 14% of luge medals won by the non-German-speaking countries Soviet Union, United States, Latvia, and Russia.

The four sports with the least competitive balance are badminton, table tennis, rhythmic gymnastics, and beach volleyball. The sport that shows the least competitive balance in this group of events is badminton, where nearly 85% of the medals in the four Summer Olympics 1996, 2000, 2004, and 2008 have been shared by China, Indonesia, and South Korea (Silver 2012).

Sometimes countries are able to sweep all the medals in one event. For instance, in Sochi the Netherlands won all the available gold, silver, and bronze medals in four speed skating events (Mallon 2014c). Another recent example is Germany that swept the medals in women singles luge at three consecutive Winter Olympics (2002, 2006, and 2010). Norway is the national leader in medal sweeps, with 11 at the Winter Olympics. According to Mallon, medal sweeps have happened 260 times at the Summer Olympics and 44 times at the Winter Olympics (Mallon 2014d). The fact that only 10 different nations managed to achieve medal sweeps in the Olympic history shows that this extreme form of specialization can only be accomplished by few nations. A medal sweep might even have negative consequences for a country in case the sport is removed from the Olympic program and the country cannot compensate the success with other sports: Williams comments on Germany's luge dominance that it is "great for Germany, arguably less great for luge, given the Olympics' propensity to look disapprovingly on sports where one or two nations become too dominant (e.g. baseball and softball)" (Williams 2014).

An effect of the specialization strategy is that individual athletes can win numerous medals, if they operate in a sport where they can participate in numerous competitions. There are 33 athletes who won 10 or more Olympic medals for their country. This list is led by the American swimmer Michael Phelps who won 22 Olympic medals for the United States in his career, among them eight gold medals in Beijing in 2008. Since Phelps won nine out of his 22 medals in relay races, the most successful individual athlete at Summer Olympic Games is Larisa Latynina. The Soviet gymnast won 18 medals in total and 14 of those medals by herself. However, Phelps does lead the list of individual gold medals with 11 individual gold medals. The most successful athlete of all time in the Winter Games is the Norwegian Ole Einar Bjørndalen who won in total 13 medals (eight golds) for his country in biathlon, nine of them by himself (Mallon 2015a).

The specialization of countries in certain sports is no coincidence, and is usually the result of a strategic approach of governments and sport governing associations, as exemplified by the United Kingdom. After a disappointing result at the 1996 Summer Olympics in Atlanta, when the UK finished 36th in the IOC medal ranking with only one gold and 15 medals in total, Britain introduced its so-called "no compromise system." This is a "resource-dependent relationship: a relationship that will only endure if the sport delivers on the Olympic stage" (Green 2007, 939). This "all or nothing" approach focuses public funding on the most successful sports that are most likely to win medals. Sports need to prove that they have a chance of a medal in the next two Games and maintain annual performance targets or their funding is withdrawn. Advocates call this approach "a merit system with a clear ambition to be the best," while for critics it is a "ruthless approach to excellence" (Green 2007, 940).

Since moving to the "no compromise" approach, the UK tremendously improved its medals output, from 36th in the medal count in 1996 to top five ranks at the 2008 and 2012 Summer Olympics. However, having medals as the only metric for apportioning public funding to elite sport is controversial and critically discussed in Great Britain. In the British newspaper the *Guardian*, Gibson calls the "no compromise" approach an "emotion-free, highly analytical funding model" that will develop a growing gap between the sports. In 2014 seven sports – basketball, synchronized swimming, water polo and weightlifting, blind football, goalball and wheelchair fencing – have had their funding withdrawn, based on their poor performances in London 2012 at the Olympic and Paralympic Games. They were no longer considered realistic medal prospects for 2016 or 2020. Gibson comments this decision by asking the following critical questions:

> Should a sport like cycling, in which competition is drawn from a handful of nations, be considered on the same basis as one like table tennis, where there is a production line of Asian talent standing in the way of a medal? ... Can it be right that a sport such as basketball, so popular in inner cities and in schools, with so much potential in legacy terms, can have its elite funding cut from almost £9m to nothing within a year?

Basketball, argues Gibson, has a grassroots base bigger than any other British Olympic team sport (Gibson 2014a).

UK Sport's chairman, Rod Carr, justified the "no compromise" approach by saying that money diverted to team sports without medal potential could impact on podium chances elsewhere. Funding basketball until 2024 would have cost GBP£33 million.

> That is an awful lot of public money with no certainty of qualification, let alone winning a medal. To invest £33m at that rate is not a good use of public money.... We have got a certain pot of money and we have to spend that widely in the best interests of winning across a wide range of sports in a limited timeframe.... Given a limitless amount of money and limitless time frame, there might be different policies.
>
> (Gibson 2014b)

The former British colony New Zealand has adopted the United Kingdom's policy of specialization, with a similar list of priority sports. New Zealand, a small country with only 4.5 million people, has the ambition to "punch above its weight" in global sports and international affairs. With so far 100 Olympic medals won (99 of them at the Summer Olympics), the country has certainly done so. Apart from cycling, New Zealand's focus is on water sports. The country won 54 of its 99 Olympic medals in sports that are done in or on the water (21 in rowing, 18 in sailing, 9 in canoeing, and 6 in swimming). Apart from water sports and particularly rowing and sailing, cycling is a targeted sport in New Zealand.

Given the small size of the country, the New Zealand government claims that the country has to be "smart and innovative" to be competitive in elite sports, since it is not competitive with the size and resources of major sport powers. "Targeting resources" means in the case of New Zealand that first of all the number of priority sports have been reduced, while other sports are receiving at the same time more funding. The agency responsible for elite sport, HPSNZ, has halved the number of athletes it supports from 950 in 2006 to 440 athletes in 2013, while at the same time "this rationing has paradoxically occurred in an environment of steadily increasing budgets, where HPSNZ's allocation doubled in the same period" (Sam 2015, 1–14, 9).

A controversial case was cutting the funding for basketball. The sport is not only popular in New Zealand, but also, given the small size of the country, relatively successful. The national basketball team qualified twice (2000, ending up at the rank of 11, and 2004, 10th) for the Summer Olympics and five times for the FIBA World Cup, with the highlight of achieving the 4th rank in 2002. According to the chief executive of HPSNZ, "no one will win if resources are spread too thinly," and if basketball were funded, "it wouldn't be fair to another sport that had a better chance of winning on the world stage" (Sam 2015, 9). According to Sam, New Zealand's emphasis on elite sport has grown, from initially occupying approximately 40% of the total sport expenditure (in 2002) to exceeding 60% of the total sport budget (in 2013). Sam comments on the focus of New Zealand and other small countries on just a small number of medal-promising sports that "any small deviation from the expected target (due to injury, sickness or luck) represents a

proportionately greater blow to their medal count, and by extension
to the legitimacy of their systems" (Sam 2015, 3).

Whereas only few countries are so radical like the UK and N⟨
completely cut funding for sports without any medal prospect
trend to specialize on the disciplines with the best medal prosp⟨
cluded in his comparative study on Olympic sporting success fro⟨⟨ ⟨⟨
in Australia, Canada, and the United Kingdom that the development in Canada

> not only reflects Australia's adoption of a targeted approach in the early 1990s
> but also the strategy adopted by UK Sport in the late 1990s in the UK – a
> strategy that has developed further into an even tougher regime with UK Sport's
> announcement of its "no compromise" funding strategy for 2008 and beyond.
>
> (Green 2007, 935)

In Canada, "Criteria were heavily weighted towards elite success, with far less
weight given to broader social objectives" (Green 2007, 933).

Japan decided in 2000 to focus its Olympic funding on athletes with medal
potential. A result was that in 2004 the country won half of its 16 gold medals in
judo (Johnson 2008). Hong Kong followed the example by classifying sports as
priority and non-priority sports: "The degree of specialization and prioritization
was further intensified in the twenty-first century and the government has continued to allocate additional funding to the 'Major Four' – badminton, table
tennis, cycling and windsurfing" (Zheng 2015, 9). Hong Kong has so far won
three medals at the Summer Olympics in 1996 in Atlanta, 2004 in Greece and
2012 in London, all of them in one of the priority sports. Only badminton has
been unable to deliver a medal for the former British colony.

Starting from the Olympic Games in 1972, West Germany introduced a new criterion for the participation of athletes in the Olympic Games: The "finals opportunity," referring to a realistic chance of reaching the final of a competition (Krüger
et al. 2015, 103). Apart from the nomination criteria of a finals opportunity for
athletes, achievement-oriented salaries for federal coaches were introduced in 1970.
In addition, in 1980 special bonuses for success were introduced (Krüger et al.
2015, 105). In 1970, the board of the German Sports Federation (DSB) decided "to
privilege sports and disciplines with better chances of success with respect to the
allocation of public as well as private funding" (Krüger et al. 2015, 106).

After being reunified, Germany shifted toward an even more success
dependent promotion scheme which led to a critical discourse in Germany with
some journalists and scholars arguing that the previous Eastern German system
of solely focusing on medal-promising sports has been adopted (WAZ Rechercheblog 2012). Comparing the present German with the past East German
system might be exaggerated, but a trend toward a stronger focus on success
cannot be neglected. The annual financial support from the ministry of the interior has two components: a basic funding and a so-called project funding. The
basic funding depends on the number of Olympic competitions and of participating athletes at the last two Games. A third criterion is the amount of medals a

ₚport has won at the last two Olympics. These three criteria are weighted in relation 1:1:3 (3 for number of medals won). While there is already in the basic funding a strong component of past Olympic success, the so-called project funding entirely depends on the prospects for success at the next Olympic Games. Preference is given to sports that can stabilize or increase their potential or medals won. Olympic sports are grouped in five different categories: A for successful sports with high potential for medals; B for sports with average potential for medals; C for sports with some potential for medals; D for sports with potential to qualify for the final round of competitions; and E for sports without potential to qualify for the finals. A is receiving the highest, E the lowest project funding ("Verbandsförderung im Olympischen Spitzensport" 2007). The Federal Ministry of the Interior negotiates with the German Olympic Sports Confederation, DOSB, over which group certain sports will be placed in. Michael Vesper, General Secretary of the DOSB, is quoted in a press article as saying: "In elite sport there is only one criteria for success which is success." The number of medals won is, according to Vesper, the main but not only criteria for financial support (WAZ Rechercheblog 2012).

China is another example of a country successfully specializing in certain events: Table tennis is an incredibly popular sport in China. Table tennis did not become an Olympic sport until 1988, however of the 88 Olympic medals awarded in the sport from 1988 until 2012, 47 have been won by China (53%), including 24 of the 28 gold medals (86%). In 2012, further regulations were introduced to limit the amount of Chinese medals that could be won. After China swept all six singles medals in Beijing, the athlete quorum per nation was reduced to two, ensuring at least one non-Chinese medal in each singles event. In London, the Chinese table tennis players achieved a maximum score, occupying both finals (Heijmans 2015b).

However, China's Olympic table tennis history started with a failure: When the sport made its Olympic debut in the 1988 Games in Seoul, Chinese players failed to win any medal in men's singles: "Players who were fed up with fixed government-funded salaries sought more lucrative careers abroad and became known as the 'overseas legion' … This loss of talent was detrimental to the Chinese squad's international performance, including its Olympic medal count" (Chen et al. 2015, 2, 6). The government introduced sport reforms, among them in table tennis "a professional league governed under a socialist system." Table tennis clubs started to pay high salaries. "The Chinese government understood that only raising salaries at home could reverse the exodus of players" (Chen et al. 2015, 5). What Chen et al. call the "Chinese model" is a reimbursement model with different pay grades depending on the players' performance in the national team. In 2008, the highest payment grade was US$162,000. In the following years, additional appearance and win bonuses were introduced. "By coupling players' pay and bonuses with their performance in the national team, the government is to some extent able to control athletes and boost their desire to compete for the country" (Chen et al. 2015, 8). This payment model aimed to avoid a scenario known from Western professional sports leagues such as the Major League Baseball (MLB) that high-paid players showed little interest in the Olympics (when baseball was an Olympic sport) due to the lack of attractive payments and the risk of injury. China's success in Olympic table tennis starting with the 1992 Games in Barcelona shows that the "introduction of Western market practices gave table tennis in China a second life and helped the country regain world dominance in the sport" (Chen et al. 2015, 2). Other measures for maintaining China's table tennis success were proposed by the country and introduced by the International Table Tennis Federation (ITTF), including a three-year waiting period for athletes to compete for a different national team, and an age limit of 28 for male and of 26 for female athletes to be permitted to go abroad (Tan and Houlihan 2012, 143).

Table tennis is the national sport in China, and is popular in many other countries in the world, with millions of people playing for fun or on a competitive level. Despite its success in table tennis, China has won most of its Olympic medals in less popular sports. An example for China's Olympic success in a niche sport is women's weightlifting. Whereas men's weightlifting belonged to the first Olympic program in 1896 (and has been regularly present at the Summer Olympics since 1920), it was not until 2000 that women's weightlifting became a sport contested at the Olympic Games. There are seven weight classes in women's weightlifting; each country is allowed to enter four categories. China won 14 out 16 possible gold medals at the four Summer Olympics in Sydney 2000, Athens 2004, Beijing 2008, and London 2012: three each in Sydney and Beijing, four each in Athens and London.

Beech describes how "the country's sports bureaucrats have developed a winning formula" to increase China's medal count: "Target less popular disciplines contested by fewer countries; choose sports that offer multiple medals, like for different weight classes; and focus on women, whose athletic efforts are underfunded in most countries." A coach of the national women's weightlifting team is quoted in the article as saying that "We saw an opportunity … and we broke the sport down very scientifically into the smallest components. No country can compare with us" (Beech 2012).

According to Beech, when women's weightlifting became an Olympic sport

> scouts had been dispatched to the countryside, where parents were more likely than their urban counterparts to release their daughters into state care. Frantic research by China's athletic czars had determined the ideal girl for the sport: she would have the stoicism that comes of a rural background; rapid reflexes, big hands and fleet feet; explosive jumping power since lifting is as much about quickness as strength; and matching height and wingspan for balance.
>
> (Beech 2012)

Women's weightlifting in China is a full-time job with practices six days a week, following a strict schedule that starts in the morning at 6.30 a.m. According to Bleech, the athletes "rarely have free time. They are allowed little life outside the discipline that was chosen for them." Food, housing, clothing, and tuition are paid for the athletes who usually leave their home at the age of 10 to live in the academy. Later, the lifters receive a state salary (Beech 2012).

The journalistic work of Beech is confirmed by research from Tan and Green on China's drive for Olympic success. According to Tan and Green, China is targeting resources on a relatively small number of sports through identifying those that have a real chance of success at the world level. Of Chinese Olympic gold medals, 75% were won in five sports: gymnastics, diving, weightlifting, shooting, and table tennis:

> In order to increase its chances of winning Olympic gold medals, China not only targeted "softer" medal sports, such as table tennis, badminton, diving, weightlifting, gymnastics and female wrestling, but also focused on women's sports such as rowing, canoeing, sailing and team sports (volleyball, soccer, softball, basketball and hockey).
>
> (Tan and Green 2008, 326–327)

Based on their interviews with 32 Chinese sport officials, Tan and Green found that China is searching for young athletes from lower socio-economic areas, such as in some of the poorer rural districts and inland provinces: "In doing so, China maximized its sport system by linking the wealthy sport resources of the south-east provinces to a potentially large talent pool in the poorer north-west provinces" (Tan and Green 2008, 328).

Cuba is another example of specialization at the Olympics. Cuba's Olympic success is remarkable, given its small population base and weak economy. The country could maintain "it's pre-eminence as a regional athletic power despite decades of erosion caused by the American trade embargo and the collapse of the Soviet Union and the Eastern bloc, formerly the island nation's primary sporting benefactors" (Longman 2014). Cuba has won most of its Olympic medals in boxing, among them 34 gold medals in that sport. According to an article in the *New York Times* that is based on interviews with Cuban athletes and sport officials, Cuba's top Olympic fighters can earn US$8,000 to 12,000 per month. Olympic gold medalists are entitled to a monthly US$300 life-long payment. For comparison: The average monthly salary in Cuba is US$20. On top of the payments, gold medalists are provided with a home and a car (Longman 2014).

An extreme example of specialization is the Olympic success of East African countries in long-distance running. Ethiopia's long-distance runners have won all 45 Olympic medals of the country. Kenya, apart from Ethiopia the most successful long-distance-running nation, has won the vast majority of its Olympic medals (79 out of 86) in athletics, most of them (68) in running. Without boycotting the 1976 and 1980 Olympic Games, Kenya could have won far more medals, since the country has been an international athletic powerhouse since the late 1960s. The same applies to Ethiopia that boycotted three Games in 1976, 1984, and 1988.

The success of Kenya and Ethiopia is often explained with genetics and high altitude training. Indeed, the majority of successful Kenyan and Ethiopian runners remain geographically clustered within the high-altitude region of the Rift Valley that runs through both countries. Ethiopia's track training takes place in the Diahemeda stadium that is 2,500 meters above sea level. However, Hamilton argues that "If altitude were the only factor involved, then all African countries with high altitude populations, as well as countries such as Nepal, Peru, and Mexico, should be producing many world class athletes" (Hamilton 2000, 391). The same author points out regarding genetic explanations for East African running success that "although many physiological and anatomical factors have been proposed to explain East African dominance, research into these variables has not yet revealed any definitive advantage for the African" (Hamilton 2000, 391).

Ethiopia and Kenya belong to the world's poorest nations, they lack basic sporting equipment and infrastructure. However, the governments of both countries are targeting running, a sport that is less cost-intensive than other sports, for Olympic success. According to a case study on Ethiopian sport by Chappell and Seifu, one of the main reasons for the success of Ethiopian runners is that they are able to be full-time athletes. Running is viewed as a viable route out of poverty. Young sports talent is identified at national championships where elite athletes are recruited into the army and security clubs. "The army provided the ideal conditions for the development of excellence.... Consequently, most of Ethiopia's world-class athletes, and other team representatives became members of army sports clubs" (Chappell and Seifu 2000, 40).

A similar structure applies to Kenya. Starting with the 1968 Mexico Games, Kenyan runners had overwhelming success at the Summer Olympics. For a long time, only male athletes won medals at the Olympic level. However, since the 1996 Atlanta Olympics, women have contributed to the medal tally for Kenya. According to a case study by Jarvie and Sikes about female Kenyan running athletes, the key to the countries' success is the teams that represent Kenya's main government institutions:

> Historically the most successful women have secured a position within an institutional team such as the prisons team, the armed forces, or the air force. This confers a significant advantage in that athletes who are affiliated to a particular state institution are provided with the relevant training and support while they compete.
>
> (Jarvie and Sikes 2012, 637)

Simiyu Njororai also refers to the contribution of the countrywide school system that generates "thousands of runners" because cross-country and track and field competitions are a major part of co-curricular activities. Distance running in Kenya has become a mass movement (Simiyu Njororai 2012, 195).

According to Jarvie and Sikes, for runners from the pioneering generation of athletes in Kenya, running was a source of personal satisfaction and a chance to travel outside of Kenya. Since the international governing body of athletics allowed athletes to receive remunerations based on athletic performance in 1982, material benefits to be gained through running is the central motivation of runners today: "Athletics represents an avenue through which some runners can radically improve the living standards of themselves and their families" (Jarvie and Sikes 2012, 636).

Apart from the natural advantages from the Great Rift Valley's altitude and the motivation that comes from living in a society in which running is popular, another Kenyan success factor might be widespread doping: "But Kenyans have clearly been relying on some unnatural advantages as well. The received wisdom is looking more than a little naïve with over 30 Kenyan athletes having tested positive for banned substances since 2012," commented the *New York Times* in August 2015 (Clarey 2015b).

Danish track cycling is yet another example for targeted efforts of a country. Cycling (and sailing) are the sports where Denmark has won most medals in the Olympic Games. Most cycling medals have been achieved on the track. Different to other mentioned examples such as speed skating in the Netherlands, and running in East African countries, this is an example for Olympic success without mass participation, but from a strict niche strategy that is concentrating on specific track cycling events. One of the keys for the recent Danish cycling successes after the year 2005 was the modernization of the one essential track in the country. Ronglan concluded in his study on Scandinavian elite sport policies:

> Danish track cycling is an example of how specific infrastructure and competence in combination with strict priorities can foster success despite a shrinking recruitment base. It is worth noting that the number of track cyclists, and the number of competing road cyclists, diminished during the recent elite sport success.
>
> (Ronglan 2014, 13)

For Ronglan, the case contradicts the widespread notion of a "virtuous cycle" that successful elite sport as such will generate mass sport, or vice versa.

Alpine skiing in Austria is another example for the specialization of a country in a specific sport. However, contrary to Danish track cycling, it is a popular mass sport in the Central European country:

> It can be shown that the period around the First World War was a key phase in the development of skiing in Austria, leading it away from the leisure activity of a privileged few and towards a mass phenomenon, and later a "national sport." In addition to the military, it was primarily schools, as the second main governmental authority that rendered skiing available to the masses.
>
> (Müllner 2013, 667–668)

While Austria did not win a single medal at the London 2012 Summer Games, it was in the top 10 of the medal table at the Winter Olympics in 2014 in Sochi. This reflects Austria's historically better performance at the Winter Olympics (218 medals won compared with 86 at the Summer Games). More than half of the medals the country has ever won at the Winter Olympics were in alpine skiing (114): "Competitive skiing constitutes the only high-performance sport in which victories and top results could be obtained on a regular basis by Austrian athletes" (Müllner 2013, 666). A main success factor was "Skiing for all" as a guiding principle of the Austrian government, promoting skiing in the military and establishing it in schools linked with policies such as the support of financially underprivileged parents, the establishment of public skiing equipment rental facilities, and the provision of group reductions for railway travel (Müllner 2013, 665).

Even the Olympic superpower, the United States, moved after the 2000 Olympic Games in Sydney toward a performance-based funding strategy that focuses on the development of Olympic medalists. This process was investigated by Binns in his dissertation "The Use of Performance Based Funding in a Sport Organization: A Case Study of the United States Olympic Committee" and reflects the trend that "Performance-based budgeting systems grew in popularity in the United States during the late 1990s as governments looked to account for the limited resources they had to spend" (Binns 2009, 3).

The rationale behind the new approach was, according to Binns, that

> Americans don't really care about the athlete that finished fourth. Americans want a winner. ... Our society is focused on results. The USOC (United States Olympic Committee) understands that, and that is one reason they have focused on performance-based funding principles.
>
> (Binns 2009, 108)

Another reason for the new performance-based funding strategy is the unique structure of elite sport promotion in the United States. Different to most other countries, the US government has never directly funded the United States Olympic Committee (USOC). Therefore, the USOC "must be very judicious with the limited funds that they have" (Binns 2009, 94). The annual USOC budget of US$150 million is made up of sponsorship and television revenue. This money is distributed to the National Governing Bodies (NGBs). For example, the successful US swimming association received over US$2.2 million in 2007, whereas the US table tennis association (that unlike swimming has no world-class athletes who are able to win medals at the Olympics) received less than US$200,000. Apart from payments from the USOC, NGBs try to generate their own income particularly from sponsors. However, those sports that have difficulties in attracting athletes and spectators face more problems to attract sponsors and are more reliant on the USOC for funds. The 45 national governing bodies rely on the USOC for between 6% and 85% of their funds (Binns 2009, 3).

The United States has increased its overall lead in the Olympic medal count since the implementation of performance-based funding in 2000: "The USOC's financial and podium performance over the past eight years shows that the performance-based funding principles are helping the USOC keep the United States at the top of international competition" (Binns 2009, 57). After winning in

Sydney "only" 91 medals (but still leading the medal ranking), the United States won 102 in 2004, and 110 medals in 2008 (more overall medals than the host country China, but less gold medals). About half of the medals were won in two sports: swimming, and track and field. In 2004, the United States won 28 medals in swimming, and 25 in track and field. In 2008, the count increased to 31 in swimming and was 23 in track and field. Binns points out that "the number of medals won by USA Swimming at the Olympics help ensure that the United States stays close to or at the top of the overall medal count" (Binns 2009, 76).

The increase in medals at the Winter Olympics after the implementation of the performance-based funding system in 2000 was even more remarkable: after winning only 13 medals each in 1994 and 1998, the United States won 34 medals in 2002 – a success that has also to be explained with the US home advantage at the Games in Salt Lake City. In 2006, the US won 25 medals. Similar to the Summer Olympics, a majority of the medals were won in only a few sports: Skiing, snowboarding, and speed skating. In 2002, the United States won 10 medals in skiing and snowboarding, as well as 11 in speed skating. Four years later, the United States won 10 medals in skiing and snowboarding as well as 10 in speed skating.

What is also unique to the United States is that sport is tightly linked to public education, in contrast to countries such as Germany where traditional sports clubs are the backbone of the elite sport system: Athletes develop in junior and high schools, and the best athletes receive college athletic scholarships. Whereas the United States does not directly subsidize Olympic sports, the government gives tax-free status to the US Olympic Committee and to university sports programs (Johnson 2008). While some of the most famous US universities are private (such as Harvard, MIT, Stanford), there are also plenty of public universities such as the universities of Berkeley, Los Angeles, Virginia, and Michigan that have ambitious, publicly funded sports programs.

Some of the countries that have not yet been successful at the Olympics are in the process of implementing the strategy of specializing. One example is India, a country with a large population base but limited Olympic success in the past. For the 2016 Summer Olympics in Rio, Sports Minister Sarbananda Sonowal said "This time, we are aiming at ten-plus medals." The ministry has devised a so-called Target Olympic Podium Scheme (TOPS) to support athletes who are medal prospects. "We have identified seven medal prospect disciplines for the coming Olympics and identified 75 core probables. Another 75 probables will be selected shortly," the minister said. The disciplines are archery, athletics, badminton, boxing, shooting, weightlifting, and wrestling ("India Targetting Ten-Plus Medals at Rio Olympics, Says Sports Minister" 2015).

Sweden is an example of a country that failed to specialize, with a result of decreasing success. The country won 483 medals at the Summer Olympics, and was always ranked in the top 10 of the medal rankings until the 1956 Games in Melbourne (when the equestrian events were held in Stockholm, the Swedish capital that hosted the entire Games in 1912). One of the reasons for Sweden's remarkable early successes was the extensive financial support to the building of sport facilities in the first half of the twentieth century:

The winners were sports that were dependent on specific weather conditions such as ice hockey and swimming which could move their activities indoors, thanks to the building of indoor ice rinks and indoor swimming pools. Similarly, the extension of sport facilities also promoted extended seasons for sports such as athletics and tennis.

(Fahlén and Stenling 2015, 5)

However, since 1956, Sweden has never returned to the top 10, finishing 55th in the IOC medal tally in Beijing in 2008, and 37th in London in 2012. According to a case study on Swedish sport policy by Fahlén and Stenling, there is a "lack of elite sport goals in government sport policy" and the increase of support for mass participation "has left elite sport in a marginal position" (Fahlén and Stenling 2015, 10).

One of the most successful small sporting nations is Finland. This success also reflects the transformation of Finland "from a poor, agriculture-dependent country, from a European perspective, peripheral country, into an affluent Nordic social welfare nation with a high standard of living supported by strong education and technology sectors" (Koski and Lämsä 2015, 2). Most of Finland's Olympic success has been achieved in track and field events (115 medals, among them 57 medals in long-distance running), wrestling (83 medals), and cross-country skiing (73 medals). These three sports account for 53% of the total number of Finland's Olympic medals (Koski and Lämsä 2015, 9).

What is interesting about the case of Finland is that the country won a vast majority of its Olympic medals in the first half of the twentieth century (1908–1952). One possible explanation for Finland's declining success in the Olympic Games is greater international competition; another one is that the interest of the Finnish youth shifted toward team sports. However, the main reason seems to be that the country did not specialize in the second half of the twentieth century in those sports that were successful in the first half of the twentieth century. Finland has not made strategic choices to invest in a few targeted sports like many other countries have done:

In Finland, probably because of the deeply rooted ideal of equality and emphasis on pluralism, the focus on targeted sports has not even been a consideration. Thus, it is no surprise that this policy is reflected in success ratings as measured by Olympic medals.... Finland's system is clearly different from the sports movement-based model of the other Nordic countries, but is also distinct from sport policy in Anglo-Saxon countries.

(Koski and Lämsä 2015, 17)

12 Early Learning (E)

If countries want to be successful at the Olympics, they need to have the capability to be innovative by adopting the latest innovations in elite sport policies around the world on issues such as talent identification, coaching, and sports facilities: "Countries have a tendency to imitate the most successful 'regimes' and then attempt to develop an improved version of the original model" (Augestad et al. 2006, 294). Furthermore, countries need to promote sports that were newly added to the Olympic program. I will first address the aspect of newly added sports, before discussing the homogenization trend in elite sport policies around the world.

The addition of women's weightlifting to the Summer Olympic program at the Sydney Games in 2000, and of short-track speed skating at the 1992 Winter Olympics in Albertville, are examples how at the Summer (women's weightlifting) as well as Winter Games (short-track) early adopters can dominate a sport and win numerous Olympic medals. Table 12.1 shows how both South

Table 12.1 Olympic Short-Track Medal-Winning Countries

Country	Gold	Silver	Bronze	Total
South Korea	21	12	9	42
China	9	13	8	30
Canada	8	11	9	28
United States	4	6	9	19
Italy	1	3	4	8
Russia	3	1	1	5
Japan	1	0	2	3
Bulgaria	0	2	1	3
Australia	1	0	1	2
Great Britain	0	0	1	1
Unified Team	0	0	1	1
North Korea	0	0	1	1
Netherlands	0	0	1	1
TOTALS	**48**	**48**	**48**	**144**

Source: Adapted from "Olympic Sports Short Track Speed Skating," *Sports Reference*, www.sports.reference.com/olympics/sports/STK/.

Korea and China have dominated the sport of short-track, and Table 12.2 shows how China has dominated the sport of women's weightlifting at the Olympics. Table 12.1 shows that South Korea and China, both relatively new winter sport nation-states, have won 50% of all Olympic short-track medals. When just looking at the gold medals won, the dominance of both countries is even more striking: 62.5% of all gold medals were won by South Korea and China.

Table 12.2 shows that China won half of all available women's weightlifting gold medals. I have given more information on China's strategic approach for success in women's weightlifting and on the South Korean success story in short-track speed skating in the chapter on specialization.

The example of women's weightlifting reflects a trend in the Olympic Games to expand the opportunities for female athletes. Table 12.3 displays when certain women's sports were added to the Olympic program. Out of 40 women's disciplines that were introduced at the Olympics, almost half of them were introduced in the last three decades: 19 women's sports have been added to the Olympic program since the Seoul Summer Games in 1988. With the addition of women's

Table 12.2 Olympic Women's Weightlifting Medal-Winning Countries

Country	Gold	Silver	Bronze	Total
China	14	1	0	15
Russia	0	7	3	10
Thailand	3	1	3	7
North Korea	2	2	2	6
Kazakhstan	3	2	1	6
Belarus	0	1	4	5
Chinese Taipei	0	2	3	5
Indonesia	0	2	2	4
Ukraine	1	1	2	4
South Korea	1	2	0	3
United States	1	0	1	2
Turkey	1	1	0	2
Columbia	1	0	1	2
Hungary	0	2	0	2
Poland	0	1	1	2
Japan	0	1	0	1
Moldova	0	0	1	1
Mexico	1	0	0	1
Greece	0	0	1	1
Canada	0	0	1	1
India	0	0	1	1
Romania	0	1	0	1
Nigeria	0	1	0	1
Armenia	0	0	1	1
TOTALS	**28**	**28**	**28**	**84**

Source: Adapted from "London Weightlifting," *Official Website of the Olympic Movement*, www.olympic.org/olympic-results/london-2012/. "Olympic Sports Weightlifting," *Olympic.it*, www.olympic.it/english/event/id_32.

boxing, the 2012 Games in London were the first in which women competed in every sport in the Summer Olympic program (in rhythmic gymnastics and synchronized swimming only female competitions take place). Also, since 1991, all new sports wishing to be included to the Olympic program must feature women's events. Ski jumping was added to the program for the first time in Sochi in 2014 (International Olympic Committee 2014a). Nordic combined (a sport in which athletes compete in cross-country skiing and ski jumping) remains the only winter discipline in which women don't compete ("Women's Ski Jumping Has Arrived … But There's Still a Hill to Climb" 2014).

Given the expansion of women's sports at the Olympics, one understands why the Vice President of the Chinese Track and Field Federation is reported as saying that "it has been our policy to concentrate on women's sport" and a swimming coach is quoted in the same article saying that "The outstanding achievements made by female athletes … have encouraged Chinese sports authorities to channel more funds and manpower to women's events than to men's, resulting in wider participation and higher technical standards among women" (Riordan and Jinxia 1996, 130–152).

Table 12.3 Introduction of Women Sports at the Olympics

Year	Sports
1900	Tennis, golf
1904	Archery
1908	Tennis, figure skating
1912	Swimming
1924	Fencing
1928	Athletics, gymnastics
1936	Alpine skiing
1948	Canoeing
1952	Equestrian sports
1960	Speed skating
1964	Volleyball, luge
1976	Rowing, basketball, handball
1980	Field hockey
1984	Shooting, cycling
1988	Tennis, table tennis, sailing
1992	Badminton, judo, biathlon
1996	Soccer, softball
1998	Curling, ice hockey
2000	Weightlifting, pentathlon, taekwondo, triathlon
2002	Bobsleigh
2004	Wrestling
2008	BMX
2012	Boxing
2014	Ski jumping

Source: Adapted from "Factsheet Women in the Olympic Movement," *International Olympic Committee*, May 2014, www.olympic.org/Documents/Reference_documents_Factsheets/Women_in_Olympic_Movement.pdf.

One of the most recent examples that the Olympic program is not static is the inclusion of rugby into the Olympic program. Rugby union was played at four of the first seven Summer Olympic Games (in 1900, 1908, 1920, and 1924). However, the competition at the 1924 Paris Games was the last time rugby union was played at the Summer Olympics. Eighty-five years later, the International Olympic Committee voted to add rugby for the programs of the 2016 and 2020 Summer Games. However, instead of traditional rugby union that uses 15 players per side, and is played in an 80-minute game, rugby returns to the Olympics with rugby sevens, a more dynamic version of the sport that is played in two seven-minute halves.

After the IOC made its decision in 2009 to add rugby sevens to the Olympic program, according to an article from the *New York Times* some countries started to immediately promote the sport: "Some countries, including Russia and China, quickly made rugby part of the physical education curriculum in schools in an attempt to fast-track the sport's development" (Bordon 2014). Canadian sports officials invest more than US$1 million a year in rugby development, and the United States has its rugby sevens players working full-time at the Olympic Training Center in Chula Vista, California. This strategy paid off, as the US men's and women's rugby sevens teams qualified for the Olympic Games in 2016 ("Olympic Rugby Sevens: USA Men, Women Qualify for Rio 2016" 2015).

In addition to quickly reacting to changes of the Olympic program, countries need to be early adopters of successful elite sport policies. The gap between countries that are successful at the Olympic Games and those that fail can be explained with the willingness (or failure) to adopt a certain model of elite sport policies. Sam writes about New Zealand's sport policy that this case of a successful Olympic country illustrates "a steady commitment to reforms" (Sam 2015, 11). On the basis of the existing literature, nine clusters of policy areas or "pillars" were identified by De Bosscher et al. to explain why nations excel in elite sport: Financial support (Pillar 1); an integrated approach to policy development (Pillar 2); sport participation (Pillar 3); talent identification and development system (Pillar 4); athletic and post career support (Pillar 5); training facilities (Pillar 6); coaching provision and coach development (Pillar 7); organization of and participation in national and international competitions (Pillar 8); as well as scientific research and sports medicine support (Pillar 9) (De Bosscher et al. 2006, 209).

The authors comment on the importance of individual pillars that "Nations might not increase their chances of success by investing in a few pillars; rather they need to find the most suitable blend of all pillars for their specific circumstances" (De Bosscher et al. 2006, 208). Finally, De Bosscher et al. conclude:

> Uncertainties over the relationship between policies and international sporting success will always remain. The reason for this is that it is impossible to set up an experiment trying to explain a causal correlation of one factor leading to success while other factors are controlled.
>
> (De Bosscher et al. 2006, 209)

One of the reasons for uncertainties about sporting success is that sport is embedded in a broader cultural context, where beliefs, norms, and values, for example those associated with social class, gender, disability, and ethnicity, have an impact on the character of sport policy: "Consequently, policy instruments are often dependent on politics and policy regimes, which implies that similar policy actions may have different outcomes in different nations" (De Bosscher et al. 2010, 571).

According to different authors, there is a trend toward homogeneity of elite sport policies among those countries that compete for medals at the Olympics. This was also one of the results of Bergsgard et al.'s comparative analysis of sport policy in Canada, England, Germany, and Norway. The authors identified the common characteristic of a "significant intensification in government involvement in sport policy" (Bergsgard et al. 2007, 150) regardless of the type of welfare regime (liberal, conservative, social democratic), the political culture (individualistic or collectivistic oriented), and whether the respective countries are federalist or unitary states:

> Our analysis suggests a significant degree of homogenization as all four countries have developed, or are in the process of developing, relatively similar high performance sport structures. The sport systems of all countries focus quite strongly and consistently upon success in international competitions, strong and relatively centralized elite sport organizations, systematic and professional coaching, the establishment of elite sport centre(s), and the use of scientific methods to improve the functioning of the whole elite sport system.
>
> (Bergsgard et al. 2007, 194)

According to Bergsgard et al., the sport systems of different countries imitate each other and converge. However, the corresponding discourses still vary considerably: "Thus it may be appropriate to conclude that structures converge, but discourses vary in the field of elite sport" (Bergsgard et al. 2007, 197).

De Bosscher et al. observed an increasing trend toward the homogeneity of elite sport policies based on a comparison of policies in the following six countries: Belgium (separated into Flanders and Wallonia), Canada, Italy, the Netherlands, Norway, and the United Kingdom. The study was based on the performances of the respective countries at the Summer Olympic Games in Athens 2004 and Beijing 2008, as well as the 2006 Winter Games in Torino. The work was conducted with a mixed research design with two main instruments, an overall sport policy questionnaire completed by the cooperating researchers in each country, and an elite sport climate survey questionnaire completed by athletes, coaches, and performance directors. A substantial difference of scores was only identified regarding the financial support of elite sport: "The study revealed that the countries with the highest absolute expenditures on elite sport and providing the highest elite sport funding for national sport organizations (pillar 1) were also the most successful ones in Olympic Summer Games" (De Bosscher et al. 2009, 129).

Apart from the financial support, the authors concluded regarding the importance of their previously published nine-pillar model that "statistical relationships are hard to determine and theory development is still at an early stage of development" (De Bosscher et al. 2009, 131). For example, the authors noticed that nations that do not perform well in one or a few policy pillars could still be successful in Olympic sports. Because of the lack of causal relationships "it is practically impossible to create a theoretical model that is totally construct valid" (De Bosscher et al. 2009, 130). However:

> the findings suggest that some pillars could be regarded as possible drivers of an effective system because they were prioritized in the most successful sample nations: financial resources (pillar 1), athletic and post-career support (pillar 5), training facilities (pillar 6) and coach development (partly pillar 7).
>
> (De Bosscher et al. 2009, 113)

In another publication, this time in conjunction with Shibli, van Bottenburg, De Knop, and Truyens, De Bosscher tried to develop a method for comparing nations' elite sport systems by measuring and comparing determinants of national competitiveness quantitatively. The nine pillars and its critical success factors (CSFs) identified in previous research (De Bosscher et al. 2006, 185–215) were operationalized through qualitative and quantitative data that were transformed into a scoring system. A pilot study with the same six sample nations as in her previous work – Belgium (separated into Flanders and Wallonia), Canada, Italy, the Netherlands, Norway, and the United Kingdom – was conducted to explore a method to measure quantitatively the determinants of competitiveness of nations at an elite sport policy level rather than to evaluate the policies themselves. A five-point scoring scale was used to assess each nation's performance for each of the nine pillars, with "one" indicating little and "five" a high level of development.

The results of the study confirmed previous research by De Bosscher et al., as well as by other authors that there is a trend toward homogeneity of elite sport policies:

> There is little variation in the scores achieved by the six sample nations against Pillar 2 [integrated approach to policy development], which perhaps endorses the point made by several authors that nations' elite sport development systems are becoming increasingly homogeneous.

The authors conclude that "the proposed measurement system should not be isolated from general descriptive information on elite sport policies," should be guided by information on the general context and quantitative findings alone are not sufficient to assess the quality of elite sport systems. The natural resources of countries and their social, cultural, and historical background need to be considered (De Bosscher et al. 2010, 587).

The previously mentioned studies that indicate a worldwide homogenizing in elite sport policies refer to developed countries. Tan and Green asked in their research on China's drive for Olympic success if and to what extent developments in China mirror experiences in respect of elite athlete development in the West. China is a relatively new Olympic superpower that was absent from the Olympic stage for 32 years until 1984 (because of its dispute with the IOC on Taiwan's recognition). Tan's and Green's work is based on interviews conducted with 32 Chinese sport officials as well as 14 interviews with Chinese sports academics. The article aimed to contribute to a better understanding of the similarities and differences of policy decisions, priorities, and outcomes in under-reported cultural/sporting contexts, and concluded "compelling evidence for policy convergence and the global homogeneity thesis" (Tan and Green 2008, 330).

Examples for the homogenous model of elite sport development are the sources of income for elite sport development found in China that reflect those found in many Western nations, among them a lottery China introduced to subsidize its elite sport system. Another example is sport colleges to allow elite athletes to train and study at the same time. According to Tan and Green, 400,000 young boys and girls are training at more than 3,000 sports schools throughout China. Furthermore, policy learning is of similar importance like in Western countries: Sport officials have the opportunity to travel abroad in order to enhance their knowledge of elite sport policies in other countries, and high-standard equipment and facilities are imported, especially from the United States. Part of the policy learning process is also to import foreign coaches, some of them even from the main rival at the Olympic Games, the United States. For example, the American Randy Huntington who coached Mike Powell when Powell jumped 8.95 meters (29 feet 4¼ inches) in Tokyo in 1991 – setting a world record that is still valid – has been coaching Chinese athletes since 2013. He helped China win its first medal in long jumping at the world championships in Beijing in August 2015 (Clarey 2015a).

Whereas there is, according to Tan and Green, a large degree of similarity between the different components that make up elite sport systems, there are "subtle 'domestic' (national) variations apparent in the implementation of these mechanisms" (Tan and Green 2008, 334). In the case of China this is the sheer dominance of the Communist Party and the central state as well as the "ideological indoctrination" in the form of "teaching on patriotism, collectivism and revolutionary heroism in order to dilute and reduce the allurements of materialism and money" (Tan and Green 2008, 333).

A homogenization of high-performance sport is also the result of a study by Digel on the eight most successful nations in the Olympic Summer Games of Atlanta in 1996. The work refers to similarities and differences between the high-performance sport systems of Australia, China, Germany, France, Great Britain, Italy, Russia, and the United States. According to Digel:

> High-performance sport is, to a great extent, a precisely controllable technological undertaking that can be compared to the manufacture of industrial products.... Each side strives to win the contest and be better than the other

or others. In such a situation, there is value in knowing as exactly as possible who is on the other side, what they are capable of, and the strategy and tactics they intend to use to prevail in the competition. In short, it is good to know the methods the opponent employs.

(Digel 2005)

An example of the global convergence of elite sport systems is, according to Digel, the "takeover of some institutions of the former GDR sport system," with the cooperation of the public school system and the elite sport sector at the center of reforms:

> Seven of the performance systems have special schools for serious sport within the public school system. The children and youth sport schools of the former GDR and the comparable schools of the former Soviet Union are reference points in this context.

(Digel 2005)

Further similarities among the examined countries are, according to Digel, that all the studied nations show a long Olympic tradition with intensive participation in recent Olympic Games; in all the countries, centralized training seems to be an essential prerequisite for success; all the systems require steadily growing budgets.

Countries have entered the sporting arms race at different points in time, but have ended up with similar governmental policies, concludes Green in his comparative study on Olympic sporting success from 1960 to 2006 in Australia, Canada, and the United Kingdom:

> In Australia and Canada (in contrast to the UK), the prioritization of elite sport achievement has been at the forefront of federal government policies over the past 25 to 30 years.... In the UK, it is only over the past decade that central government has promoted a far more positive policy discourse around, and allocated increasingly large amounts of public money for, elite sport development.

(Green 2007, 921)

It applies to all the investigated cases that

> governments in all three countries have, to a greater or lesser extent, intervened directly in the elite sport development process requiring substantial changes ... (for example professional management, high-quality coaching and talent identification programs) as a condition of grant aid.

(Green 2007, 922)

The three countries have come to terms with what are according to Green the assumed requirements of modern elite international sport:

This suggests that athletes must now train full-time and must be supported by an entourage of coaches, trainers, sports scientists, administrators and so on, and that Olympic and other international success requires a well-funded, bureaucratic and highly technical elite athlete development system.

(Green 2007, 923)

Even in countries with a traditionally more egalitarian approach and opposition to elitism such as Norway, over the last decades elite sport efforts have been in line with general international tendencies: Ronglan gives the following examples in his study on the elite sport policies in Denmark, Norway, and Sweden: Construction of elite sport facilities, targeted talent development programs, support for full-time athletes, provision of professional coaching, and sports medicine support service have become integrated in elite sport efforts of these countries. He concludes, "This captures a broad trend of convergence, which also applies to Scandinavian countries' elite sport efforts" (Ronglan 2014, 2).

According to the study of Kårhus on Norway, "ideas about elite performance have become mainstream" (Kårhus 2014, 11). In 2006, elite sport was introduced into the Norwegian national curriculum available as a five-hours-per-week elective subject to students and at the academic pre-tertiary school level. Before 2006, the only option for promising elites to integrate the promotion of their sporting talent into their education was visiting a private school, the Norwegian College of Elite Sport. The requirement was that the students should be capable of winning medals in international championships, and subsequently several Norwegian winners from the Winter Olympics and World Cups are former NCES students. According to Kårhus, "the introduction of an elite sport subject for the most physically able students exemplifies how powerful discourses of sport and political populism might have underpinned the elite sport interests in the policy of education" (Kårhus 2014, 10).

The existence of a homogenization of the elite sport systems in Western nations was also the result of another case study on Norway by Augestad et al. The authors focused in their work on the Norwegian elite sport institution Olympiatoppen (OT) that was founded in 1988. The work was a combination of an in-depth study of the Norwegian system with a comparative approach, based on 57 interviews in Norway. OT is, according to Augestad *et al.*, highly centralized and similar to the elite sport systems in other nations, such as Australia and France that focus on a small number of sports that have the possibility of achieving international success. How countries imitate the more successful ones can be seen by the diet regime developed by the OT that "strongly resembles the Australian model" (Augestad et al. 2006, 294). This means according to the three authors that similarities between nations are in relatively abstract categories such as scientification and centralization, but there are important variations when it comes to details.

However, in spite of the similarities, there are also local variations in the context of the various elite sport development systems. In the case of Norway, high altitude chambers (which are not illegal according to international rules) are prohibited, and there are restrictions on talent identification concerning children under 13 years of age, as well as rules aimed at preventing children from specializing in one particular sport too early. This

> may partly explain why Norway does not achieve success at international level in sports such as gymnastics, figure skating, and rhythmic sport gymnastics. International success in these sports requires a huge investment in special training during the athlete's early years.
>
> (Augestad et al. 2006, 306)

According to a study on elite athletics by Truyens et al., "it seems that although a list of crucial organizational resources and first-order capabilities in athletics can be identified, there remains a diversity of ways to combine and organize them in higher-order capabilities" (Truyens et al. 2013, 26).

Local variations in elite sport policies is a phenomenon that is also referred to in literature as "glocalisations which reflect a homogenized (global) response to generic (macro) factors impacting on success but with heterogeneous applications (local adaptations) when it comes to the unique national situation and competitive environment" (De Bosscher et al. 2015, 368).

De Bosscher et al. conclude in their latest publication that even successful countries do things differently, and as such can continue to learn from each other: "The challenge remains to find the right blend of system ingredients and processes that will work best for given nations in their own context and culture" (De Bosscher et al. 2015, 390).

13 Naturalization

This chapter discusses the naturalization of foreign-born athletes. Different to the policies summarized in the WISE formula in Chapters 10–13, the approaches of naturalization and hosting the Olympic Games are not accessible strategies for all countries, and therefore are not included in my success model. While in some cases the naturalization of foreign-born athletes and hosting the Olympic Games might contribute to Olympic success, their overall contribution as an explanation of success and failure at the Games is insignificant.

Regarding the naturalization of foreign athletes, a vast majority of countries mainly invests into domestic talents to achieve Olympic success. However, there are also nation-states that take what I call "the passing lane" by importing and naturalizing foreign talents to achieve a competitive advantage.

At the Olympic Games, athletes represent a country of which they are a citizen, and citizenship is determined by the countries themselves. Some nation-states determine citizenship based on birthplace (*jus soli*); but most countries are more restrictive and base it on ancestry (*jus sanguinis*). However, even among the countries with rules of *jus sanguinis*, some have introduced policies that fast-track citizenship for foreign-born elite athletes in order to "buy" Olympic success.

Horowitz and McDaniel have investigated in their work how immigrant athletes impact Olympic medal counts. They looked for medals won by athletes born in a different country than the one for whom they competed, and classified them as "non-native medals." Horowitz and McDaniel focus in their research on the four Olympic Summer Games in 2000, 2004, 2008, and 2012. Their work contained two interesting findings: They determined that countries that featured non-native medal winners won more medals on average in 2000, 2004, 2008, and 2012 than countries whose medals were won exclusively by native-born athletes. Furthermore, they noticed that countries with higher GDP levels displayed greater probability of attracting foreign talent.

Horowitz and McDaniel constructed a data set of non-native medal winners among the 7,269 medalists at the 2000, 2004, 2008, and 2012 Games. Table 13.1 shows that in 2000, 100 athletes (5.6% of medal-winning athletes) won individual medals or were on a medal-winning team for a country different from the one in which they were born. There were 115 (6.3% of medal-winning athletes) such athletes in 2004, 92 (4.9% of medal-winning athletes) in 2008, and 120 (6.8% of medal-winning athletes) in 2012.

Table 13.1 Immigrant Medal-Winning Athletes in the Summer Olympics

Year	Total Medal-Winning Athletes	Immigrant Medal-Winning Athletes	Percent
2000	1,785	100	5.6
2004	1,840	116	6.3
2008	1,874	92	4.9
2012	1,770	120	6.8

Source: Adapted from Horowitz and McDaniel (2015).

European countries accounted as a destination for most of the athletes born in a different country, and many medal-winning athletes migrated intercontinentally within Europe. Horowitz and McDaniel also compared the percentage of immigrant medal winners with the general world's migrant population of 2.9%: "The percentage of medal winners who are immigrants is statistically significantly higher than the percentage of the world's international migrant population" (Horowitz and McDaniel 2015, 19).

There are differences among sports if it comes to the naturalization of foreign-born athletes. Table tennis as well as middle- and long-distance running might belong to the most extreme examples. I start with discussing the case of table tennis: "Many major international table tennis competitions became competitions among Chinese table tennis players competing for different countries" (Horowitz and McDaniel 2015, 38).

Heijmans investigated the Olympic history of table tennis, a sport that has been in the Summer Games program since the 1988 Games in Seoul. Of the 666 Olympic table tennis competitors in all Games between 1988 in South Korea, and 2012 in London, at least 91 of them have been born in China: "Combined with the Chinese competitors, this means that about a fifth of all table tennis Olympians are Chinese!" (Heijmans 2015b). The number might be even larger than 91, but Heijmans did not find official birth data for some Olympic table tennis competitors, and this includes for example the Swiss player Dai-Yong Tu.

The 91 naturalized China born competitors represented 24 different nations, half of them (45) were from these five countries: Hong Kong (11 competitors), Canada (10), Singapore (9), Australia (8), and the United States (7). An extreme example is Singapore's women table tennis team that won silver in Beijing 2008. All three women were born in China and later naturalized by Singapore (Heijmans 2015b).

Similar to Chinese athletes in table tennis, there is in track and field significant migration of athletes from Kenya to other countries. This occurs particularly in middle- and long-distance running. Simiyu Njororai investigated in two journal articles athlete labor migration from the athletics powerhouse Kenya to other countries (Simiyu Njororai 2010, 443–461; Simiyu Njororai 2012, 187–209). Kenya has become a net exporter of athletic talent. According to the data from the International Association of Athletics Federations (IAAF), from 1998 to 2008 228 athletes changed allegiance, out of whom 18 Kenyans changed their citizenship to represent other countries. Out of the 18 Kenyans, eight athletes moved to the Middle East: five athletes became citizens of Qatar and three of Bahrain. However, the data excludes athletes who moved to Qatar and Bahrain before they had formally registered with Athletics Kenya. According to Simiyu Njororai, more than 40 athletes had moved to Middle Eastern countries compared to the eight reflected on the IAAF list (Simiyu Njororai 2012, 197). According to Campbell there were over 38 nationality transfers from Kenya to Qatar in 2005 alone (Campbell 2011, 45–60).

While Qatar and Bahrain want to raise their international profiles with sporting success, for the athletes there are two main motives to change citizenship and compete for these countries: The first is economical, given the poverty in Kenya and the wealth of the Gulf countries: "The unbalanced nature of global wealth and sporting corporate power has created movement of sporting talent from less paying to higher paying clubs and now nations" (Simiyu Njororai 2010, 443). However, apart from economic there are also sport-related reasons. In Kenya, there is a concentration of world-class middle- and long-distance runners. But at international competitions such as the Olympics, only three athletes from one country can compete. This means that many world-class runners from Kenya are not eligible to compete at the Olympic Games (the same applies to table tennis players from China). Competing for another country makes it easier for them to enter major sporting events.

Three factors might limit the future emigration of athletes: First of all, migrant athletes often face hostility from teammates of the host country and the local people often prefer homegrown local athletes to win medals: "Only then would this give them the feeling of national pride and a sense of national identity" (Simiyu Njororai 2012, 200). Some of the athletes who moved to Bahrain and Qatar only represent these countries at the Olympic Games, and spend the majority of their time in Kenya and at the international athletic camps set up by their agents.

A second reason is possible mistreatment, such as the withholding of payments, promised bonuses, and passports of Kenyan-born athletes in the Middle East. One Kenyan runner who migrated to Bahrain even lost his citizenship after competing in Israel. Qatari club and national team coaches told me that naturalization does not mean that the naturalized athletes get the same privileges as other Qatari citizen. Naturalized athletes often get provisional passports that do not remain with them, and are only used for travel to international competitions (Reiche 2014, 6).

A third reason for limiting future emigration is the cultural transformation that is expected but is often not given much significance by the athletes and their families. There are no historical or cultural ties between Kenya and the countries Qatar and Bahrain. While Kenya is a secular country, with more than 80% of the population being Christian, Islam is the state religion in Bahrain and Qatar, with most Qataris belonging to the strict Wahhabi sect.

Some migrant athletes even undergo name changes, for example, the previous world champion in steeplechase running, Stephen Chrerono, who is now competing for Qatar as Saif Saaeed Shaheen (Simiyu Njororai 2010, 443–461; Simiyu Njororai 2012, 187–209). Other examples are the following athletes paired with their Qatari given name: David Nyaga: Daham Najim Bashir, Albert Chepkurui: Hassan Abdullah, James Kwalia Moses Chirchir: Al Badri Salem Amer, Thomas Kosgei: Ali Tharer Kamel, Daniel (Nicolas) Kemboi Kipkosgie: Salem Jamal, Richard Yatich: Musbarak Shaami (Campbell 2011, 45–60).

While the naturalization of foreign athletes is a popular tool around the world to achieve Olympic success, not every country is dealing with this part of its sport politics in a transparent way. I give two examples, one of a country that is very open about its naturalization politics, Singapore, and another one that tries to hide respective efforts, Qatar.

Singapore introduced the Foreign Sports Talent Scheme (FSTS) in the early 1990s with the aim of identifying and facilitating the migration and naturalization of foreign-born athletes. Naturalized athletes are most common in the Singapore badminton and table tennis squads, but are also present in other sports. Most FSTS athletes have come from China. According to Houlihan and Zheng, there is

> divided domestic opinion with the national media clearly treating success by Singapore-born athletes much more positively. There have also been domestic expressions of concern that the domination of Chinese-born athletes in some sports, table tennis in particular, is contrary to the implicit policy of ethnic balance in Singapore public life.
>
> (Houlihan and Zheng 2014, 10)

In contrast to the example of Singapore, Qatar tries to hide its naturalization efforts. It is not communicated in any Qatari policy document that I reviewed for the work on my article "Investing in Sporting Success as a Domestic and Foreign Policy Tool: The Case of Qatar." When I asked a leading representative of the Qatar Olympic Committee for the country's policy of naturalization, while doing field work in Doha in January 2014, he was at first not willing to discuss the matter with me, telling me I would be impolite to ask and it would be not a relevant issue. After I gave several examples for Qatar's naturalization, he told me: "Qatar is just doing what everybody is doing" (Reiche 2014, 6).

Two of the four Qatari Olympic medal winners were not born in the country. Mohamed Suleiman, who won an Olympic bronze medal for Qatar in 1992, was born in Somalia. Said Saif Asaad, who won an Olympic bronze medal for Qatar in 2000, was born in Bulgaria as Angel Popow.

Naturalizations will most likely continue in the future, even if Qatar has heavily invested in domestic talent identification and elite sport infrastructure. However, international sport associations have started to complicate nationality transfer. The IOC introduced a three-year waiting period before an athlete can compete for a new country (Campbell 2011, 45–60; Poli 2007, 646–661).

Campbell comments on Qatar's policy of naturalizing foreign athletes: "In the case of Qatar, where citizenship might be understood to be by blood, naturalizing transnational athlete migrants contradicts citizen criteria" (Campbell 2011, 52).

14 Home Advantage

One factor that is often linked with Olympic success is the home advantage. Countries that host the Summer and Winter Olympic Games usually win more medals than at previous Games abroad. Tables 14.1 and 14.2 show the performance of the host countries at the Summer and Winter Olympic Games starting in 1988. I begin with the Games in 1988 since the 1980 and 1984 Games were affected by political boycotts (the absence of some if its main rivals explains the huge number of medals the United States won in 1984). The tables show that the United States at the 1996 Summer Games, and Italy at the 2006 Winter Games could not improve their performance while hosting the Games (but remained more or less at their previous level of medal winnings). Apart from these two cases, countries did improve their performance while hosting the Games, and some of these improvements were quite significant. This applies particularly to those host countries that were not Olympic powerhouses before hosting, such as South Korea, Spain, and Greece. For them, hosting the Olympics in 1988, 1992, and 2004 was connected with major sporting successes. Greece, where the ancient Olympics took place, was the first nation to host the modern Olympic

Table 14.1 Home Advantage at the Summer Olympic Games

Summer Olympics Host Country	Medals Won While Hosting Games	Medals Won at Prior Three Games		
South Korea – 1988	33	1976 – 6	1980 – 0	1984 – 19
Spain – 1992	22	1980 – 6	1984 – 5	1988 – 4
United States – 1996	101	1984 – 174 (Hosted)	1988 – 94	1992 – 108
Australia – 2000	58	1988 – 14	1992 – 27	1996 – 41
Greece – 2004	16	1992 – 2	1996 – 8	2000 – 13
China – 2008	100	1996 – 50	2000 – 59	2004 – 63
Great Britain – 2012	65	2000 – 28	2004 – 30	2008 – 47
Brazil – 2016	?	2004 – 10	2008 – 15	2012 – 17

Sources: Adapted from "A Map of Olympic Medals," *New York Times*, August 4, 2008, www.nytimes.com/interactive/2008/08/04/sports/olympics/20080804_MEDALCOUNT_MAP.html?_r=1&. "London 2012 Olympics Medal Tracker Overall," *ESPN Summer Olympics*, http://espn.go.com/olympics/summer/2012/medals.

Table 14.2 Home Advantage at the Winter Olympic Games

Winter Olympics Host Country	Medals Won While Hosting Games	Medals Won at Prior Three Games		
Canada – 1988	5	1976 – 3	1980 – 2	1984 – 4
France – 1992	14	1980 – 1	1984 – 3	1988 – 2
Norway – 1994	26	1984 – 9	1988 – 5	1992 – 24
Japan – 1998	10	1988 – 1	1992 – 7	1994 – 5
United States – 2002	34	1992 – 15	1994 – 13	1998 – 131
Italy – 2006	11	1994 – 20	1998 – 10	2002 – 13
Canada – 2010	26	1998 – 15	2002 – 17	2006 – 24
Russia – 2014	33	2002 – 13	2006 – 20	2010 – 15
South Korea – 2018	?	2009 – 11	2010 – 14	2014 – 8

Sources: Adapted from "A Map of Olympic Medals," *New York Times*, http://2010gzmes.nytimes.com/medals/map.html. "Sochi 2014 Olympics Medal Tracker Overall," *ESPN Winter Olympics*, http://espn.go.com/olympics/winter/2014/medals.

Games in 1896. Out of the 111 medals that Greece has won in the history of the Summer Olympics, 62 of them were won at the 1896 and 2004 Games, about 56% of all medals Greece has ever won.

However, even leading Olympics countries sometimes heavily benefit from hosting the Games. While the United States retained a high medal count at the Summer Olympics 1996 in Atlanta (although winning slightly fewer medals than four years earlier), it greatly benefitted from hosting the 2002 Winter Olympics in Salt Lake City. After winning only 13 medals at each of the Winter Olympics in 1994 in Lillehammer, Norway, and 1998 in Nagano, Japan, the United States won 34 medals while hosting in 2002.

China increased the number of medals won from 63 in 2004 in Athens, to 100 at its home games in Beijing in 2008; Great Britain improved from 47 medals in 2008 in Beijing to 65 in 2012 in London; Australia enhanced from 41 medals in Atlanta in 1996 to 58 medals in Sydney in 2000; France even increased its medals won from two at the Winter Games in 1988 in Alberta to 14 medals at the home Games in 1992 in Albertville; and Japan doubled its medals from five in 1994 in Lillehammer to 10 in 1998 in Nagano.

Russia's performance in Sochi 2014 is another clear example of the home advantage of more established sporting countries: Russia won 33 medals, 13 of them gold, and ended up being the most successful nation in the medal ranking. However, just four years earlier at the 2010 Games in Vancouver, Canada, Russia only won 15 medals (three of them gold), and was 11th in the medal ranking. Russia's performance in Sochi was better than many of its other Winter Olympic appearances: In 2006 in Turin, Italy, Russia won 22 medals (eight gold) and was 4th in the medal ranking. In 2002 in Salt Lake City, USA, Russia won 13 medals (five gold) and was 5th in the medal ranking. In 1998 in Nagano, Japan, Russia won 18 medals (nine gold) and was 3rd in the medal ranking.

Reasons given for the home advantage in academic literature are that "host countries can tailor facilities to meet the needs of their athletes and may gain an edge if home crowd enthusiasm sways judges" (Bernard and Busse 2004, 414). In addition, "athletes of the host countries are more adapted to the climate or the host countries are more inclined to select events in which their athletes have a comparative advantage" (Lui and Suen 2008, 15). Finally, host countries usually put more resources into Olympic success. Rathke and Woitek give for the host's advantage the explanation that "Hosting the Olympic Games considerably increases the public support for (and therefore the money and effort invested in) sports in the years before the Games" (Rathke and Woitek 2008, 521). For example, after London's successful bid to host the 2012 Summer Games, an extra GBP£200 million of public money was provided for elite sport development leading up to 2012 (Green 2007, 940). The Canadian government approved in 1982 the "best ever" campaign for the 1988 Calgary Winter Olympics and the creation of the country's first multi-sport training centre in Calgary. The federal government committed CAD$25 million for ten winter Olympic sport organizations to ensure that Canada would have a "best ever" performance in 1988 (Green 2007, 931).

Balmer et al. investigated the host advantage at the Winter Games from 1908 until 1998 and concluded, based on a comparison of the medals or points won by a hosting country with the medals or points won by the same nation-state when visiting other Olympic Games, "significant evidence of home advantage was identified" (Balmer et al. 2001, 137). However, the authors observed differences among the disciplines at the Winter Games: "Grouping events based on whether they were subjectively judged or not demonstrated that subjective judgments as a form of assessment produced significantly greater home advantage than events with objectively measurable performance or outcome (e.g. time, goals or distance)" (Balmer et al. 2001, 137). Examples for disciplines that depend on subjective judgments are figure skating and freestyle skiing, where the outcome is determined entirely by the scores of judges; ski jumping also features an element of judging (style marks), as does Nordic combined. Balmer et al. speculate that:

> This finding may reflect the better performances of athletes competing in front of a supportive partisan audience. However, this would result in consistently elevated home advantage over all events, whenever crowds were present. An alternative explanation is that the judges responded more positively to crowd noise when judging home competitors' performances.
>
> (Balmer et al. 2001, 137)

The same authors published a paper on the significance of the home advantage at the Summer Olympic Games between 1896 and 1996. Only male data were analyzed, and a points system was used, with three points allocated for a gold medal, two points for silver and one point for bronze. Five event groups were selected for the study: Athletics and weightlifting (predominantly objectively judged), boxing and gymnastics (predominantly subjectively judged), and team games (involving subjective decisions). The results confirmed the previous Winter Olympic Games findings:

> Highly significant home advantage was found in event groups that were either subjectively judged or rely on subjective decisions. In contrast, little or no home advantage (and even away advantage) was observed for the two objectively judged groups. Officiating system was vital to both the existence and extent of home advantage. Our findings suggest that crowd noise has a greater influence upon officials' decisions than players' performances, as events with greater officiating input enjoyed significantly greater home advantage.
>
> (Balmer et al. 2003, 469)

While the host effect is only temporary, Kuper and Sterken noticed that this is a factor that is not limited to the Games hosted by the respective country:

> At the recent versions of the Games countries that will host the next version of the games perform better. Korea doubled its medal share at the 1984 games and hosted the Olympics in 1988. Australia performed significantly better at the Atlanta Games in 1996. And Greece doubled its medal normal share at the Sydney 2000 Games. This is a time-to-build argument: it takes long run planning to create a group of optimal performing athletes.
>
> (Kuper and Sterken 2003, 4)

Successful home games also result in a virtuous circle. As Green wrote on the Australian success at the Sydney Games in 2000, "to not support the country's elite athletes after the success at Sydney 2000 was politically unthinkable" (Green 2007, 942).

In a paper on the home advantage at the Olympic Games that I wrote with Stephen Pettigrew, we argue that the academic literature largely ignores the importance of participation rates in explaining the home advantage (Pettigrew and Reiche 2016). We argue that prior work on this topic has two major shortcomings. First, these studies fail to define an appropriate comparison for estimating the impact of hosting the Games. Most of the studies estimate the home advantage by comparing host countries to all other (e.g. Johnson and Ali 2000; Kuper and Sterken 2003). In other words, the research estimates the home advantage by comparing host countries like Great Britain to non-hosts. Other studies compare hosts only to their previous success, but do so by pooling across many years (Lui and Suen 2008, 1–16). Such research compares Great Britain's medal count when it hosted in 2012 to its medal count in 1896, when it did not. Rather than comparing hosts to all other countries, we compared the medal counts of Olympic hosts to their own medal count in the previous Olympics four years earlier.

Second, previous work largely neglects the fact that the qualification rules for athletes from host countries are significantly less strict, resulting in more medal opportunities for the host country. For example, Great Britain had 530 athletes competing at the London Games in 2012, compared to 304 in Beijing in 2008. In Sochi in 2014, 215 athletes represented Russia, compared to 175 in Vancouver four years earlier.

Our work accounts for these two shortcomings of the empirical literature. We find weak to no evidence of a hosting advantage in the history of the Olympic Games. In particular, there is not a statistically significant increase in the number of total medals or gold medals won by a country when they host. We do find huge increases in the number of athletes for host countries. When we account for increased participation by looking at the ratio of medals to athlete, we find that the home advantage decays to almost zero.

Our paper examined the history of the Olympic Games after World War II. We started with the 1952 Summer Games in Helsinki (Finland) and the Winter Games in the same year in Oslo (Norway), and included all 16 Summer Games through 2012 in London and all 17 Winter Games until Sochi in 2014 in our analysis. The size of the host country's team grows significantly in the year that they host. Of our data set of 33 Summer and Winter Games after World War II, there is only one instance (the United States in the 1980 Winter Games) of a country decreasing its number of participants in the year that it hosted, compared to the previous Games. In Summer Games, on average, the host country's team is 162.2 athletes larger than in the previous Summer Games. In Winter Games, the difference is 28.1 athletes.

The main reason that host nations have larger teams is that the qualification standards for the host country are substantially easier. For team events, the host countries do not have to participate in qualification tournaments. For example, South Korea's men's and women's ice hockey teams will make their Olympic debuts in 2018 when Pyeongchang is the host city (Klein 2014). Great Britain's men's and women's handball teams team made their Olympic debut in London in 2012, 76 years after the sport was introduced at the Olympics (Walker 2012).

Automatic qualification also applies to individual sports. In the triathlon, for example, 55 men and 55 women could qualify for the Summer Olympics 2012, with a maximum of three starters per country. The United Kingdom had one guaranteed starter in both competitions, with the option of further participants depending on the British results in the qualification events (International Triathlon Union 2012).

The importance of automatic qualification rules is clear. While the German men and women's soccer teams were toward the top of the FIFA rankings, neither team qualified to participate at the London 2012 Olympics (Ahrens 2012). Great Britain participated in soccer for the first time since 1960, despite both of its teams being outranked by Germany. Similarly, Germany has had tremendous success in handball in recent years, with regular victories at European club competitions and a world championship in 2007, but it did not qualify for handball events in London. Great Britain qualified despite having never participated in the event at previous Games.

Automatic qualification therefore increases the opportunities to win medals for the host country. In 2012, Great Britain had a team that was 74% larger than it was in 2008 (304 athletes in 2008, 530 in 2012) and turned the increase in participation into 18 additional medals (47 in 2008; 65 in 2012).

From the nation-states that are ranked in the top 10 of the all-time Olympic medals ranking, only the former German Democratic Republic never hosted the Games. Seven countries from the top 10 hosted the Summer as well as the Winter Games. The three countries that hosted Summer but not Winter Games are Sweden, the United Kingdom (which does not have favorable winter sport conditions), and China, which is a relatively young winter sport nation that was awarded the 2022 Winter Olympics by the IOC in July 2015. However, only 19 countries ever hosted the Summer Olympics (data includes all Games until 2020), and only 12 have hosted the Winter Olympics (data includes all Games until 2018).

Our finding is especially important given the politics of the bidding process for the Olympics. In total, only 23 countries ever hosted either the Summer and/ or the Winter Olympics. The Olympic powerhouse, the United States, is also the country that hosted the Olympics most often (eight times in total). No other country hosted more Summer Olympics (four times), and no other country was more often the host of the Winter Games (four times as well) (see Tables 14.3 and 14.4). The remaining 182 National Olympic Committees that were recognized by the International Olympic Committee in July 2015 have never hosted

Table 14.3 Summer Olympic Games Host Countries

Summer Olympics Host Country	*Number of Games Hosted*
United States (St. Louis, 1904/Los Angeles, 1932/Los Angeles, 1964/Atlanta, 1996)	4
Great Britain (London, 1908/London, 1948/London, 2012)	3
Greece (Athens, 1896/Athens, 2004)	2
France (Paris, 1900/Paris, 1924)	2
Germany (Berlin, 1936/Munich, 1972)	2
Australia (Melbourne, 1956/Sydney, 2000)	2
Japan (Tokyo, 1964/Tokyo, 2020)	2
Sweden (Stockholm, 1912)	1
Belgium (Antwerp, 1920)	1
Holland (Amsterdam, 1928)	1
Finland (Helsinki, 1952)	1
Italy (Rome, 1960)	1
Mexico (Mexico City, 1968)	1
Canada (Montreal, 1976)	1
Russia (Moscow, 1980)	1
South Korea (Seoul, 1988)	1
Spain (Barcelona, 1992)	1
China (Beijing, 2008)	1
Brazil (Rio De Janeiro, 2016)	1

Sources: Adapted from "Olympic Dates and History," *World Atlas*, www.worldatlas.com/aatlas/ infopage/olympic.htm. "Olympic Games Countries and Host Cities," *Top End Sports*, www.topend sports.com/events/summer/hosts/list-countries.htm.

Table 14.4 Winter Olympic Games Host Countries

Winter Olympic Host Country	Number of Games Hosted
United States (Lake Placid, 1932/Squaw Valley, 1960/Lake Placid, 1980/Salt Lake City, 2002)	4
France (Chamonix, 1924/Grenoble, 1968/Albertville, 1992)	3
Switzerland (St. Moritz, 1928/St. Moritz, 1958)	2
Norway (Oslo, 1952/Lillehammer, 1994)	2
Italy (Cortina d'Ampezzo, 1956/Turin, 2006)	2
Austria (Innsbruck, 1964/Innsbruck, 1976)	2
Japan (Sapporo, 1972/Nagano, 1998)	2
Canada (Alberta, 1988/Vancouver, 2010)	2
Germany (Garmisch-Partenkirchen, 1936)	1
Yugoslavia (Sarajevo, 1984)	1
Russia (Sochi, 2014)	1
South Korea (PyeongChang, 2018)	1

Sources: Adapted from "Olympic Dates and History," *World Atlas*, www.worldatlas.com/aatlas/infopage/olympic.htm. "Olympic Games Countries and Host Cities," *Top End Sports*, www.topend sports.com/events/summer/hosts/list-countries.htm.

the Olympics. While some emerging countries such as South Africa and India might be hosts in the future, a vast majority of countries will never be able to host the Games due to economic, geographic, climate, or other factors. From the perspective of these small or less developed countries, our findings should be encouraging. We cannot say whether they would receive a hosting bump in their medal count, since we have no data upon which to base that prediction. We can say, however, that large, economically prosperous countries, by virtue of hosting the Games, are not receiving a large hosting boost in their medal count which small countries are precluded from receiving. While host nations have a significantly larger Olympic team than in years when they are not hosting, they do not do a good job of winning additional medals with those extra athletes. This is perhaps largely a consequence of the fact that these extra participants will tend to be of lower quality, given that the qualification rules are more lax for host nations.

While our research has proven that there is no statistically significant home advantage at the Olympic Games in general, there might be a home advantage in the history of specific events. For example, at the Sochi Winter Olympics in 2014 Russian figure skater Adelina Sotnikova surprisingly won the gold medal over South Korean Yuna Kim. Many experts heavily criticized the result from the competition in Sochi and argued that it was the result of the judges being influenced by the home crowd ("Yuna Kim Sochi Scandal" 2014).

15 Conclusion

An increasing number of countries have the ambition to be successful at the Olympic Games. While there are, as presented in Chapter 2, different methods of defining success, all of them (number of gold medals, total number of medals, medals weighted, medals in relation to GDP, population, etc.) have one similarity: they solely measure success in terms of medals. While some of the rankings take the different starting conditions of countries into consideration (such as wealth/poverty, size, etc.), they all focus on the outcome. The same applies to the official Olympic targets of most countries: they are concerned with a certain position in the medal ranking or a certain number of medals won.

My argument that is summarized in Figure 15.1 is that, apart from the outcome (medals won, position in medal ranking), countries should also take the process that leads to their successes and failures into consideration. Furthermore, the popularity of the winning or failing sports is a factor that matters for societal acceptance of elite sport policies.

While people all over the world might be proud when their country succeeds in the Olympic Games, there is always an invisible level of the medal rankings: Which medals were won and how were the models won?

Grix and Carmichael classify success obtained in the most popular sports of a country as " 'quality' medals" (Grix and Carmichael 2012, 81). Research shows that success in the most popular sports of a country is more important for the national identity (Haut 2014, 70). Brazil does not only want to end up in the top 10 of the Rio Summer Olympics medal ranking. Another officially claimed aim of the 2016 host country is winning the gold medal in the men's soccer event. Formulating such a goal (winning a medal in the most important sport of a country) is not yet common in the world; only soccer-mad Nigeria has claimed the same ambition as Brazil to win gold in the men's soccer competition in Rio. It is consequent to give special emphasis to the most popular sport of a country, as done by Brazil and Nigeria. But for most countries it's just about winning medals, regardless of the popularity of the respective sports.

For example, there are only 8,000 members in the German luge federation ("Bob- Und Schlittenverband Für Deutschland" 2015). Germany is the leading country in luge at the Winter Olympics, but the public interest in that sport is limited in Germany, despite their Olympic success. Far more popular in the

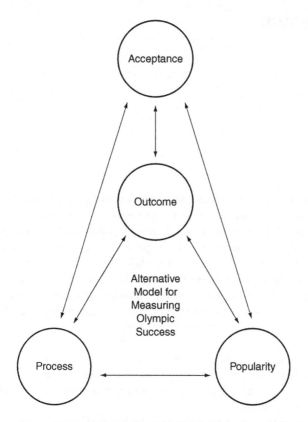

Figure 15.1 Alternative Model for Measuring Olympic Success.

country is skiing. The German skiing federation has 650,000 members, 81 times more than the luge federation (Deutscher Skiverband n.d.). There are similar examples from summer sports: For example, the German Archery Federation has only 6,000 members (the federation does not publish membership statistics, the number is from an interview with the head of the German archery federation) and has won so far two Olympic medals (Bogensport-extra n.d.). The German table tennis federation has 590,000 members, 98 times more members than the archery federation, and won so far five Olympic medals (Deutscher Tischtennis Bund 2015). The German tennis federation won seven Olympic medals and has even 250 time more members than the archery federation: 1.5 million members, which is, according to the federation's website, the largest national tennis federation in the world (Deutscher Tennis Bund 2015).

Medal rankings and the medal targets of countries, such as Germany's target for Rio 2016 to exceed the number of medals won at the London 2012 Summer Olympics (44), do not consider the different popularity of sports. It is not rational that every medal counts the same, while the popularity of sports is so different.

Countries such as Germany should value in their evaluations successes in popular sports such as skiing and tennis more than in niche sports such as luge and archery. But currently, concern is just about the number of medals won. It also does not matter whether only few sports win most medals, as is currently the case even in the most developed countries, or if a broad variety of sports contribute to the medal count of a country.

In addition to the popularity of sports, also the process that leads to medal winning is important. For Ronglan it is not the total number of medals that is crucial, but which medals (outcome legitimacy) as well as how they are achieved (Ronglan 2014, 14). For example, if doping contributed to Olympic success, this might affect political aims such as increasing national pride and gaining soft power that are discussed in depth at the beginning of the book. In communist states occurred "longevity, structural organization, explicit and systematic cheating and the abuse of minors" (Dimeo 2013, 200). However, other countries such as West Germany and Australia also had doping cultures, albeit of a different nature. Particularly in open societies, public acceptance is vital for the support to the elite sport system, and there is a public expectation to fight "the Dark Side of Sport" which includes, apart from doping, abuse, violence, corruption, and match fixing (Petroczi 2009, 349–352). For example, consequences of the 1988 Seoul Olympics, where the Ben Johnson drugs affair blighted the games, were a "moral crisis in high-performance sport in Canada" (Green 2007, 932). But even in the autocratic GDR, there was a "decline of citizens' acceptance of the lavishly funded elite sport program" (Grix 2008, 408).

While in Norway, for example, there are usually restrictions on talent identification concerning children under 13 years of age, and rules aiming to prevent children from specializing in one particular sport too early, in China athletes leave their families at the age of 10 to live in academies, and to focus every single day on a specific sport such as weightlifting (Augestad et al. 2006, 293–313; Beech 2012). The Chinese approach would certainly cause an outcry in liberal Western societies.

This book has discussed *why* nation-states are aiming for Olympic success and *how* some countries managed to become more successful than others. What the book has not done is to question in general the desire for elite sport success, and to discuss whether it is good or bad for human development. Some authors are very critical of elite sport investment. Grix and Carmichael, for example, conclude in their paper "Why do Governments Invest in Elite Sport? A Polemic" that "the rationale for investment in elite sport remained and remains unclear, under-researched and generally uncritically accepted" (Grix and Carmichael 2012, 75).

A growing number of countries, particularly developed countries and nation-states with emerging economies, are becoming more and more ambitious when it comes to the Olympic Games, and are heavily increasing their elite sport budgets. For example, Houlihan and Zheng argue, "once the governments identify elite sport success as a policy objective they are locked onto a path from which it is increasingly difficult to deviate" (Houlihan and Zheng 2013, 343). Houlihan and Zheng point out that:

> Given that most of the countries that traditionally finish in the top 20 of the Olympic Games or the top 10 of the Winter Olympics are participating in this sporting arms race, there should hopefully be an awareness that a high proportion of every increase in funding is absorbed in maintaining rather than improving the country's relative position.
>
> (Houlihan and Zheng 2013, 334–335)

De Bosscher et al. come to similar conclusions in their work: "The finding suggest that as nations strive for success there are diminishing returns on investment such that it is necessary to continue investing in elite sport simply to maintain exiting performance levels" (De Bosscher et al. 2008, 123).

The question is whether the vast investments undertaken by countries can be justified. Potential positive domestic benefits of Olympic success like national pride and cohesion are difficult to prove and to rebut. The same applies to international targets such as gaining legitimacy and soft power. In the end, it all depends on the domestic discourses around elite sport investments, and the perception of its benefits. Interestingly, there seem to be no cases in the world where there is large societal pressure to question in general elite sport investments. While protests against hosting mega-sporting events such as the FIFA World Cup and the Olympics have become common, such as those that occurred recently in Brazil, the host of 2014 FIFA World Cup and the 2016 Summer Olympics, there are not similar visible movements that call for a reduction or abolishment of investments into elite sport, in spite of the increasing budgets for Olympic success in many countries. However, there are certainly critical questions that should be asked:

- On the domestic level, should the money that is invested into elite sport instead be invested into other areas such as education, health, or mass sport participation that might be of larger benefit for society?
- From an international perspective, does "the global sporting arms race" (Bingham and Shibli 2008) promote a development that contradicts Olympic values such as contributing to peace, harmony, and a better understanding among countries?

Answering the first question might depend on the context, particularly on the stage of development of a country, as well as that developed countries like Germany and Norway can more easily afford and justify participating in "the new gold war" (Johnson 2008) than countries such as Brazil and India, which still face mass poverty. However, this does not mean that countries such as Brazil and India should not aim for Olympic success. It might be wise for those countries to focus on historic strengths (such as soccer in Brazil and field hockey in India) and invest in new sports (such as rugby sevens), such as by adding them to the PE curriculum in schools, rather than entering an expensive competition with developed countries in established and costly sports such as equestrian and sailing.

It remains to be seen whether Houlihan and Zheng are correct in their prediction that "at some point in the medium-term future, the government of one of the major sports powers will step off the policy path, facing the challenge of justifying its decision to its electorate/public" (Houlihan and Zheng 2013, 352).

Regarding the second question about "the global sporting arms race," what sport certainly can do is bring people from all over the world together. For example, while there were political tensions between the United States and Iran, and hardly any contact between government officials took place (before the relations improved in 2015 with the historic Joint Comprehensive Plan of Action, JCPOA, which aims to ensure that Iran's nuclear program will be exclusively peaceful), there was contact between Iranians and Americans in wrestling, an Olympic sport with a long tradition that is popular in the United States as well as in Iran. US athletes participated in competitions in Iran, and Iranian athletes competed in wrestling events in the United States. When the International Olympic Committee considered removing wrestling from the program of the 2020 Games in Tokyo, Iranian and American athletes fought together to maintain the sport in the program of the Summer Olympics. According to US wrestling coach Zeke Jones, "Wrestling has brought closer the people of Iran and the US" ("Olympic Wrestling Becomes Common Ground for US and Iran" 2013).

Countries are becoming obsessed with Olympic success, formulating more and more ambitious targets for the Olympics (such as winning more medals than at the previous Games while at the same time the competition between countries is increasing and more nation-states are participating and winning medals), and a continuous increase in national budgets for elite sport success is taking place around the world. My concern is that in such an environment, the potential of the Olympics to not only bring people together but also contribute to a better understanding among them might gradually disappear and be replaced by jingoism, an aggressive form of nationalism. This is why I believe that the International Olympic Committee should consider measures to condemn extreme forms of nationalism at the Games.

John Gleaves and Matthew Llewellyn make in their paper "Ethics, Nationalism, and the Imagined Community: The Case Against Inter-National Sport" a suggestion against "cases where sport nationalism exacerbated national chauvinisms, xenophobia, or various prejudicial biases" (Gleaves and Llewellyn 2014, 2). They propose to no longer make the Olympics a contest between national teams. The current system that National Olympic Committees and federations nominate the athletes that can compete at the Olympics leads to the fact that some of the best athletes or teams are excluded from the competition and left at home:

> For example, the fourth best men's table tennis player from China is also the fourth best table tennis player in the world. If China can only send three

table tennis players to an international tournament, then some talented athletes are left home simply because of their nationality, not their athletic merit.

(Gleaves and Llewellyn 2014, 13)

Athletes who can qualify on their athletic merit should not be omitted because of their national affiliation. This process would, according to Gleaves and Llewellyn, deny athletes and fans the ability to derive elite sport's most meaningful narrative: the best athletes competing against the best. The authors argue that with their model, the national origin of athletes would matter much less than their performance, and the expensive national arms race as well as nationalism at the Olympics might end.

While I agree with Gleaves and Llewellyn that their suggestion would on the one hand increase the quality of the competitions from a pure sporting point of view, on the other hand the Olympics would become less inclusive. Excluding athletes from less competitive countries ignores that "issues of identity and cultural representation are valuable ends that can be pursued through sport" and "that inter-national sport sometimes leads to significant moral discourse within and between national communities," as Iorwerth and Hardman write in their response to Gleaves and Llewellyn (Iorwerth and Hardman 2015, 14).

If athletes from specific countries would dominate certain events (such as Chinese table tennis, South Koreans archery, Germans luge, etc.), this would significantly affect the international character of the Games. But "cross-cultural conversation is the pragmatic starting point for human progress and cooperation" (Iorwerth and Hardman 2015, 12). It is also questionable how a model that would lead to a larger dominance of some nation-states in their national sport(s) could be considered as a measure to combat nationalism. On the contrary, I would argue it could reinforce the belief in national supremacy and exceptionalism.

My suggestion is to keep the basic structure of the Olympics with the International Federations who make the rules, approved by the IOC, and the National Olympic Committees, that nominate the athletes, but to abolish the strict organization of the Olympic events along national lines. I suggest introducing events that allow for teams composed of athletes from different countries. A good example that could be easily adopted by the IOC comes from the International Table Tennis Federation (ITTF). The ITTF took in 2014 the decision that players from different associations were allowed to form doubles pairs. At the 2015 table tennis World Championship in Suzhou, China, athletes from different countries were paired for the first time, for example Ma Long from China and Timo Boll from Germany. According to ITTF President Thomas Weikert, the new policy had the intention to "strengthen the good international relations between our national associations" ("Ma Long & Timo Boll to Team Up at 2015 World Table Tennis Championships" 2015). If such mixed teams were to become common in different Olympic sports, this might become an effective measure to promote cooperation among countries (internationalism) and mutual respect in a common community (cosmopolitanism). My suggestion could also ensure that the best athletes are present at the Olympics, a valid concern raised by Gleaves and Llewellyn. For example, in team sports such as volleyball only a limited number of countries can qualify for the Olympics. In the women's as well as the men's event only 12 nation-states can participate. But the sport is popular in far more than 12 countries in the world. This means that many world-class players who failed to qualify with their country won't be present at the Games, and their absence might also limit the interest of the respective domestic audiences. The International Federations and the IOC should consider allowing one foreigner in each team, making the event more inclusive by involving athletes from more countries in the event. If such mixed teams win medals, this should be also reflected in the medal count by awarding points to all nationalities that contributed to success.

Such reforms for the future of the Olympic Games might preserve honorable objectives such as contributing to a better international understanding that were once formulated when the modern Olympic Games began their unique success story, and became the greatest sporting event in the world. After moving from the Cold to the Gold War, the Olympics should now move toward an event that encourages peace instead of war of any kind.

References

Ahrens, Peter. 2012. "Olympia-Krise Der Ballsportarten: Daheim Sein Ist Alles." Accessed August 19, 2015, www.spiegel.de/sport/sonst/olympia-krise-der-ballsportarten-daheim-sein-ist-alles-a-813070.html.

Alperovich, Amichai. 2008. *Israel in Der Olympischen Bewegung*. Deutsche Sporthochschule Köln.

Anderson, Richard. 2012. "Olympic Success: How Much Does a Gold Medal Cost?" BBC News. Accessed June 2, 2015, www.bbc.com/news/business-19144983.

Andreff, Wladimir. 2013. "Economic Development as Major Determinant of Olympic Medal Wins: Predicting Performances of Russian and Chinese Teams at Sochi Games." *International Journal of Economic Policy in Emerging Economies* 6 (4): 314–340.

Armbrecht, Anne. 2015. "Stillstand Im Deutschen Spitzensport." *Frankfurter Allgemeine Zeitung*, October 2.

Around the Rings. 2015. "Hickey Dismisses Fears Over Threat to European Games." Accessed August 7, 2015, http://aroundtherings.com/site/A__50716/title__Hickey-Dismisses-Fears-Over-Threat-to-European-Games/292/Articles.

Augestad, Pål, Nils Asle Bergsgard, and Atle O. Hansen. 2006. "The Institutionalization of an Elite Sport Organization in Norway: The Case of 'Olympiatoppen'." *Sociology of Sport Journal* 23 (3): 293–313.

Baimbridge, Mark. 1998. "Outcome Uncertainty in Sporting Competition: The Olympic Games 1896–1996." *Applied Economics Letters* 5 (3): 161–164.

Bairner, Alan. 2015. "Assessing the Sociology of Sport: On National Identity and Nationalism." *International Review for the Sociology of Sport* 50 (4–5): 375–379.

Balmer, Nigel J., Alan M. Nevill, and A. Mark Williams. 2001. "Home Advantage in the Winter Olympics (1908–1998)." *Journal of Sports Sciences* 19 (2): 129–139.

Balmer, Nigel J., Alan M. Nevill, and A. Mark Williams. 2003. "Modelling Home Advantage in the Summer Olympic Games." *Journal of Sports Sciences* 21 (6): 469–478.

Banda, Davies. 2010. "Zambia: Government's Role in Colonial and Modern Times." *International Journal of Sport Policy* 2 (2): 237–252.

Barney, Robert K. and Michael H. Heine. 2014. " 'The Emblem of One United Body … One Great Sporting Maple Leaf': The Olympic Games and Canada's Quest for Self-Identity." *Sport in Society* (ahead-of-print): 1–19.

BBC News. 2009. "Huge Bolivian Glacier Disappears." Accessed February 17, 2015, http://news.bbc.co.uk/2/hi/8046540.stm.

Beech, Hannah. 2012. "China's Gold Standard." *TIME*, July 19.

Belson, Ken. 2015. "I.O.C. Adds Four Events to Roster of 2018 Winter Games." *New York Times*, June 8.

Berdahl, Jennifer L., Eric Luis Uhlmann, and Feng Bai. 2015. "Win–Win: Female and Male Athletes from More Gender Equal Nations Perform Better in International Sports Competitions." *Journal of Experimental Social Psychology* 56: 1–3.

Bergsgard, Nils Asle, Barrie Houlihan, Per Mangset, Svein Ingve Nodland, and Hilmar Rommetvedt. 2007. *Sport Policy: A Comparative Analysis of Stability and Change.* Routledge.

Bernard, Andrew B. and Meghan R. Busse. 2004. "Who Wins the Olympic Games: Economic Resources and Medal Totals." *Review of Economics and Statistics* 86 (1): 413–417.

Bian, Xun. 2005. "Predicting Olympic Medal Counts: The Effects of Economic Development on Olympic Performance." *The Park Place Economist* 13: 37–44.

Bickerton, James and Alain-G. Gagnon. 2011. "Regions." In *Comparative Politics*, edited by Daniele Caramani, 367–391. Oxford University Press.

Billings, Andrew C. 2008. *Olympic Media: Inside the Biggest Show on Television.* Routledge.

Bingham, Jerry and Simon Shibli. 2008. *The Global Sporting Arms Race: An International Comparative Study on Sports Policy Factors Leading to International Sporting Success.* Meyer & Meyer Verlag.

Binns, James T. 2009. "The Use of Performance Based Funding in a Sport Organization: A Case Study of the United States Olympic Committee." Accessed January 20, 2015, http://oai.dtic.mil/oai/oai?verb=getRecord&metadataPrefix=html&identifier=ADA505164.

Blanchard, Christopher. 2014. "Qatar: Background and U.S. Relations." Accessed August 26, 2015, www.fas.org/sgp/crs/mideast/RL31718.pdf.

"Bob- Und Schlittenverband Für Deutschland: Historie." 2015. Accessed May 22, 2015, www.bsd-portal.de/index.php?id=426.

Bogensport-extra. n.d. "Interview Mit Wolfgang Kalkum Präsident Des Deutschen Bogensport-Verbandes 1959 E.V." Accessed May 22, 2015, www.bogensport-extra.de/interviews/205-interview-mit-wolfgang-kalkum-praesident-des-deutschen-bogensport-verbandes-1959-ev.html.

Bordon, Sam. 2014. "Speeding Up and Shrinking, Rugby Extends Reach." *New York Times*, December 8.

Bravo, Gonzalo and Jorge Silva. 2014. "Sport Policy in Chile." *International Journal of Sport Policy and Politics* 6 (1): 129–142.

Campbell, Rook. 2011. "Staging Globalization for National Projects: Global Sport Markets and Elite Athletic Transnational Labour in Qatar." *International Review for the Sociology of Sport* 46 (1): 45–60.

Carter, Thomas F. 2008. "New Rules to the Old Game: Cuban Sport and State Legitimacy in the Post-Soviet Era." *Identities: Global Studies in Culture and Power* 15 (2): 194–215.

Castro, Suélen Barboza Eiras de, Fernando Augusto Starepravo, Jay Coakley, and Doralice Lange de Souza. 2015. "Mega Sporting Events and Public Funding of Sport in Brazil (2004–2011)." *Leisure Studies*: 1–18.

Cha, Victor D. 2009. *Beyond the Final Score: The Politics of Sport in Asia.* Columbia University Press.

Chappelet, Jean-Loup. 2010. "Switzerland." *International Journal of Sport Policy and Politics* 2 (1): 99–100.

Chappell, Robert and Ejeta Seifu. 2000. "Sport, Culture and Politics in Ethiopia." *Sport in Society* 3 (1): 35–47.

Chen, Yu-Wen, Tien-Chin Tan, and Ping-Chao Lee. 2015. "The Chinese Government and the Globalization of Table Tennis: A Case Study in Local Responses to the Globalization of Sport." *The International Journal of the History of Sport* (ahead-of-print): 1–13.

Clarey, Christopher. 2015a. "American Coaches Have a Field Day, But for Other Countries." *New York Times*, August 25.

Clarey, Christopher. 2015b. "Atop Medal Table at Worlds, Kenya is Also Under a Cloud." *New York Times*, August 24.

Cornelissen, Scarlett. 2010. "The Geopolitics of Global Aspiration: Sport Mega-Events and Emerging Powers." *The International Journal of the History of Sport* 27 (16–18): 3008–3025.

D'Agati, Philip A. 2011. *Nationalism on the World Stage: Cultural Performance at the Olympic Games*. University Press of America.

D'Agati, Philip. 2013. *The Cold War and the 1984 Olympic Games: A Soviet-American Surrogate War*. Palgrave Macmillan.

Danziger, James N. 2012. *Understanding the Political World: A Comparative Introduction to Political Science*. 10th edn. Pearson.

De Bosscher, Veerle, Jerry Bingham, and Simon Shibli. 2008. *The Global Sporting Arms Race: An International Comparative Study on Sports Policy Factors Leading to International Sporting Success*. Meyer & Meyer Verlag.

De Bosscher, Veerle, Paul De Knop, Maarten Van Bottenburg, and Simon Shibli. 2006. "A Conceptual Framework for Analysing Sports Policy Factors Leading to International Sporting Success." *European Sport Management Quarterly* 6 (2): 185–215.

De Bosscher, Veerle, Simon Shibli, Hans Westerbeek, and Maarten Van Bottenburg. 2015. *Succesful Elite Sport Policies. An International Comparison of the Sports Policy Factors Leading to International Sporting Success (SPLISS 2.0) in 15 Nations*. Meyer & Meyer Sport.

De Bosscher, Veerle, Paul De Knop, Maarten Van Bottenburg, Simon Shibli, and Jerry Bingham. 2009. "Explaining International Sporting Success: An International Comparison of Elite Sport Systems and Policies in Six Countries." *Sport Management Review* 12 (3): 113–136.

De Bosscher, Veerle, Simon Shibli, Maarten van Bottenburg, Paul De Knop, and Jasper Truyens. 2010. "Developing a Method for Comparing the Elite Sport Systems and Policies of Nations: A Mixed Research Methods Approach." *Journal of Sport Management* 24 (5): 567–600.

Den Butter, Frank A.G. and Casper M. Van Der Tak 1995. "Olympic Medals as an Indicator of Social Welfare." *Social Indicators Research* 35 (1): 27–37.

Deutscher Skiverband. n.d. "Über Uns Der DSV." Accessed May 22, 2015, www.deutscherskiverband.de/ueber_uns_der_dsv_zahlen_fakten_de.html.

Deutscher Tennis Bund. 2015. "Wir Über Uns – Deutscher Tennis Bund." Accessed May 22, 2015, www.dtb-tennis.de/Verband/Wir-ueber-uns.

Deutscher Tischtennis Bund. 2015. "Sport Und Organisation – Deutscher Tischtennis Bund E.V." Accessed May 22, 2015, www.tischtennis.de/dttb/sport_und_organisation/.

Digel, Helmut. 2005. "Comparison of Successful Sport System." Accessed December 2, 2014, www.coachr.org/comparison_of_successful_sport_systems.htm.

Dimeo, Paul. 2013. "Sport Under Communism: Behind the East German 'Miracle'." *Sport in History* 33 (2): 199–201.

"Does the U.S. Lead the Winter Olympics – Or Does Germany? | WCAI." 2014. Accessed August 21, 2014, http://capeandislands.org/post/us-leads-winter-olympics-or-does-germany.

Dorsey, James 2014. "The Turbulent World of Middle East Soccer: Qatar's Sports-Focused Public Diplomacy Backfires." Accessed June 13, 2014, http://mideastsoccer.blogspot.com/2014/02/qatars-sports-focused-public-diplomacy.html.

Dorsey, James. 2015. "Setting Benchmark in Battle for Statehood: Palestine Plays in Asian Cup." Accessed January 20, 2015, www.huffingtonpost.com/james-dorsey/setting-benchmark-in-batt_b_6406964.html.

Dousti, Morteza, M. Goodarzi, H. Asadi, and M. Khabiri. 2013. "Sport Policy in Iran." *International Journal of Sport Policy and Politics* 5 (1): 151–158.

Dyreson, Mark. 2009. *Crafting Patriotism for Global Dominance: America at the Olympics*. Routledge.

Emrich, Eike, Markus Klein, Werner Pitsch, and Christian Pierdzioch. 2012. "On the Determinants of Sporting Success: A Note on the Olympic Games." *Economics Bulletin* 32 (3): 1890–1901.

Ernst & Young. 2015. "Rapid-Growth Markets Soft Power Index: Soft Power Variables – EY – Global." Accessed June 12, 2014, www.ey.com/GL/en/Issues/Driving-growth/Rapid-growth-markets-soft-power-index-Soft-power-variables.

Fahlén, Josef and Cecilia Stenling. 2015. "Sport Policy in Sweden." *International Journal of Sport Policy and Politics*: 1–17.

Farkas, Christoph. 2015. "Eishockey Als Widerstand Reminiszenz an Ein Spiel, Das Nicht Unterzukriegen War: Berlin-Weißwasser, Weißwasser-Berlin, Zwanzig Jahre Lang." *Frankfurter Allgemeine Zeitung*, September 23.

Fernandes, António José Serôdio, Fernando Jose dos Santos Tenreiro, Luis Felgueiras e Sousa Quaresma, and Victor Manuel de Oliveira Maças. 2011. "Sport Policy in Portugal." *International Journal of Sport Policy and Politics* 3 (1): 133–141.

Games of Small States of Europe. 2015. "History." Accessed August 17, 2015, www.luxembourg2013.lu/index_en.htm.

Gibson, Owen. 2014a. "The Great Funding Debate: Has Britain's Medal Chase Gone Too Far?" *Guardian*, March 18.

Gibson, Owen. 2014b. "This is a Very Dark Day for Sport." *Guardian*, March 19.

Gleaves, John and Matthew Llewellyn. 2014. "Ethics, Nationalism, and the Imagined Community: The Case Against Inter-National Sport." *Journal of the Philosophy of Sport* 41 (1): 1–19.

Green, Mick. 2007. "Olympic Glory Or Grassroots Development? Sport Policy Priorities in Australia, Canada and the United Kingdom, 1960–2006." *The International Journal of the History of Sport* 24 (7): 921–953.

Grix, Jonathan. 2008. "The Decline of Mass Sport Provision in the German Democratic Republic." *The International Journal of the History of Sport* 25 (4): 406–420.

Grix, Jonathan. 2013. "Sport Politics and the Olympics." *Political Studies Review* 11 (1): 15–25.

Grix, Jonathan and Fiona Carmichael. 2012. "Why Do Governments Invest in Elite Sport? A Polemic." *International Journal of Sport Policy and Politics* 4 (1): 73–90.

Hamilton, B. 2000. "East African Running Dominance: What is Behind it?" *British Journal of Sports Medicine* 34 (5): 391–394.

Harkness, Geoff. 2012. "Out of Bounds: Cultural Barriers to Female Sports Participation in Qatar." *The International Journal of the History of Sport* 29 (15): 2162–2183.

Haut, Jan (Ed.). 2014. *Leistungssport Als Konkurrenz Der Nationen. Sozio-Ökonomische Bedingungen Und Effekte*. Universaar.

Heijmans, Jeroen. 2014. "Unrecognized States at the Olympics." Accessed January 20, 2015, http://olympstats.com/2014/11/04/unrecognized-states-at-the-olympics/.

Heijmans, Jeroen. 2015a. "Countries Winning Medals in Just a Single Sport." Accessed August 27, 2015, http://olympstats.com/?s=Countries+winning+medals+in+just+a+single+sport+.

Heijmans, Jeroen. 2015b. "One in Every Five Table Tennis Olympians is Chinese." Accessed June 16, 2015, http://olympstats.com/2015/04/25/one-in-every-five-table-tennis-olympians-is-chinese/.

Heijmans, Jeroen. 2015c. "The Unluckiest Countries at the Olympics." Accessed January 20, 2015, http://olympstats.com/2015/01/05/the-unluckiest-countries-at-the-olympics/.

Hellborg, Anna-Maria and Susanna Hedenborg. 2015. "The Rocker and the Heroine: Gendered Media Representations of Equestrian Sports at the 2012 Olympics." *Sport in Society* 18 (2): 248–261.

Heywood, Andrew. 2013. *Politics*. 4th edn. Palgrave.

"High Achievers to Get Olympic Games Cash, Non-Performers to Miss Out." 2015. Accessed January 20, 2015, www.dailytelegraph.com.au/sport/more-sports/performing-athletes-to-get-olympic-cash/story-fnducgor-1226526118764?nk=23d3b2a724cbe24a4af63dc01bac8333.

Horne, John and Garry Whannel. 2012. *Understanding the Olympics*. Routledge.

Horowitz, Jonathan and Stephen R. McDaniel. 2015. "Investigating the Global Productivity Effects of Highly Skilled Labour Migration: How Immigrant Athletes Impact Olympic Medal Counts." *International Journal of Sport Policy and Politics* 7 (1): 19–42.

Houlihan, Barrie and Jinming Zheng. 2013. "The Olympics and Elite Sport Policy: Where Will it all End?" *The International Journal of the History of Sport* 30 (4): 338–355.

Houlihan, Barrie and Jinming Zheng. 2014. "Small States: Sport and Politics at the Margin." *International Journal of Sport Policy and Politics* (ahead-of-print): 1–16.

Hunter, John. 2003. "Flying the Flag: Identities, the Nation, and Sport." *Identities: Global Studies in Culture and Power* 10 (4): 409–425.

"India Targetting Ten-Plus Medals at Rio Olympics, Says Sports Minister." 2015. First-post. Accessed February 19, 2015, www.firstpost.com/sports/india-targetting-ten-plus-medals-rio-olympics-says-sports-minister-2104559.html.

Institut für Forschung und Entwicklung von Sportgeräten. 2015. "Philosophie." Accessed August 28, 2015, www.fes-sport.de/philosophie.htm.

International Olympic Committee. 2014a. "Sochi 2014 Facts and Figures." Accessed September 22, 2015, www.olympic.org/Documents/Games_Sochi_2014/Sochi_2014_Facts_and_Figures.pdf.

International Olympic Committee. 2014b. "Women in the Olympic Movement." Accessed November 21, 2014, www.olympic.org/Documents/Reference_documents_Factsheets/Women_in_Olympic_Movement.pdf.

International Sports Press Association. 2015. "USA, Russia and Germany Ranked Top Three Countries in Elite Sport Ranking." Accessed October 13, 2015, www.aipsmedia.com/index.php?page=news&cod=17052&tp=n#.VhzAq87ji1s.

International Triathlon Union. 2012. "Olympic Qualification 101 – How Athletes and Countries Get to London 2012 | Triathlon.Org." Accessed May 26, 2015, www.triathlon.org/news/article/olympic_qualification_101.

"IOC Grants Full Olympic Recognition to Kosovo." 2014. Accessed January 20, 2015, www.usatoday.com/story/sports/olympics/2014/12/09/ioc-grants-full-olympic-recognition-to-kosovo/20128911/.

Iorwerth, Hywel and Alun Hardman. 2015. "The Case for Inter-National Sport: A Reply to Gleaves and Llewellyn." *Journal of the Philosophy of Sport* (ahead-of-print): 1–17.

Jarvie, Grant and Michelle Sikes. 2012. "Running as a Resource of Hope? Voices from Eldoret." *Review of African Political Economy* 39 (134): 629–644.

Johnson, Daniel K.N. and Ayfer Ali. 2000. "Coming to Play Or Coming to Win: Participation and Success at the Olympic Games." *Wellesley College Dept. of Economics Working Paper* (2000–10).

Johnson, Ian. 2008. "The New Gold War – WSJ." Accessed January 20, 2015, www.wsj.com/articles/SB121763204928806141.

Kalifa, Tamir. 2015. "In Israel, Migrants Find a Home, through Running." *New York Times*, April 24.

Kang, Jiyeon, Jae-On Kim, and Yan Wang. 2015. "Salvaging National Pride: The 2010 Taekwondo Controversy and Taiwan's Quest for Global Recognition." *International Review for the Sociology of Sport* 50 (1): 98–114.

Kårhus, Svein. 2014. "What Limits of Legitimate Discourse? The Case of Elite Sport as 'Thinkable' Official Knowledge in the Norwegian National Curriculum." *Sport, Education and Society*: 1–17.

Khatri, Shabina. 2013. "Qatar, US Sign 10-Year Military Cooperation Pact during Official Visit." Accessed August 26, 2015, http://dohanews.co/qatar-us-sign-10-year-military-cooperation-pact-during-official-visit/.

Kinsella, David, Bruce Russett, and Harvey Starr. 2012. *World Politics: The Menu for Choice*. Cengage Learning.

Kiviaho, Pekka and Pekka Mäkelä. 1978. "Olympic Success: A Sum of Non-Material and Material Factors." *International Review for the Sociology of Sport* 13 (2): 5–22.

Klein, Jeff. 2014. "South Korea is Awarded Berths in 2018 Olympic Tournaments." *New York Times*, September 19.

Koski, Pasi and Jari Lämsä. 2015. "Finland as a Small Sports Nation: Socio-Historical Perspectives on the Development of National Sport Policy." *International Journal of Sport Policy and Politics* (ahead-of-print): 1–21.

Krüger, Michael. 2015. "Global Perspectives on Sports and Movement Cultures: From Past to Present–Modern Sports Between Nationalism, Internationalism, and Cultural Imperialism." *The International Journal of the History of Sport* 32 (4): 518–534.

Krüger, Michael, Christian Becker, and Stefan Nielsen. 2015. *German Sports, Doping, and Politics: A History of Performance Enhancement*. Rowman & Littlefield.

Kummels, Ingrid. 2013. "Anthropological Perspectives on Sport and Culture: Against Sports as the Essence of Western Modernity." In *Sport Across Asia: Politics, Cultures, and Identities*, edited by Katrin Bromber, Birgit Krawietz, and Joseph Maguire, 11–31. Routledge.

Kuper, Gerard Hendrik and Elmer Sterken. 2003. *Olympic Participation and Performance since 1896*. University of Groningen.

Lee, Ping-Chao and Bai-Sheng Li. 2015. "Does China Matter? Taiwan's Successful Bid to Host the 2017 Summer Universiade." *The International Journal of the History of Sport* 32 (8): 1044–1056.

Longman, Jere. 2014. "Cuban Athletes Cheer as Nations Drop Fists." *New York Times*, December 22.

Longman, Jere. 2015. "Women's World Cup: First Opponents to Face the Fury of U.S. Players? Older Siblings." *New York Times*, June 14.

López de D'Amico, Rosa. 2012. "Policy in Venezuela." *International Journal of Sport Policy and Politics* 4 (1): 139–151.

Lui, Hon-Kwong and Wing Suen. 2008. "Men, Money, and Medals: An Econometric Analysis of the Olympic Games." *Pacific Economic Review* 13 (1): 1–16.

"Ma Long & Timo Boll to Team Up at 2015 World Table Tennis Championships." 2015. Accessed May 21, 2015, www.ittf.com/press_releases/PR/PR1.asp?id=85.

McCree, Roy. 2009. "Sport Policy and the New Public Management in the Caribbean: Convergence Or Resurgence?" *Public Management Review* 11 (4): 461–476.

McDougall, Alan. 2013. "Sport Under Communism: Behind the East German 'Miracle'." *Sport in Society* 16 (6): 841–843.

McLaughlin, Douglas W. and Cesar R. Torres. 2014. "A Veil of Separation." *International Journal of Applied Philosophy* 28 (2): 353–372.

Maguire, Joseph and Robert Pearton. 2000. "The Impact of Elite Labour Migration on the Identification, Selection and Development of European Soccer Players." *Journal of Sports Sciences* 18 (9): 759–769.

Mair, Peter (Ed.). 2011. *Democracies*. Oxford University Press.

Majumdar, Boria and Nalin Mehta. 2010. *India and the Olympics*. Routledge.

Mallon, Bill. 2014a. "Most Sports Winning Medals by Nations." Accessed November 19, 2014, http://olympstats.com/2014/02/12/most-sports-winning-medals-by-nations/.

Mallon, Bill. 2014b. "Nations with Most Olympic Medals but No Golds." Accessed June 2, 2015, http://olympstats.com/2014/08/25/nations-with-most-olympic-medals-but-no-golds/.

Mallon, Bill. 2014c. "Netherlands Speed Skating Medal Sweeps." Accessed November 12, 2014, http://olympstats.com/2014/02/18/netherlands-speed-skating-medal-sweeps/.

Mallon, Bill. 2014d. "Olympic Medal Sweeps." Accessed November 12, 2014, http://olympstats.com/2014/01/13/olympic-medal-sweeps/.

Mallon, Bill. 2014e. "Olympic Medals Won by Nations: A Deeper Analysis." Accessed November 24, 2014, http://olympstats.com/2014/07/14/olympic-medals-won-by-nations-a-deeper-analysis/.

Mallon, Bill. 2015a. "Individual and Team Olympic Medal Records." Accessed June 16, 2015, http://olympstats.com/2015/01/26/individual-and-team-olympic-medal-records/.

Mallon, Bill. 2015b. "International Women's Day." Accessed June 17, 2015, http://olympstats.com/2015/03/08/international-womens-day/.

Menary, Steve. 2007. *OUTCASTS! The Lands that FIFA Forgot*. Know The Score.

Ministry of Education, Culture, Sports, Science and Technology. 2015. "Promotion of Sports." Accessed July 22, 2015, www.mext.go.jp/english/sports_promotion/index.htm.

Moosa, Imad A. and Lee Smith. 2004. "Economic Development Indicators as Determinants of Medal Winning at the Sydney Olympics: An Extreme Bounds Analysis." *Australian Economic Papers* 43 (3): 288–301.

Morgan, William J. 1999. "Patriotic Sports and the Moral Making of Nations." *Journal of the Philosophy of Sport* 26 (1): 50–67.

Müller, Martin. 2011. "State Dirigisme in Megaprojects: Governing the 2014 Winter Olympics in Sochi." *Environment and Planning A* 43: 2091–2108.

Müllner, Rudolf. 2013. "The Importance of Skiing in Austria." *The International Journal of the History of Sport* 30 (6): 659–673.

Nassif, Nadim. 2015. In Discussion with the Author. September 25.

Nassif, Nadim and Mahfoud Amara. 2015. "Sport, Policy and Politics in Lebanon." *International Journal of Sport Policy and Politics* (ahead-of-print): 1–13.

"The NBS Summer Seminar: Understanding the Olympic Games." 2012. Accessed June 12, 2014, http://newbooksinsports.com/2012/07/26/the-nbs-summer-seminar-understanding-the-olympic-games/.

Novikov, A.D. and A.M. Maximenko. 1972. "The Influence of Selected Socio-Economic Factors on the Level of Sports Achievements in the Various Countries (using as an Example the 18th Olympic Games in Tokyo)." *International Review for the Sociology of Sport* 7 (1): 27–44.

"Nowhere to Call Home; Statelessness." 2014. *The Economist*, May 17, 58.

Nye, Joseph S. 2004. *Soft Power: The Means to Success in World Politics*. Public Affairs.

Nye, Joseph S. 2014. In Discussion with the Author. October 7.

NYTimes.com. 2008. "The Medal Rankings: Which Country Leads the Olympics?" Accessed August 21, 2014, http://beijing2008.blogs.nytimes.com/2008/08/23/the-medal-rankings-which-country-leads-the-olympics/?_php=true&_type=blogs&_r=0.

Olympic Charter. 2015. Accessed August 21, 2014, www.olympic.org/documents/olympic_charter_en.pdf.

Olympic Council of Asia. 2014. "17th Asian Games Incheon 2014 – Medals." Accessed March 18, 2015, www.incheon2014ag.org/Sports/Medals/MenuMedalStanding?lang=en.

"Olympic Medal Count – 2014 Sochi Winter Olympics." 2014. Accessed June 23, 2015, http://espn.go.com/olympics/winter/2014/medals.

"Olympic – Overall Medals by Country." 2014. Accessed August 21, 2014, www.olympic.it/english/medal.

"Olympic Rugby Sevens: USA Men, Women Qualify for Rio 2016." 2015. Accessed June 19, 2015, www.si.com/more-sports/2015/06/14/olympic-rugby-sevens-usa-qualify-rio-2016.

"Olympic Wrestling Becomes Common Ground for US and Iran – RT Sport." 2013. Accessed May 21, 2015, http://rt.com/sport/wrestling-us-iran-olympic-613/.

Onyestyák, Nikoletta. 2013. "Monarchy, Socialism and Modern Capitalism: Hungary's Participation in Three London Olympic Games." *The International Journal of The History of Sport* 30 (7): 757–773.

Ostapenko, Nikolai. 2010. "Nation Branding of Russia through the Sochi Olympic Games of 2014." *Journal of Management Policy and Practice* 11 (4): 60–63.

Persson, Emil and Bo Petersson. 2014. "Political Mythmaking and the 2014 Winter Olympics in Sochi: Olympism and the Russian Great Power Myth." *East European Politics* 30 (2): 192–209.

Petroczi, Andrea. 2009. "The Dark Side of Sport: Challenges for Managers in the Twenty-First Century." *European Sport Management Quarterly* 9 (4): 349–352.

Pettigrew, Stephen and Danyel Reiche. 2016. "Hosting the Olympic Games: An Overstated Advantage in Sports History." *The International Journal of the History of Sport*: 1–13.

Pfau, Wade Donald. 2006. "Predicting the Medal Wins by Country at the 2006 Winter Olympic Games: An Econometrics Approach." *Korean Economic Review* 22 (2): 233–247.

Pfister, Gertrud. 2010. "Outsiders: Muslim Women and Olympic Games: Barriers and Opportunities." *The International Journal of the History of Sport* 27 (16–18): 2925–2957.

Pierluisi, Pedro. 2015. "Statehood is the Only Antidote for what Ails Puerto Rico." *New York Times*, July 10.

Poli, Raffaele. 2007. "The Denationalization of Sport: De-Ethnicization of the Nation and Identity Deterritorialization." *Sport in Society* 10 (4): 646–661.

Potwarka, Luke R. and Scott T. Leatherdale. 2015. "The Vancouver 2010 Olympics and Leisure-Time Physical Activity Rates Among Youth in Canada: Any Evidence of a Trickle-Down Effect?" *Leisure Studies*: 1–17.

Powell, Anita. 2012. "African Countries: Olympic Medals seem Elusive." The Root. Accessed May 11, 2015, www.theroot.com/articles/world/2012/08/african_countries_olympic_medals_seem_elusive.1.html.

Qatar National Development Strategy 2011–2016. Accessed January 11, 2013, Qatar_NDS_reprint_complete_lowres_16May.Pdf.

Qatar Winter Sport Committee. n.d. "About Qatar Winter Sport Committee (QWSC)." Accessed February 17, 2015, http://pointstreaksites.com/view/qataricehockeyfed/about-272.

Rathke, Alexander and Ulrich Woitek. 2008. "Economics and the Summer Olympics: An Efficiency Analysis." *Journal of Sports Economics*: 520–537.

Reiche, Danyel. 2014. "Investing in Sporting Success as a Domestic and Foreign Policy Tool: The Case of Qatar." *International Journal of Sport Policy and Politics* (ahead-of-print): 1–16.

Reinsch, Michael. 2013. "Die Stille Suche Nach Der Perfekten Maschine." *Frankfurter Allgemeine Zeitung*, May 25, 28.

Riordan, James and Dong Jinxia. 1996. "Chinese Women and Sport: Success, Sexuality and Suspicion." *The China Quarterly* 145: 130–152.

Riordan, James and Robin E. Jones. 1999. *Sport and Physical Education in China*. Taylor & Francis.

Romero, Simon. 2007. "Bolivia's Only Ski Resort is Facing a Snowless Future." *New York Times*, February 2.

Ronglan, Lars Tore. 2014. "Elite Sport in Scandinavian Welfare States: Legitimacy Under Pressure?" *International Journal of Sport Policy and Politics* (ahead-of-print): 1–19.

Ryan, Stephen. 2005. "Nationalism and Ethnic Conflict." In *Issues in World Politics*, edited by Brian White, Richard Little, and Michael Smith. 3rd edn, 137–154. Palgrave Macmillan.

Saaty, Thomas L. 2010. "Who Won the Winter 2010 Olympics? A Quest into Priorities and Rankings." *Journal of Multi-Criteria Decision Analysis* 17 (1–2): 25–36.

Sam, Michael P. 2015. "Sport Policy and Transformation in Small States: New Zealand's Struggle Between Vulnerability and Resilience." *International Journal of Sport Policy and Politics* (ahead-of-print): 1–14.

Sam, Michael P. and Steven J. Jackson. 2015. "Sport and Small States: The Myths, Limits and Contradictions of the Legend of David and Goliath." *International Journal of Sport Policy and Politics* (ahead-of-print): 1–9.

Shearer, Derek. 2014. "To Play Ball, Not Make War." *Harvard International Review*. Accessed January 20, 2015, http://hir.harvard.edu/archives/7309.

Shibli, Simon, Veerle De Bosscher, Maarten van Bottenburg, and Hans Westerbeek. 2013. "Alternative Measures of Performance in the Olympic Games." Accessed January 20, 2015, http://easm.net/download/2013/ALTERNATIVE MEASURES OF PERFORMANCE IN THE OLYMPIC GAMES.pdf.

Silver, Nate. 2012. "Let's Play Medallball." *New York Times*, July 12.

Simiyu Njororai, Wycliffe W. 2010. "Global Inequality and Athlete Labour Migration from Kenya." *Leisure/Loisir* 34 (4): 443–461.

Simiyu Njororai, Wycliffe W. 2012. "Distance Running in Kenya: Athletics Labour Migration and its Consequences." *Leisure/Loisir* 36 (2): 187–209.

Ski Dubai. n.d. "Ski Dubai Resort Overview." Accessed February 17, 2015, www.skidubai.com/ski-dubai/resort/.

Smith, Alan. 2015. "Team GB Will Not Enter Football Teams for 2016 Rio Olympics." *Guardian*, March 30.

Sotiriadou, Kalliopi Popi and David Shilbury. 2009. "Australian Elite Athlete Development: An Organisational Perspective." *Sport Management Review* 12 (3): 137–148.

"South Korea, Netherlands Ink Skating Accord." 2014. *Reuters*, November 4.

Spiegel Online. 2014. "Deutscher Spitzensport Bekommt 15 Millionen Euro Mehr Fördergelder." Accessed August 18, 2015, www.spiegel.de/sport/sonst/deutscher-spitzensport-bekommt-15-millionen-euro-mehr-foerdergelder-a-1002810.html.

"Sport and Recreation New Zealand (SPARC) — Ministry of Justice, New Zealand." Accessed July 17, 2015, www.justice.govt.nz/publications/global-publications/d/directory-of-official-information-archive/directory-of-official-information-december-2011/alphabetical-list-of-entries-1/s/sport-and-recreation-new-zealand-sparc.

Stanton, Andrea L. 2012. "'Pioneer of Olympism in the Middle East': Gabriel Gemayel and Lebanese Sport." *The International Journal of the History of Sport* 29 (15): 2115–2130.

Stanton, Andrea L. 2014. "Syria and the Olympics: National Identity on an International Stage." *The International Journal of the History of Sport* 31 (3): 290–305.

Tan, Tien-Chin and Mick Green. 2008. "Analysing China's Drive for Olympic Success in 2008." *The International Journal of the History of Sport* 25 (3): 314–338.

Tan, Tien-Chin and Barrie Houlihan. 2012. "Chinese Olympic Sport Policy: Managing the Impact of Globalisation." *International Review for the Sociology of Sport* 48 (2): 131–152.

Tcha, Moonjoong and Vitaly Pershin. 2003. "Reconsidering Performance at the Summer Olympics and Revealed Comparative Advantage." *Journal of Sports Economics* 4 (3): 216–239.

Tozer, Malcolm. 2013. "'One of the Worst Statistics in British Sport, and Wholly Unacceptable': The Contribution of Privately Educated Members of Team GB to the Summer Olympic Games, 2000–2012." *The International Journal of the History of Sport* 30 (12): 1436–1454.

Truyens, Jasper, Veerle De Bosscher, Bruno Heyndels, and Hans Westerbeek. 2013. "A Resource-Based Perspective on Countries' Competitive Advantage in Elite Athletics." *International Journal of Sport Policy and Politics* (ahead-of-print): 1–31.

"The Turbulent World of Middle East Soccer: Qatar's Sports-Focused Public Diplomacy Backfires." 2014. Accessed June 13, 2014, http://mideastsoccer.blogspot.com/2014/02/qatars-sports-focused-public-diplomacy.html.

Van Tuyckom, Charlotte and Karl G. Jöreskog. 2012. "Going for Gold! Welfare Characteristics and Olympic Success: An Application of the Structural Equation Approach." *Quality & Quantity* 46 (1): 189–205.

"Verbandsförderung im Olympischen Spitzensport." 2007. Accessed November 18, 2014, www.dosb.de/fileadmin/fm-dosb/arbeitsfelder/leistungssport/Konzepte/Foerderkonzept_beschlossen_08_12_07.pdf.

Waardenburg, Maikel and Maarten van Bottenburg. 2013. "Sport Policy in the Netherlands." *International Journal of Sport Policy and Politics* 5 (3): 465–475.

Walker, Peter. 2012. "London 2012: Team GB Receive a Harsh Welcome to Olympic Handball." Accessed May 26, 2015, www.theguardian.com/sport/2012/jul/30/london-2012-team-gb-olympic-handball.

WAZ Rechercheblog. 2012. "Olympia: Das System Plansport – Millionen Für Medaillen." Accessed November 19, 2014, www.derwesten-recherche.org/2012/07/das-system-plansport-millionen-fur-medaillen/.

Weed, Mike. 2009. "The Potential of the Demonstration Effect to Grow and Sustain Participation in Sport." *A Review Paper for Sport England.*

Williams, Olli. 2014. "Olympic Links: 1 December, 2014 | Frontier Sports." Accessed July 24, 2015, http://frontiersports.co.uk/2014/12/olympic-links-1-december-2014/.

"Women's Ski Jumping Has Arrived … But There's Still a Hill to Climb." 2014. Accessed November 21, 2014, www.usatoday.com/story/sports/olympics/sochi/2014/02/11/sarah-hendrickson-usa-women-ski-jumping-future-winter-games/5399797/.

Won, Hyung-Joong and Eunah Hong. 2015. "The Development of Sport Policy and Management in South Korea." *International Journal of Sport Policy and Politics* 7 (1): 141–152.

World Curling Federation. 2014. "Hong Kong and Qatar Confirmed as Conditional Members of WCF." Accessed February 17, 2015, www.worldcurling.org/hong-kong-and-qatar-confirmed-as-conditional-members-of-wcf.

Yamamoto, Mayumi Ya-Ya. 2012. "Development of the Sporting Nation: Sport as a Strategic Area of National Policy in Japan." *International Journal of Sport Policy and Politics* 4 (2): 277–296.

"Yuna Kim Sochi Scandal: South Korean Figure Skater Robbed of Gold in Russia's Controversial Olympics." 2014. Accessed May 27, 2015, www.ibtimes.com/yuna-kim-sochi-scandal-south-korean-figure-skater-robbed-gold-russias-controversial-olympics-1557134.

Zaccardi, Nick. 2014. "Thomas Bach Hopes Mixed-Gender Events in Nanjing Impact Olympics (Video)." OlympicTalk. Accessed June 17, 2015, http://olympictalk.nbcsports.com/2014/08/27/thomas-bach-hopes-mixed-gender-events-in-nanjing-impact-olympics-video/.

Zheng, Jinming. 2015. "Hong Kong." *International Journal of Sport Policy and Politics* (ahead-of-print): 1–18.

Index

Page numbers in *italics* denote tables, those in **bold** denote figures.